Journeys

Journeys

An Anthology of Adult Student Writing

2022

Literacy Minnesota

First Edition
Printed in the United States of America

ISBN 978-1-7337440-5-8

Cover Design: Heather Cook

Table of Contents

Introduction from the Executive Director

Dear Reader,

As the new interim Executive Director of Literacy Minnesota, it has been a joy to see the magic that happens in Adult Basic Education classrooms. Watching and listening to learners from here and around the world come together to create community is a powerful reminder about the importance of literacy. It is a basic need just like food, housing, and transportation.

The writers in *Journeys* are all working to create a future for themselves that has possibilities and brings more hope to their families. As a resident, I am hopeful because of the energy, grit, determination, and positivity each person brings to make our respective communities a good place to live and work. Literacy changes each of our lives.

Some adult learners have left all that is near and dear to them in their homeland because of war, famine, lack of food or jobs, and violence. Others are in Minnesota to be near family, build community, and seek educational opportunities. All of the learners are in pursuit of their maximum potential and even better lives for themselves and their loved ones. The writers in this edition are testimonials to the resilience and strength of the human spirit. The determination shared in these stories is palpable and speaks to hope.

We believe that *Journeys* continues to fill a unique need in the community of Adult Basic Education teachers and learners, because it:

- Gives Adult Basic Education learner-writers a chance to share their stories and have their voices heard.
- Is a classroom tool for Adult Basic Education teachers and others working with students to build their literacy and literary skills.
- Highlights the richness and critical importance of the literacy work being done across communities.
- Introduces new readers to the stories of others who are on journeys like – and unlike – their own.

This thirty-third annual edition of *Journeys* features the work of 371 authors and artists representing Adult Basic Education programs across the state of Minnesota. I am grateful for these courageous authors who have shared their stories with us. I know you will enjoy each and every one.

Renae Oswald-Anderson
Interim Executive Director

In the Past

Featured Author

Yukie Nelson

BROOKLYN PARK, MN

Yukie was born in Matsumoto in Japan. It is a very beautiful place with high mountains and rivers. Yukie's family moved to the suburbs of Tokyo when she was one year old. She has an older brother and a younger sister. Yukie's sister, Yoko, lives in Australia and her brother, Kazu, still lives in Japan. Yukie has lived in Minnesota since 2011 with her two children. They miss their family so much because they all live so far away and can hardly meet.

When Yukie moved to the USA, she could not speak English well. Her children were little at the time, and they loved to help her with her English. The children are now teenagers and still like to help with English. Yukie is wanting to provide good opportunities for her children in this country. One of these opportunities is playing the violin and saxophone in the school programs and band and orchestra.

In the future, Yukie would like to be a translator and interpreter for Japanese and English. She and her family dream of going to different places on vacations.

Family Road Trip to Michigan

The coronavirus had spread all over the world since the end of 2019 and it has changed our normal lives. We were anxious and were receiving sad news every day. I was thinking of visiting Japan with my children during spring break, but I suddenly had to go to Japan for a family emergency in February. My mother was in a coma and never woke up again. She passed away in May.

During the pandemic, I have been able to continue working because I was an essential worker. I had to stay home for two weeks when a coworker had Covid-19. I needed something fun and happy during this difficult time. I decided to take this opportunity to get a puppy for my family! Her name is Roxie, and she is very cute, but we quickly learned she was a very smart troublemaker and she quickly got used to our family!

There were so many events happening in 2020 and when it came to an end, I said, "Goodbye, 2020." I still really wanted to go to Japan in 2021, but I thought international travel was still made very difficult by the pandemic. Instead, I thought about traveling by car during summer break. That was a good idea for keeping a social distance and taking Roxie with. I wanted to see a beautiful ocean, but it is a long way to drive from here to the ocean. I found a beautiful, crystal clear lake with Caribbean blue and green waters. The lake was Torch Lake in Michigan.

One way distance was 600 miles and twelve hours. The Mackinac Bridge in Michigan is an amazing architectural feat and incredible view during every crossing of the bridge. The road trip was tiring, but if we could find a beautiful place, we could stop and take a picture. We finally arrived in Torch Lake. It was the same blue and green waters that I saw in the photos. The place was not the Caribbean, but Torch Lake was an amazing and beautiful place. I've never seen such a beautiful lake before! We found some favorite beaches and swam together. Roxie wanted to swim with us too. She followed us and her swimming was amazing for her first time! It was our adventure and fun first family road trip. The kids and I are talking about the next family road trip in 2022 already!

Yukie Nelson is 45 and originally from Japan.

Starting a School

JORGE SANCHEZ MARIN, MINNEAPOLIS, MN

Hi, my name is Jorge. I was born in a very poor town in Mexico. I remember my first years of education. There were no schools, no electricity, no water, and no roads or infrastructure, but the people of the town were organizing themselves to come up with a solution to all of these problems. First, they found a person who had a space in their house to use as a classroom. It was one of my uncles who had an extra room, and he decided to lend it to us to use as a classroom. Then they had to find a teacher, so they went to the municipality to talk with the president and asked him to send a teacher to this little town, and they achieved that. We had a teacher, but no furniture. The teacher had to walk for like an hour to my uncle's house and she only did it for a few weeks.

Then they sent another teacher who had a car, and he only did that for a few months because the roads were in very bad condition, so we ended up with no teacher and later without a classroom. People had to start from the beginning. This time it was one of my cousins who had an empty two-room house, so they decided to use it as a classroom. They brought furniture, a teacher, and it was up and running, until one day, I saw the teacher come with a truck. She took all the furniture and never came back. That was when the people of my town became serious about having a real school, so they petitioned the president for a school. That is when the first school was established in my town, and I was a part of the construction team. I was eight.

Jorge Sanchez Marin is 35 and originally from Mexico.

My Favorite Childhood Vacation

SHELLY DOREEN BRESNAHAN, ST. PAUL, MN

To start off, I was fifteen years old and my mom and I took a vacation to Daytona, Florida for a week. We went to the Minneapolis-St. Paul International Airport to catch the flight which was on a 747 airplane. We got settled into our seats, then the plane took off into the clouds and my ears started to pop. I had to chew some gum and my mom looked at me and asked me if I was alright. I said, "I'm okay." As we stepped off the plane, my mom said, "I'm going to rent a car so that we can get around." I was beyond excited to see a whole different state. My mom and I first stopped to get something to eat at McDonalds. I got a Quarter Pounder with cheese, fries, and a drink. When we got done eating, we went back to the hotel so we could rest up.

The next day, we went to Daytona Beach for a couple of hours. It was my very first time near the ocean. Eek. The best thing I enjoyed was the art fair. I was able to look around at what was going on from table to table. I watched people paint such incredible wall hangings. I was stunned at the capability of this one lady who painted a painting of the Florida sun coming up above the ocean. I became so adapted to Florida in just that one week that I told my mom I wished I did not have to go back to Oakdale, Minnesota. Oh, I keep my memories.

Shelly Doreen Bresnahan is 55 and originally from Maplewood, MN.

"Where Are You, Manavi?"

MANAVI KOUNOU, ST. PAUL, MN

My husband is a truck driver and I have been traveling with him since my arrival in the USA in May 2021. When I was in Lomé, Togo, I kept my husband company on the phone everywhere he went. He told me about the road, mountains, bridges, et cetera. That made me want to lead a tourist life, and at the same time spend time with him as his wife.

We go almost everywhere except the West. We haven't been there because my husband says there are too many mountains. Delivery often happens at midnight or 1 a.m. When it strikes midnight, I go to bed and my husband keeps driving. We have bunk beds but sleep together in one bed. Sometimes we don't eat breakfast because we don't wake up early. We shower daily at a truck stop, whenever we need fuel.

Sometimes if we are tired and cannot stop for a long time, we take a five-to-ten-minute break to rest on the shoulder of the road. We play music, sing, and dance just to overcome fatigue and then we continue down the road. Sometimes when we do not have an immediate return load, we go walking or we take an Uber to another village or go shopping. We have fun. But as husband and wife we argue some, too.

When we leave our house, we do one, two, or three weeks and then we are home to rest for five days to one week. I don't want to be a trucker, I just want to keep my husband company and discover other cities and states. I have seen many places in the east, north, and south of the U.S. I know this will no longer be possible if I have a child and a job, but for the moment, I take advantage of the opportunity to see America and be with my husband. If a baby is born, I will take my leave as a trucker's assistant.

I am also taking Hubbs Center for Lifelong Learning ESL level six classes while in the truck. Each day my class asks, "Where are you Manavi?" I sometimes have trouble with the internet, but I always attend my online class. I don't like to stay still. I am supporting my husband even though the trucker life can be stressful.

Manavi Kounou is 32 and originally from Togo.

Story of My Life in Thailand

WAH EH, ST. PAUL, MN

My name is Wah Eh and I was born in a Thailand refugee camp. I came to America when I was eleven years old, almost twelve years old. Now I live in St. Paul, Minnesota. The thing that I remember most about being in Thailand is when my house was close to the river. When it was about to be summer, my dad took the rock out of the water and put it around the side like river polo, so whenever people want to swim they go swim there. The second thing I remember is playing with my friends. It was fun. We played rock, jump rope, hide and seek, ran to chase each other, and we played a lot of things that are fun. I really miss living in Thailand.

Wah Eh is 17 and originally from Thailand.

A Love of Nature and Architecture

IRINA GANELES, NEW HOPE, MN

This is the fifth time in twenty years I have stood in this place. I was here during a summer and a winter. I saw this view both in the bright rays of the midday sun and in the rays of the sunset. I'm here tonight during a full moon.

I am not inclined to mysticism, but I feel like I am standing on the edge of the Earth, and on the other side of this truly grand canyon begins another world, another planet, another dimension, another universe.

I see stone ledges carved out by a gigantic stonecutter with some magical tools. I see stone figures carved with a skillful sculptor's chisel. The colors on the canvases of Roerich and Gauguin seem to fade when I see the colors of the greatest artist—Nature!

I was born in Minsk, the capital of Belarus, formerly part of the Soviet Union. Minsk was completely destroyed during World War II. By the time of my growing up in Minsk, there was not a single old building worthy of the interest of local historians.

I was lucky twice. First, my father, whose memory I am in awe of, lived in Minsk in his youth before the war. He was fond of photography and managed to save several albums with interesting photographs of old Minsk.

Second, my school geography teacher. My love for nature and my genuine interest in local history and old architecture is undoubtedly to the merit of my unforgettable teacher.

After graduating from university, I got a job that resulted in numerous business trips. I admired the nature of the unique Lake Baikal. I saw the snow-capped peaks of the gigantic mountains in Central Asia and the Caucasus and the quiet, melancholic nature of the Baltic coast in the west of Russia.

But I was especially pleased with walking tours of beautiful Russian cities. I was sure that I could not see anything more beautiful, but a little more than twenty years ago, by the will of fate, I ended up in the United States of America.

By this time, I have visited over twenty states.

I fell in love with North American architecture. I found a unique local history gem right here—this is the city Stillwater, where on weekends, I spend many hours hiking and admiring the excellent architecture. I can recommend to anyone who shares my interests to go to this city.

Irina Ganeles is 69 and originally from Belarus.

Moving to a New Country

ANONYMOUS, ST. PAUL, MN

I am from Thailand. When I knew I would be able to move to the U.S. I was very excited, but at the same time I got very nervous because I did not know what would happen to me. My uncle didn't want to come, so he tried to run away. But my cousin and I wanted to go and have a better life.

We decided to borrow a motorcycle from other people and we had to pay 150 baht. After that we left right away to go find my uncle. When we got there, we tried to talk with my uncle and my uncle refused to move to the U.S. He said he was scared to move. People around him told him that if he moved to the U.S., they would give you crocodiles to eat. That's why my uncle didn't want to come. And my aunt told us, "You guys can go home now. I'll talk to your uncle later tonight."

When we went back to my uncle's house a few days later, my aunt and my uncle were back home. My uncle decided to go to the U.S., so I came with my uncle's family.

Route 66 to the Promise of Disneyland

DARRELL RAVITZ, BROOKLYN CENTER, MN

I'm eighty-four years old and have always loved to travel by car. One of my favorite memories was in 1951, when my mom, dad, sister Joan, and I took a road trip, driving from Minneapolis, Minnesota to Los Angeles, California. I was thirteen years old and had always dreamed about traveling on Route 66.

We left the Twin Cities in our 1950 Buick Century and picked up Route 66 near Tulsa, Oklahoma. Joan and I entertained ourselves in the backseat by reading comics and Burma Shave signs along the way.

Your shaving brush
Has had its day
So why not
Shave the modern way
With
Burma Shave

In Flagstaff, Arizona, it was snowing lightly. We were going to drive across Death Valley, but we had to travel at night because it was too hot during the day. There was no air conditioning so we had an early form of AC, a tube coming from a cooler filled with ice into the car.

We made it to Los Angeles and met our cousins. My cousin Dolly had connections to Columbia Pictures and she got us into the Walt Disney Studios, where we were able to hear a broadcast of Dragnet on the radio. We met Jack Webb and Ben Alexander, the stars of the show.

When we were leaving the studio, we saw the very first prop that was made especially for Disneyland in Anaheim, California. It was a stagecoach at about sixty percent of a full-size coach. Our tour guide swore us to secrecy, saying, "Don't tell anyone!" At this time, Disneyland was still in the planning stages. I remember thinking, "This is going to take a long time!" Four years later, on July 17, 1955, Disneyland became a reality.

Knott's Berry Farm in Buena Park, California was a lot of fun. Knott's started as a small berry farm and grew into a huge family amusement park with lots of rides. I was exhausted, in a good way, when we finally left the park. Another highlight was a visit to the tar pits at La Brea, one of the world's most famous fossil localities with natural asphalt. We saw fossils of mastodons and other extinct animals.

When we left for home, we drove through the Rocky Mountains out of Denver, Colorado on a two-lane highway at fifty miles per hour. The trip back was uneventful. We were all exhausted and eager to get home.

Darrell Ravitz is 84 and originally from Minneapolis, MN.

Tippy

MARGARET JOHNSON DAVIS, BROOKLYN CENTER, MN

Our dog Tippy was a black lab. He had a white spot on his chest. He was a very good dog. When we lived on Queen Avenue in Minneapolis, he was very friendly when others came over to our house. Tippy was also a good watchdog. When all the family was together, Tippy was very happy! He loved when we pet him. Every time we ate dinner, Tippy would sit by the table and beg. When Tippy was older, he had some health problems. One day in May, he ran off. Afterwards it snowed. He was fourteen years old. Sadly, we never found him again.

Margaret Johnson Davis is 63 and originally from Minneapolis.

El Dia de Mi Boda, My Wedding Day

KARLA MONTES WALDINA, MAPLEWOOD, MN

I was recently married on September 11th at 4 p.m. of this year (2021) to Roberto Maldonado. My husband and I decided on a one-day celebration because it would cost too much money to have a celebration for more then one day. We have a large family, on my husband's side of the family there is about eighty. Roberto and I were married by Pastor Cesar.

We were married here in the United States in Ellendale, Minnesota on a hobby farm. The ceremony was outside on a nice sunny day with simple decorations and a canopy. The yard was completely beautiful and green. We hired a decorator and someone to put lights all around and some torches. Plus, we had a DJ who played some Spanish and some English music. One song that I remember is "Mil años" (One Thousand Years) in Spanish.

I had three bridesmaids, and my Matron of Honor was Elsa, my husband's cousin. She lives with us and we are very close. There were also two groomsmen, a flower girl who again was a cousin of my husband, and my son Braden who is six years old and was the ring bearer. His suit matched Roberto and he looked very handsome.

I wore a long white dress with a train, it was a little tight from when I first had it fitted. Comfortable heels and earrings. Roberto was wearing a blue tux with a white shirt and a blue vest. His tie was brown and blue and his shoes were brown. He looked handsome too.

After the ceremony, there was food. I told my mother-in-law I didn't want her cooking and doing all that work, but she did it anyway. This was much cheaper. Roberto's mother cooked baked pork, rice, potatoes, tamales, and there were different drinks. Modello, Dos Equis XX, Heineken, Flor de caña. There was Capri Sun for the kids and soda for those that preferred it. Roberto and I sat at a special table made only for us.

Karla Montes Waldina is originally from Honduras.

I Remember

LAWRENCE KYI, ST. PAUL, MN

I remembered when I was a child, I had a lot of friends. One day, my friends and I were planning to go to the forest and hunt birds. The next day, I woke up early and packed up food for lunch and prepared to go to the forest. After that, I went to pick up my friends and we went to the forest together. We went together and while we walked, we sang funny songs and we played with each other before we got to the forest.

Lawrence Kyi is 23 and originally from Thailand.

My First Two Years in the USA

HALIMA KHATUN, COON RAPIDS, MN

I came to America in the fall of 2019 at midnight. My husband's older brother received us from the airport. We didn't know he came to Minnesota, so we were surprised that day when we saw him, because he lives in California.

After the next morning, we started our USA life. My brother-in-law took us to the driver's license office. We were photographed in that office but I didn't know why we went there. But at last, I saw they gave a driving written test book to my husband. That day we went to another office and we got our social security number from this office. Then one or two days later, we went to the Adult Education Center and we took our admission test. I got level two and my husband got level three. Teacher Lorna was my level two teacher. She was my first teacher in America. At first, I had trouble understanding in class. She helped me in many ways. Now I am level four. I respect and love all my teachers. I think they are very helpful.

After one week, my son was admitted to a new elementary school. He loves his class very much. At that time, my husband, nephew, and his wife helped us very much. In 2021, we were moving to a new apartment, so my son changed his previous school. Now he studies at another elementary school. I work at my son's school as a substitute. At first we started our class in person but when Covid-19 started, we have been taking our class online. For a few months, my son took his class online. Right now he goes to school every day in person.

We were very happy to see the first direct snowfall after coming to America. We have never seen snowfall before. From 2020, I started my work. I like and respect my work so much. We love America and respect their rules and law. This is the America I have seen in a short time.

Halima Khatun is 38 and originally from Bangladesh.

Grandmother Hattie's House

MARVIN GAYDEN, ST. PAUL, MN

My grandma's house was an orange and red brick one-story house on the West Side of Chicago. In her house, she had three of her own children, my mom Febbie, my auntie Jean, her sister, and my uncle Jessie. Four of her ten grandchildren were also in the house, including me. I was her favorite: you can ask anyone. She loved to cook for all of us. Grandma Hattie made a lemon meringue pie that was spectacular!

There was nothing like it. I never even liked pie until I tasted grandma's. Hattie cooked everything from scratch. No matter what, she was using recipes. On holidays, she would play music to match the holiday. Grandma Hattie Bass was a church-woman, with a large collection of church hats. When she passed, she had hats that were still in the box and my aunties argued over these hats.

She had a hard time saying no to people. Grandma was five feet, six inches with light brown skin, with long black hair that she would use a hot comb on and that turned gray as she grew older. Grandma was an Avon lady; she was a very people person. I don't think she ever even swore. She was seventy-nine when she passed on March 17, 2018 in St. Paul, Minnesota in my own mother's house after moving to Minnesota, because she no longer could live on her own in Chicago. After she passed, the family had her buried in a cemetery on the West Side of Chicago so that she could be next to my grandfather and aunts. When I am famous, I will buy her an even larger tombstone with the words "live forever."

Marvin Gayden is 32 and originally from Chicago, IL.

Memories of Home

SOWDA YUSUF, NEW HOPE, MN

I was born and raised in a small town in Somalia known as Diinsoor. It is a beautiful town that is surrounded by beautiful mountains.

My earliest memories are of me walking around in our house which was 5,000 square meters. We had a very attractive yard and a small forest surrounded the house. I always enjoyed being there with my parents and siblings. Our house consisted of four rooms: a living room, guest room, kitchen, and two toilets.

One day early in the morning, my father called my mother and told her that he decided to sell the house but promised he would buy another one for us. He said he would start a business with the remaining capital, so she agreed. However, when we heard the rumors, we were disappointed and cried badly. I used to enjoy the fresh air and the sounds of the winds.

When we moved to our new house, I felt lonely because I missed my close friends, school, and the Islamic center that was nearby. However, there's a proverb that says, "Man plans Allah's purposes." I believe there was a reason behind us moving from our old house to the new house, because I found my husband there, as we were neighbors. I thank the almighty Allah for blessing me with my husband.

I would like to conclude, always bear in mind that almighty Allah knows what is better for us all.

Sowda Yusuf is 34 and originally from Somalia.

Life in a New Country

WALTER DAVID PEREZ GUTIERREZ, MINNESOTA

I have lived in the U.S. for two years.

The first place I lived was Florida.

The first person I met was my friend Angel.

I had to learn how to use a bus card, and to say words such as how much, go ahead, et cetera.

My first winter was horrible, I have never felt so cold. I remember I had only one sweater. I felt so sad.

Walter David Perez Gutierrez is originally from Honduras.

Vacation

ANONYMOUS, WOODBURY, MN

Three years ago, I went to New York City for vacation. I took a city bus to see the Statue of Liberty. Once I arrived, I could see the statue in the distance. It was tall and surrounded by water. There were many skyscrapers also in the distance. The first thing I did was take a picture. Then I got on a ferry with a lot of people. The ferry took us closer to the statue. The closer we got, the larger she became. The ferry guy told us about different facts. The harbor was full of ships. The ships were noisy. After the ferry, we headed back to where we came from.

We saw the skyscrapers in downtown. It felt amazing because I wanted to spend time walking around the buildings. We went inside the World Trade Center and took the elevator. At the top, we saw the bottom of the city and the water. I could see all kinds of skyscrapers. I was so excited. We also went to Koreatown for shopping and food. We ate Korean barbecue, and it tasted greasy and delicious. It was my first time at a Korean barbecue restaurant. We also went to a Korean bakery store where they sold desserts. I went to a bath and body store. I couldn't buy anything because the airport doesn't allow me to fly with liquids. After New York, we went back to Minnesota. My trip to New York was okay, but maybe next time in the future I will go to South Korea.

Persuasive Writing

MAGNOLIA, WORTHINGTON, MN

Today I can tell how I like to spend my time as a family in summer.

We love to go for a picnic. My husband and I cook together, while the kids play at the park. It fills us with joy to see them having so much fun. We all enjoy the nature and the beauty of the green. I love to see them laugh! It makes my day.

Later on, we talk about memories and the fun we had together. How we love and respect each other. For me, spending time as a family is the best of all. I wouldn't change anything.

Magnolia is 35 and originally from Guatemala.

My Grandmother's House

TANYA TROMBLEY, MAPLEWOOD, MN

I remember my grandmother's house in Forest Lake. It had gray siding and the bottom part of it was rock. It had five bedrooms and two bathrooms and a two-car garage. The house was in the woods. There was a bedroom that had purple colored walls and was named Tanya's room. If I looked out the bedroom window, I would see trees everywhere and small animals, such as rabbits, squirrels, and chipmunks. I would go see my grandpa and grandma a lot and I would stay in that room. I spent most of my time watching TV or going on the computer. Grandma and Grandpa sold it over four years ago.

My grandmother is a crafty woman, she makes cards and other arts and crafts. She is a nice and caring person and is now living in Wisconsin. I don't get to see my grandmother much because of Covid, but before, I got to see her a couple times a year, mostly in the summertime. My grandfather was a good man too, who would make other people laugh. Sometimes I think he would purposely antagonize my grandmother, he knew what buttons to push! She would get so pissed and he would just laugh about it, but they were married for more than sixty years. He did not really have any hobbies but he was my favorite grandfather on both sides. My grandmother's house was a warm house that made me feel loved.

Tanya Trombley is 39 and originally from the United States.

My Name

ANONYMOUS, ST. CLOUD, MN

I first write my name

I write this in Ethiopia,
in school

I am seventeen, it's not hard,
but I am not fast

Then I come to America
At twenty-eight or twenty-nine

I write my name a little more
I write my name in ESL class
I write slow
I write bad

I have eight children

They all write fast,
Faster than *hooyo*

A Memory of My Childhood in Morocco

AMINA A., APPLE VALLEY, MN

I was born in Casablanca, Morocco. I lived in a beautiful house with my parents, one sister, and two brothers. I have a particular memory of my childhood when I was a teenager that is very nice.

When I was at home, I played a lot in the garden with my siblings and teenage neighbors. At school, I had a lot of friends. We talked about very fun stories that happened for each one of us and all these stories made us laugh a lot. In the summer, I went with my family and some cousins to the beach in Casablanca. We played volleyball, swam a lot, and sunbathed. It was fantastic.

Remembering this part of my life makes me very happy.

Amina A. is 63 and originally from Morocco.

A Little about Me

MESERET HAILU, ST. PAUL, MN

I was born and raised in the Ethiopian Tigray region. I come from an Orthodox Christian family where my parents taught me about Ethiopian culture, my religion, and Christian rules. As a kid, I always dreamed of going to school and being a doctor, not just a wife and mom. I always dreamed big, but one day everything fell apart. My parents were not rich enough for my five sisters and me to go to university.

When I was about seventeen years old, my dad came up with an idea for me to have a better life. My parents wanted to arrange a marriage for me. If I said no, that would mean I was disrespecting them. I was shocked when I found out the man they had chosen for me was twenty years older than me. I was mad at my family.

Finally, my parents convinced me that this would be the best thing. So I got married and became pregnant soon after. My husband lived in Minnesota, so after his three-month vacation in Ethiopia, he went back to Minnesota, and began the process of getting us into the USA. For three years, we communicated by video and texting. The funny thing was, we didn't communicate well. I didn't know very much about him because of the distance between us. We seemed to fight with each other for no reason. At last, the process was complete and my daughter Adonay and I came to Minnesota. After all, God helped us be together.

I will never forget the moment I met him after the three-year wait. I feel like he is my everything because I don't have any family members in America. We work hard to communicate and understand each other. We have three children and bought a house. He is supportive of whatever I do. I am thankful that he is in my life. He is a pastor. I love the way he teaches our children. My parents were right, I am very happy. I am grateful for all that has happened to me. I thank God that I am in America, that I am a working mother and going to school, and that I can help my family. We pray for our family in Ethiopia. The situation right now is very worrisome. We are grateful for what we have and what happened to us. Thank you for this opportunity to share my story.

Meseret Hailu is 25 and originally from Ethiopia.

My Wedding

RODA JAMA, WOODBURY, MN

I was married on September 1, 2012. It was a beautiful sunny day. My husband is Saalim Mahumed. We had a three-day celebration in Bloomington, Minnesota at the Crowne Plaza by the Mall of America. The building was brown and gold and had hotel suites.

The first day is called Mecher and it was only for the men, and lasted from 12 p.m. to 4 p.m. at a mosque in Minneapolis. My cousins were there to represent me. If my dad or brother were here they would have "given me away." My cousins agreed to the marriage for me. There was an imam to perform the ceremony at the mosque. On this day, I was at home. On the first day, I wore a blue and red dress. Saalim wore a traditional Muslim gown for men, he was in white from head to toe. I would meet Saalim on the second day.

The second day there was the Aroos of men and women. It went on from 10 p.m. to 4 a.m. The Aroos was held at the hotel and I wore a white dress like Cinderella with white and black shoes. Saalim was wearing black and white on this night. During this celebration and on the third day, we ate rice, fish, chicken, and veggies which were cooked by the hotel chef and served at tables. I also had a three-layer cake. Saalim would have had food with the men on the first day.

We had a DJ and video recording guy with one singer name Abdi, on both the second and third day. I remember one song was called "Faxiya Fisk" that was played during the night. I had four bridesmaids to help me out so I would not get out of control. They all wore red dresses in different designs. Two of my bridesmaids were not Somali so they did not attend the Buraabur.

On the last day, day three, there are only women. It is called a Buraabur and went on from 10 p.m. to 4 a.m. On this day, I wore a *haia* sari, an Indian sari which was white. The only men there were the DJ and the photographer.

In 2014, we went on a honeymoon to Chicago and London. I am thankful for this marriage because I gained four beautiful children.

Roda Jama is 37 and originally from Somalia.

Shocked

SURER IBRAHIM, ST. CLOUD, MN

It was Ramadan, so I had to eat before sunrise. It was 3 a.m. I was in the kitchen eating when I heard crying. I looked out the window and said, "What is happening?" I saw a young child walking in the road. I opened the window and said, "Stop, baby!" in Somali. He didn't hear me, so I ran downstairs and I didn't have shoes on. I went outside and didn't see him. I listened and heard him crying again. He was in tall grass. I picked him up and hugged him.

He didn't have shoes or a diaper on, just a sweater. He wasn't Somali. He was Hispanic, so I didn't know his language. I worried about taking him to my house, so I knocked on doors to see if someone knew who he was. A man and a woman answered the door and they called the police. The police tried to find the child's house. They found a girl asleep in a home with the door open. The child was her brother. The parents were out drinking and didn't come back until 5 a.m.

Surer Ibrahim is 52 and originally from Somalia.

My Grandmother's House

STELLA KEMBABZI KIMMET, ST. PAUL, MN

I think we all have a beautiful place in our minds, I have a wonderful place that made me happy a lot of times. But sometimes I think that I am the only person who likes this place and I am asking myself if this place will still be the same as I remember when I go back to visit.

This place is meaningful to me because it's at my grandmother's place, where I spent most of my holidays and it's part of my childhood, where I grew up. It's in the backyard of my grandmother's house in the farm.

My mother, my dad, and I were living in a small town called Kibiito. Kibiito is a populated town. This town is populated because of its industrial area where people come from different villages to do their trading. I did my schooling here, kindergarten, primary school, and high school. But during my holidays, my mother used to send me to my grandma's house.

My grandmother's place sits on six acres of land, surrounded by beautiful scenery. In the front yard, there's a view of Mt. Rwenzori. I was always sitting in the window of my grandma's house, exploring with my eyes the trees around the yard, looking for a clean and a quiet place; I found one on a small hill on the farm where cows, goats, and sheep grazed.

It's about 150 feet from my grandma's house, and when you look way down, there was a water stream running from the mountain, passing through my grandmother's farm. There were pine trees on the left side, just near to the stream, and on the right side, there was a mango tree just a few feet from the stream. It had beautiful branches and had ready yellow mangos. The mango tree leaves were big and green, some were shiny because of the reflection from the sun. I would sit down under the mango tree and looked around each corner and wondered at how beautiful this place looked. There were wild flowers with different colors, butterflies flying from one flower to another, bugs, insects making different sounds, birds singing, the sound from the pine trees when wind blows, and the sound of the river flowing.

I was so amazed by the place and ever since then, that place has taken a place in my heart.

Stella Kembabzi Kimmet is 24 and originally from Uganda.

This Is My Lived Experience

ALEJANDRA SANDOVAL, NEW BRIGHTON, MN

It is a life experience where I had to live in a difficult moment. In this story, 'we' are my husband, my friend, her father, and me.

I was born in Michoacán, Mexico, and my husband is from Mexico City. One of the wedding requirements is some marriage talks to know if we are really sure of the next step. That meeting, the priest made us do an activity that to date we both continue to remember frequently, and it was that they blindfolded us and he guided me to walk up and down without having to fall and vice versa. Over the years, I had to live this experience with one of my best friends and her father.

We have twenty-seven years of marriage. This experience was when we were married for eleven years. Due to work issues, we had to move to the city of Chihuahua to live for a few years. It changed our lives in every way. The place is the desert, it is very close to the Chihuahuan desert. My birthplace is Michoacán, Mexico where all that is seen is life, green and leafy.

So life tests us with many serious health problems, financial problems, great emotional instability, and we are in crisis. My best friend's father suggests that I do an activity with my friend, the three of us in a cave where the only light that exists is the little light that filters through the rocks.

I have learned that nothing can be controlled, fears make us take wrong steps. Fear paralyzes us and shows us the most difficult side of what we are experiencing. Likewise, it was that passage through that cave full of darkness that reflected the light that fear did not allow me to see. The cave was full of entrances and exits that lead to unknown places. But you could only walk forward. After spending three to four hours inside this place, I lost my fear of the dark. I don't know if I would experience this life experience again.

Here I learned the value of being able to see, observe everything beautiful that surrounds us, because that blackness that darkens does not compare to anything.

It has been fifteen years since this experience and I am grateful for having experienced this experience, because over time I apply it whenever I have an obstacle, fear, or doubt.

Alejandra Sandoval is 50 and originally from Mexico.

Family Love

ESIN NOURBAKHSH, FRIDLEY, MN

I loved him, I love him, and I will love him forever.

I grew up in a small city. In our culture, the father is the ancestor. What your father says will happen, it is respected, you need to be careful when you talk to him. You can't talk about everything with your father. You have to be careful of your movements. You must not do anything without your father's permission. In short, the society I lived in was a closed and conservative society. After we moved to the big city, a lot of things changed in our lives, but we couldn't change some things for the whole family. I could never say, "I love you" to my father and my mother. Of course, they didn't tell me either. In fact, they did not tell my other brothers. I don't remember them hugging me and kissing me. However, the thing that a child needs most is love, but this has never been shown to us, because of society's ridiculous rules. Children are spoiled and uncontrolled when shown love. When they didn't show love, we did the same. There was always a distance between us. We could never be sincere enough. I have always shown, and will show love for my child so that he does not experience this deficiency.

The last time I talked to my father was four months ago, when I video chatted with him on WhatsApp. I wanted to tell him that I love him. Something inside me said maybe this is the last chance. But I couldn't. I cried a lot when I hung up the phone. I told him that I loved him many times, but he didn't hear me. Three days later, I lost him. When I told my mother later, she said, "He loved you too, but he couldn't tell you." I tell my mother that I love her often now, and she tells me that she loves me too. But not being able to tell my father such a short and important sentence. I think this will remain a pain in my heart.

However, love must be shared, because when it is shared, it becomes bigger and becomes solid.

Esin Nourbakhsh is 46 and originally from Turkey.

About My High School in Ethiopia

GENET GEMTA, MINNEAPOLIS, MN

My country is Ethiopia. In our country, high school starts in seventh grade. I was twelve years old when I started seventh grade. All subjects are in English, which is different than in elementary. All subjects are in Amharic in elementary.

In seventh grade, science is divided into three subjects: physics, chemistry, and biology. Social studies is divided into two, history and geography. Also we have our language Amharic, math, and English.

And to get to school, I just walk. It is not far from my home. We went to school 8 a.m. to 12:45 p.m. one week and the next week we went from 1 p.m. to 5 p.m. and had lunch at home. At that time, there were not many schools. Our class was very big. There were fifty to sixty students in class. These days, there are more schools but there are more students too.

Genet Gemta is 55 and originally from Ethiopia.

What I Am Thankful For

DIAR LOR, BROOKLYN PARK, MN

This life is beautiful but so short. I remember when I was a little girl, I wanted to grow up as soon as I could. The last twenty-eight years have just flown by very quickly, but I'm very appreciative of myself.

I know life is difficult sometimes, but I'm glad I had all the good and bad experiences. Anyway, the past is just a memory for me. Now the important thing is the future: what do I want to do, how far do I want to go, how much do I want to change to become a better person, and how much happiness do I want to give to myself and others? So I just let the past go and am happy. People say it is never too late to change yourself. It doesn't matter how old you are, how bad an experience you had, you still can change your life to become a new life, be better, and love what you do. So I would like to give a big THANKS to myself for getting through everything in my life and becoming who I am right now. Like I said, life is short, just live happily and be thankful for everything that comes in our life.

Thanks to my dear self.

Diar Lor is 29 and originally from Laos.

Scary and Sweet

LILI LOPEZ, MINNEAPOLIS, MN

When I was a little girl, I lived in Mexico. One day, I was at my grandma's house and my grandma told me, "Go bring water from the well."

I told my grandma I would go in a bit, but she insisted I should hurry up and go before noon otherwise the goblins would appear. I did not believe my grandma. I walked for five minutes and all of a sudden I heard voices, but there was nothing there. All I saw was a tree. All of a sudden I see the branches of the tree moving like someone was playing. Honestly, I got so scared, I ran so fast that I forgot the water from the well! That day was the day I knew that goblins existed!

One of my other memories was when I went to get wood from the mountain with my friends. As we were walking, we saw a cherry tree, which was like seeing a hidden treasure. We stopped and decided to eat some cherries from the tree, however, what we didn't know was when we ate the fruit, our mouths and our hands would get stained. When I got back home my mom saw me and got scared and yelled, "What happened to you?"

I told her, "Nothing, we just ate some cherries."

She then started to laugh and took me to a mirror and said, "I think you're ready for Halloween!"

Lili Lopez is 45 and originally from Mexico.

My Personal Life

ANONYMOUS, ST. PAUL, MN

I'm from Burma. There was a war in Burma. It was really hard to live there because the Burmese military came to our village and burned down the houses. Many people had to flee through the jungle and also to the Thai refugee camps. When I was two and a half years old, my parents were crossing to the Thai border and went to live in the Thai refugee camp because the Burmese military came to the village almost all the time. I lived in the Thai refugee camp two and a half years, then I started going to school. I went to school in the Thai refugee camp for eight years.

My family moved to here when I was fourteen and now we have lived in America three and a half years, but I don't know how to speak English fluently yet and I don't understand everything in English yet. I'm continuing to learn English now.

My Childhood

ANONYMOUS, ST. PAUL, MN

I am from Morocco which is located in North Africa. I grew up in El Jadida, a touristic city. It has historical monuments like forts, castles, and Portuguese harbors. When I was six years old, I went with my grandma to the school. It was very large, with a beautiful garden. There, I met my best friend Nora. We walked to school every day, which began in September and ended in July.

In summer, we had two months vacation, so my family visited my grandparents who lived in the countryside. My grandparents owned a big house with a large field. Every summer, we were meeting with uncles and their children. We used to spend time running and playing games; "*kash-kash*" was my favorite game, it meant hide and seek. We played until it got dark. These were wonderful childhood memories!

On the Day My Son Was Born

ANONYMOUS, ST. CLOUD, MN

On the day Faysal was born, everyone smiled.
The weather was rainy.
Everyone said, what a beautiful boy
because he was so beautiful and nice.

A Second Chance

ANA CAROLINA LEMES, BROOKLYN PARK, MN

When I was thirteen years old, teenagers often went to the most famous amusement park in Goiania. When I was ready to go, my dad dropped me off there and I found Carollina, my friend since I was seven years old. On this day, we were very happy to spend time together because we hadn't seen each other for a while. But she didn't expect that our day would end in just fifteen minutes.

We went on our first ride, a ride with cars that went very fast in a circle and tipped from side to side… and then I woke up a week after this. I was in a coma for a week because the adrenaline caused by the ride knocked me out. I went to the hospital, but no doctor could diagnose me. I was a thirteen-year-old girl that had a seizure and half of her body paralyzed. After doing many exams, the doctors had an answer. They thought I had meningitis that morning and the ride made it worse.

I remember almost everything that happened while I was in the coma. However, I was also having hallucinations. In my head, I was being tortured by kidnappers. I thought I was tied up in the bed and my family was seated in modern electric chairs stacked on each other. I tried many times to stand up and save them, but I couldn't.

My aunt stayed with me a long time in the intensive care unit. When I saw her sitting next to me, I said to her, "Can you drop them? Or should I stand up?" She answered me, laughing, "Who? Only you and I are here." I don't remember what happened after this. When the drugs' effects wore off, I woke up from the coma.

My family told me what happened and when I saw my friend Carollina, she told me her version. When we were on the ride, I thought I told her that I wasn't feeling well, and I saw her yelling for the machine operator to stop the ride. She said that I never talked to her in that moment, but she was yelling for help.

It was terrible for me, my friend, and my family. I only can think how life is a precious thing that God gave us. I escaped from the meningitis, and I have a second chance in this life.

Ana Carolina Lemes is 25 and originally from Brazil.

What I Am Thankful For

MARIAN AHMED, MINNEAPOLIS, MN

I'm a thankful survivor of Covid-19. I got Covid-19. I was so sick and I thought that I couldn't make it. I was very ill and I didn't want to go to the hospital because I was watching what was happening to a lot of people. The hospitals were overwhelmed and some people didn't get good care because I believe doctors and nurses also were overwhelmed. I was scared to go to the hospital and said to myself, "They will put me on a breathing machine, and I'm going to die over there, and I cannot see my family." That was another scary thing that could happen to me. I was talking to myself, wondering what to do.

In the end, I decided to stay home with my family, whatever the outcome. I told my family that if I die, I will die here. I don't want to go to the hospital. It seemed like a crazy idea but that was what I told my mind. The reason I stayed home when I was sick with Covid-19 is that I was very scared to leave my kids behind. Some of my friends brought food. They put it at the door and I picked it up from the door. So I didn't see my friends because I didn't want to give them my virus. I was praying a lot to God to give me good health. I'm thankful to God I'm living and breathing today. Another thing that I'm thankful for is to have my husband that took care of me when I was sick and also took care of the whole family. He works so hard every day and provides for us what we need for our house. I am always thankful for him and for my family, and I will remember all the good things that he did for us. I'm lucky to have him in my life. He is one of the best people I know.

Marian Ahmed is 49 and originally from Somalia.

Singapore

HIEP DUC BUI, MAPLEWOOD, MN

The most beautiful place in the world is Singapore. I had the opportunity to travel to Singapore two years ago. I saw many trees in the city and the air was very clean and pure. Singapore is a small country, with five million people and small islands, an area of 500 square kilometers. In Singapore, I did not see any rubbish in the streets. This is a modern country with many skyscrapers and every building has a lot of trees. The roads are very wide and restaurants are everywhere. I enjoyed the food in Singapore and I did a lot of sightseeing.

Hiep Duc Bui is 40 and originally from Vietnam.

Scary Memory

SABRIN AL SHARMANI, WAITE PARK, MN

When I was nine years old, I used to live in my country, in Yemen. I was going to school when I saw a man come to me and ask me where Abdul Latif's house was. I didn't know who Abdul Latif was. He told me, "Come. I will tell you who this person is." I said, "No, I want to go to my school." Then he said, "I will drive you to your school. Look at my car. We will go there. I have chocolates and toys in the car. Come with me." I told him, "No, I don't want to go with you." He told his friend, "Come and bring the car."

When he said bring the car, I got scared and I cried and was screaming for help. When people saw me screaming, they came to me. The man got scared and said, "She is my daughter." I told the people, "No, he is not my father." When people knew that he was not my father, they caught him and his friend. They beat them and called the police. The police took them to prison and a policeman told me I did something good when I told people that I needed help. The policeman took me back to my school.

Sabrin Al Sharmani is 26 and originally from Yemen.

Ethiopia

ANONYMOUS, ST. CLOUD, MN

Ethiopia
temperature different
walking, farming, eating fruit
birds are beautiful here
raining

An Unforgettable Trip

LINDA CHACON, MAPLE GROVE, MN

When I went back to my country for the first time, I was pregnant and my older son was ten months old. There were direct flights to my country, but for economic reasons, we booked a flight that had a layover. I was so nervous because I was going to travel without any help, but I was so happy to go back to my country and enjoy time with my family.

The day came and my husband felt sad. It was a stressful flight, taking care of my belly and my little boy in my arms all the way. When we arrived in El Salvador, it was a happy moment. We had a good time there. I ate fresh fruit and vegetables, enjoyed traditional food, enjoyed the beautiful beaches, and had a good time with family and friends. When the time came to return to the United States, it was hard to separate the family again.

I never thought that traveling back could be more stressful and dangerous than the flight out.

At that time, Hurricane Isaac was hitting the city of Miami where we were going to transfer flights. Because of the storm, we lost the second flight and we needed to wait until the next day. My husband was worried and talked with the airline. They helped me to get a hotel and food. This was a blessing.

The hotel was located outside the airport and it was so difficult to get the transportation there. I needed to carry my little baby in my arms, a backpack, and my big suitcase.When a man saw me in my difficulties, he offered his help. He really was an angel that God sent me.

I like to be early for my flight and for this reason, I looked at the clock and calculated two hours before departure time. Because I was stressed and tired, I forgot to change the hour from one place to another. When I arrived, I was just on time to catch the flight. God took care of me and my babies. This was another blessing.

Before this trip, my husband and I were thinking about what to name our unborn baby. We wanted a name with two vowels together and we decided to name him Isaac. I will never forget that experience, especially because now I have a cell phone that can change the hour automatically.

Linda Chacon is 48 and originally from El Salvador.

Memory of My Best Friend

THAN THAN, ST. PAUL, MN

Memories come to mind. I remember when I went to high school. This time I was fifteen years old. I play soccer at school but I am not good. I play midfield but I score more forward. My friend says, you're good at sports. I tell him, bro, I am not good at sports. I say, thank you bro. Then he kept telling me and talking bad on me. I was mad at him and punched his face, then I go home. When I'm at home, I still think about when I punched his face. After, I think I fell asleep. I woke up at morning. I brushed my teeth and after that I went to school. I saw him and apologized to him. I'm sorry, my friend. He said, it's ok my friend. Then I went back to class. On memories day, he tells me, you remember when you punched my face, bro? I said yes. He told me, don't forget all your life when you punch my face. I told him I never forgot all my life. He told me, I think I will be your friend forever. After I left this school, I never saw him again. I never forgot him.

Than Than is 21 and originally from Thailand.

I Love Apples

HANAD MOHAMED, MINNEAPOLIS, MN

When I was young, I lived in Somalia. I liked to eat apples but I never had enough. Then I came to the United States. The first week I ate a lot of apples, like three a day. In the months since then, every time I went into the grocery store, I bought a red apple. I still like it. It is my favorite fruit. It is found in different colors like green, red, yellowish, and golden colors. Apple fruit can be consumed daily. A famous saying is "An apple a day keeps the doctor away."

Hanad Mohamed is 44 and originally from Somalia.

Memories with My Friend Benito

MANUEL SANCHEZ, MINNEAPOLIS, MN

I came from Ecuador in 2007 to Chicago, Illinois, USA. My brother-in-law Luis received me in his apartment. I lived there for one year. My first job in the USA was as a line cook at two restaurants. One restaurant was called Rud Criss. I had two jobs at that moment.

Then I decided to move to Minneapolis, Minnesota. I had experience cooking, so it was easy to find a job. I found a job in Minneapolis at a steakhouse. There was a man from my country, Ecuador. His name was Benito. He showed me all the things from the restaurant. At the end of the night, we used to take the same bus to get home.

The time passed. One winter night, we were waiting for the bus. At the bus stop, it was so cold. We were not wearing scarves that night. Suddenly, he put his tongue on the metal of the pole holding the bus stop sign, it stayed stuck for seconds. He pulled it away and said, "Ouch!"

We saw there was a piece of his tongue on the metal. The bus arrived and we went home.

The next day, I saw Benito at the job. I asked him, "How is your tongue?"

He said, "It hurts."

I asked, "Why didn't you go to the hospital?"

Benito said, "It will be okay."

He could eat only ice cream and soups during that time. After one week, he got better. We were coworkers for three years.

I still live here in Minneapolis. I like it because there is not too much traffic and it is quiet. My friend Benito now lives in Ecuador.

Manuel Sanchez is 40 and originally from Ecuador.

USA

SHAR NAY MOO, ST. PAUL, MN

Flashback to when I started my journey to the U.S. I was happy because I never saw an airplane before and also wanted to see my friends because they already lived in the USA. I am so happy to see them, because they came to pick me up at the airport and I am happy to see they are here.

Shar Nay Moo is 21 and originally from Myanmar.

A Rooster's Tale

CLARE SIERRA, SAVAGE, MN

Growing up, I lived with my family on our farm, which was south of Decorah, Iowa. It was a noisy place because our three roosters crowed night and day. I'd wake up in the middle of the night to a chorus of cock-a-doodle-doos.

Our trio of roosters each had their own personality and each had their own territory. Cornelius, the meanest of the lot, lived in the barn. The other two occupied the hog house and the garage.

Cornelius did three things really well. He strutted around, showing off his long, white, beautiful tail, he crowed a lot, and he courted the chickens. The chickens were very productive after a visit from Corny.

My sisters and I lived in fear of him. We'd be chasing him for fun and he'd do an about-face and attack us, leaving claw marks on our faces and arms. Finally, we got fed up with Corny. He'd watch from up high in the rafters of the barn and could see outside the barn doors. He was always on patrol during the day, but at night he would sleep on top of the cattle chute that ran out of the barn. One August night at midnight, my sisters and I snuck out to the barn. I reached up and grabbed Corny by the tail. He was so startled that he ran off squawking, and I was left with a fistful of his tail feathers, his pride and joy.

The next day I went off to college. We didn't know where Corny had fled to, but we thought up many possible scenarios. He could have died and gone to heaven, where he spent his days pecking people. Or, his tail could have regrown but not to its previous glory. Or he ended up in the stew pot.

And that is the end of my rooster tale.

Clare Sierra is 65 and originally from Decorah, IA.

Deer Accident

ABDI SALAT, ST. CLOUD, MN

A deer hit my car in 2017 when I was going to work in the morning at 2:20 a.m. I saw a deer on my driver's side. When I saw it, I started to drive slowly. The deer jumped to the front of my car and hit the front light and bumper. When the deer hit my car, I pushed down the brake and held the steering wheel with both hands. I was still in the car and I was thinking of standing outside, but it was a two-way road and it was narrow. There was no space to pull the car off the road. I called the police and the police came and took my license and insurance information. After that, I drove slowly to the parking company close to the road. I thanked Allah for saving my life.

Abdi Salat is 33 and originally from Somalia.

Unforgettable Place

HAY DREE, ST. PAUL, MN

I used to live in Karen State. This is a beautiful place. I had my house there and I also had a paddy field to farm near my house. There is a river that

I always went swimming in. That is a small river. There are a lot of mountains.

Sometimes I followed my father and my brothers when they went fishing. Every evening, my brothers, my friends, and I went to the forest and brought some equipment for hunting rats and birds with slingshots. Every morning, my father went fishing and he got some fish for my siblings to cook and bring to school for lunch. We shared our lunch with our friends and they also shared their lunch with us. Every weekend, we went to the forest to hunt the birds and sometimes we went fishing.

I enjoyed being there in Kawthoolei. I would like to be an architect and I plan to build beautiful houses there. I plan to go back there and live there and help my villagers. I love that place because that is my childhood place.

Hay Dree is 21 and originally from Kawthoolei (Karen State).

Valorous

THAT THAT AUNG, ST. PAUL, MN

I was once valorous when I saw a burglar. At that time, my family were all asleep. I was not sleeping and while I was using my phone, I heard a sound in the living room. I was too afraid to go to the living room, but I went there after I heard the sound no more. However, the burglar was gone and he had stolen our things such as our TV and my computer.

That That Aung is 21 and originally from Myanmar.

My Life

BIPLAB SARKER, NEW BRIGHTON, MN

My name is Biplab Kumar Sarker. I was born in 1978. I went to school and passed the secondary school certificate (S.S.C.) in 1993. After that, I got admitted to the Agriculture Training Institute and passed the Diploma in Agriculture in 1998. Later on, I joined a high school as an assistant teacher. At that time, I completed a Bachelor's degree in Agricultural Education. In 2004, I resigned from my school job, and I got a government job as a Sub-Assistant Agriculture Officer. That year, I got married.

I came to the USA in 2016 first. After that, I started work at the Electramatic company, but I didn't feel good. I always felt worried about my family and job. As a result, I went back to my country in 2017 and joined my government job again. After some days, I didn't feel good about my green card and opportunities to live in the USA. So I came to the USA again for the second time in 2018. After one year, I prepared a visa for my family, and I went to Bangladesh to bring my family in 2019. Finally, we came together to the USA on March 18, 2020.

Biplab Sarker is 43 and originally from Bangladesh.

Car Accident

MUSE DINI, ST. CLOUD, MN

When I was driving my car two years ago in Waite Park, I came to a four-way stop. I stopped and then drove. Little did I know that the other driver didn't stop. He bumped into my car on purpose. Then my airbag went off. I hurt my chest and had a hard time breathing. The other driver wasn't hurt. He had two children in the car, but they weren't in car seats. He ran with his two children and called someone to take them immediately. Later on, the police came. No cameras were found in the intersection. No witnesses were found. The other driver said that he had stopped at the four-way stop so neither of us got a ticket. My insurance paid $4,000 to have my car fixed.

Muse Dini is 47 and originally from Somalia.

Favorite Season

EH MU, WORTHINGTON, MN

I am from Burma. I came to the USA on February 2, 2009. I have lived almost twelve years here, but I like the summer season the most. When the cool season is gone, back to the summer. It is a happy time because we can go out to the park, play with kids, and we walk around the town with kids.

We go out with friends and bring food. We share their food. It brings back where I came from. Summertime is the best. A lot of fresh vegetables and fruits. That is why I like it. Every time I ate without vegetables, I feel like I have an empty stomach. Every time I ate with vegetables, my stomach feels full all day. That is why I like summer. In summertime, vegetables and fruits are cheap, and many kinds of vegetables are here for us to buy at the summer market. I like the summer market because vegetables are from my home country. We always used them too.

Eh Mu is 35 and originally from Myanmar.

Choices I've Made

IKRAN IBRAHIM, MINNESOTA

In my life, I've made many choices. Each of them are fun.

I moved to my aunt's house. I went to play with my cousins. So I lived in my aunt's house for seven days. One day, me and my cousins were bored. We planned to make a big cake. We started to make the cake. It was the first time we did cake, but it wasn't what we wanted it to be. We felt sad because the cake was burnt. After that we went outside, it was running day. We got to play outside 3 p.m.–5 p.m. That was a very fun day.

But now I miss them because we always played together.

Ikran Ibrahim is originally from Somalia.

Memories

STEPHEN GACH, WORTHINGTON, MN

I remember my relationship with my ox when I was a little boy.

My uncle called me after the ox name, he called me, *jokgeer*. So when I turned fourteen years old, his cow gave birth to little calf. It was the color he used to call me with. Then he was thanking the lord for what he was promised and he gave me that colorful calf as a gift! I thank my uncle for that special gift he has given to me. I like that ox and we have a good relationship. I gave him a bath to make its color white and cleaned. The ox loves me as I love him. We have a good relationship, I and my ox. I take care of my ox and have a very strong relationship. You have to have a good relationship with your ox as I do. I thank a lot my uncle, Ruot Luak.

Stephen Gach is 48 and originally from Sudan.

My Stories about the Police

BRENDA ROMERO, MINNEAPOLIS, MN

I was always afraid of the police. I was afraid that I would be put in jail, and so I prayed that I would never be put in a police car and never put in jail. One day, when I was driving to my job in Waconia, my tire blew out and I had to stop along the highway. Soon, a car with flashing lights pulled up. The State Patrol! I was so grateful when the officer took me in his police car, not to jail, but to my job! Later, I got help to fix my car, but the police helped me.

A few years later, I was delivering newspapers in my car, but when I stopped at a red light, my car stopped running. I called my sister, Esperanza, to help me, but she did not answer. Soon, a policeman came. He was very nice and tried to help me. He didn't ask me for my license or my insurance or my papers. He just helped me and asked me if I was okay. He pushed my car a long way into a church parking lot, a safe place, so Esperanza could come help me.

We don't have to be scared of the police. They help us. That is their job.

Brenda Romero is 44 and originally from Mexico.

Two Strangers Changed My Life Forever

NAWLAHHSERPAW (THOO THOO) MOODOH, WORTHINGTON, MN

I was two weeks old when my mother died. I was the youngest child in my family.

Due to the difficult situation, my dad gave me up and my aunty and uncle took me to their village and took care of me as their own. They taught me how to be good, strong, and depend on myself. They raised me as their own and led me the right way. "It hurts."

I remember once, we didn't have enough food to eat. We have only little cups of rice. Still, my parents share to our neighbors. My parents always pray for me and my family. They always told me when I get a chance to talk to them, "my daughter, always put God first in your life, pray over and over for your family, your kids, your neighbors, your country."

For two months, my mom is in heaven now. Her kind heart is still in my mind. If it wasn't for two strangers, I think I could not be on Earth, because my biological father gave up on me.

My adopted parents are my heroes. My adopted dad is still alive in my village and hiding in the valley because of the Myanmar military coup. Many conflicts are currently in my village right now. All villagers are hiding.

This is why two strangers changed my life forever.

Nawlahhserpaw (Thoo Thoo) Moodoh is 32 and originally from Myanmar.

What I Am Thankful For

LIDIA CAZARES, BROOKLYN PARK, MN

Two years ago, I lived an experience, I can say, of hope, strength, and miracle.

I started to feel a little pain in my left breast. Some days I'd ignored it, but I started to feel pangs, and my husband told me, you have to go to the doctor. I did go to the specialist and they gave me a sonogram. After a week, they called me to inform me that I had to go to the hospital to get a biopsy.

After two weeks from the biopsy, I received the terrible call.

They asked for me, and my body started to shake. I remember they told me, "We have your results from the laboratory and you have breast cancer." I couldn't listen. I didn't know why my ears couldn't feel any sound. After a long time, I started to cry and cry and decided to call my husband and tell him the news. I know he cried, and I didn't want to tell my kids, but my husband convinced me to give them the terrible news.

In the beginning, I just told my two older kids, they were devastated but they didn't demonstrate it to me. I know they suffered a lot but they were very strong. I felt that I would die, all the time I said it to my kids, to everybody. But my husband, my kids, my family, and friends started to say, "You won't die. You are a very strong woman and you believe in a powerful God."

And yes! I started to think differently and I talked with God and I said,

"If you give me the life that you can take away, I can tell you thank you for the family that you have given me."

I started to feel different and I just was grateful and never grumbled.

In the beginning, they just told me they have to remove it, but they didn't tell me about plastic surgery. After one month, I had to go to the surgeon because she wanted to talk to me, and she told me, "I have good news for you; you are a candidate for reconstruction. I will remove everything inside and the plastic surgeon will reconstruct your breast."

I am still in treatment that causes loss of hair and fatigue, but I am alive and I am grateful to my God, family, and friends because they never left me alone.

Lidia Cazares is 50 and originally from Guatemala.

Our Road to Happiness

PLACIDO OROZCO GARCIA, ST. PAUL, MN

I am from Petalán, Mexico. I have three sons and three daughters. My family came to the U.S. on May 14, 2005 to look for good jobs and a good future. I started to work for a lawn services company. Eleven years later, I started my own gardening and snow removal business. My business has been running for more than five years. My sons and daughters have all finished high school and are working. My family is very happy in Minnesota. We love this country!

Placido Orozco Garcia is 60 and originally from Mexico.

Bus Fare Lesson

FARAH MINHAS, COLUMBIA HEIGHTS, MN

I came to the USA with my young children. As they started school, I started going to the adult education center. Things were different and new for me. I remember going to a function with my children. We got on the bus, but I did not have bus fare in change, so I put ten dollars in the machine and waited for the money to be returned. The driver told me it's gone; you must put in the right amount of change. I was sad, I reflected that if only I had coins with me, I wouldn't have lost money. However, we arrived safely, and my children had fun.

As time passed, I opened a licensed day care and went to evening classes at the education center. I am happy, and I give full attention to my day care. I listen, hug, and share love with each one of my kids. Life goes easier now.

Farah Minhas is 50 and originally from Pakistan.

Memories

TA MWE HTOO, ST. PAUL, MN

I remember when I was a child, me and my friend were playing kick ball every afternoon. And sometimes we played different things. We have a different kind of game for every single month. Sometimes we went to the jungle where we go eat under a cave and if we found a bird, we killed it.

Ta Mwe Htoo is 19 and originally from Thailand.

My Happy Life

SEIDA USMAN, MINNEAPOLIS, MN

I remember when I came to America from Saudi Arabia for the first time on November 2, 2012. I lived in Saudi Arabia for sixteen years. When I arrived in New York City with transit, I was surprised. I saw many people in the airport. It was very crowded. People were running, trying to catch their flights. There were many big buildings and lights that I've never seen in my home country.

I was happy when I got the chance to go to America. After my three-hour flight from New York, I arrived in Minnesota. I was so happy. I saw my family for the first time in sixteen years! The first time I saw snow was the first day here in Minnesota. That was a very special day for me.

After that day, I started a new life in Minnesota. I can remember when I started at the Columbia Heights/Fridley Adult Education Center. I was happy when I learned the English language. Then I started my job.

I am very happy now because I am with my family and I have two good jobs.

Seida Usman is 41 and originally from Ethiopia.

The Huong River

NAM QUOE TRAN, LITTLE CANADA, MN

To me, one of the most beautiful places in the world is the Huong River, a little river in my country of Vietnam. I used to go swimming there with my friends after school when I was a little boy.

Nam Quoe Tran is 48 and originally from Vietnam.

My Favorite Season Is Winter

CHRISTIE LATRAILLE, ST. PAUL, MN

During the winter season, I wanna sometimes have a get-together on Christmas Eve at a hall or ballroom, or even rent a church for my entire family and friends, and all the second cousins to get together like a reunion. I been trying to do a headcount of all my second cousins, including my parents, nephews, sisters, including step-brothers, all of my two sisters' nieces and nephews, and all of our ex-boyfriends.

My activity for leisure in the winter is roaming around outside in a heavy winter snowstorm while wearing heavy boots, high-class snow pants, and a matching jacket with a matching hat. A Tommy Hilfiger outfit. Beautiful areas that I intend on going to in the winter are areas that have a lot of trees, recreation parks, or areas on busy streets with a lot of lights.

Highland Park and Ford Parkway are nice and

I notice all the differently shaped snowflakes while daydreaming and admiring the heavy snow. The best times in the winter season are around December 19–January 14 and March 1–13. The wintertime helps out with my asthma and my lungs, and being outside. Recreation helps, but being inside, I need a window open.

Christie Latraille is 41 and originally from the United States.

A Bad Fall

AYAN ISSE, WAITE PARK, MN

When I was nine months pregnant, I went shopping and to the laundromat. When I came back home, I fell down on the ice in the parking lot of my apartment building. Then I felt pain. Someone in my family picked me up and took me to the hospital. When I arrived at the hospital door, my baby started coming out. I was happy that my baby came out safely.

Ayan Isse is 33 and originally from Somalia.

The Ice House

WAHNITA FELIEN, MINNEAPOLIS, MN

Journey with night stars, silvery moon, ice crystals tingling.

Moaning cries from ice cracking, crunching with each step.

Underfoot, a loud thunderous roar, (The big one) ice smooth as glass

Ripped with fractures in all directions, excitement, anticipation, frightful awe.

Dim light, the moon's soft glow, a shadowy form in the distance. A little

House, sturdy wood, comforting. The little house, The Ice House.

Promises, promises, promises of fresh fish, tasty crappies, or delicious walleye, savory

Aroma, walleye, sauteed in butter and spices. A delight to the palette.

A light glowing in the tiny ice house window, anticipation rising, closer, closer, nearing

Our journey's end, or perhaps only our journey's beginning?

Wahnita Felien is 77 and originally from Preston, MN.

They Took Our Country/*Dhulkii waa lala waregey*

SULEKA AHMED, ST. PAUL, MN

As we know in Somalia there is a group of people not controlled by the government. Some other people don't agree so they started to flee to the next country. They were looking for a safe place to maintain their life and family. One family moved in the middle of night, mom and dad with three kids, they didn't have anything to eat or drink. They arrived in the new city Kismayo, the kids passed away, the two parents became weak from malaria. Dad was the one who worked in a small business. Mom was a housewife. After a few weeks they heard city people say, we're scared to come, new people may come and control us. So they fled to Kenya. Mom died in a boat, Dad landed in a new land but he became mentally ill, all day he called his kids and his wife. He liked to work with water to supply houses, then he got served food.

They still make war in our country. We recommend stopping supporting them and servicing our community.

Suleka Ahmed is 51 and originally from Somalia.

From There to Here: Journeys to the U.S.

Featured Author

Nelsy Bruns

PERHAM, MN

I am Nelsy Bruns of Perham, Minnesota. I am from Colombia where salsa is not eaten; it is danced! I am a daughter of Ramon and Dolly Montoya. I have ten siblings. From my mom and Grandma Rosmira I inherited love for God, family, and traditions.

I didn't go to university for long. I think passion is very important. I worked in Colombia for 26 years, where I was a purchasing manager.

My favorite hobbies are reading spirituality books, traveling, fishing, and swimming. I love cats. I like to live quietly without grudges. In my spirituality, I have learned that happiness is within us and doesn't depend on anything external. Life is how each one decides to look at it, and I have decided to see more beauty.

From the USA, I learned to have a passion for the art of painting, writing, and tennis shoes. I like to show who I am. That's why I go through life simply. For me the most beautiful thing in every human being is inside of the heart and not the wrappers.

I consider myself a good daughter, mother, sister, friend, and wife. I like to be loyal. I enjoy being consistent with what I say, with what I think, and with what I do. I chose "Tears of Blood" for my writing because I want to show reality.

Thanks to those who are working hard on this project, helping us to discover the best of us.

Thanks to Juanjo, Edward, Leah.

God bless the United States of America.

Tears of Blood!

People cannot imagine how it feels in a country where we weren't born. We've abandoned our families, houses, jobs, friends, and pets. English isn't our native language. Often, people make fun of us. English isn't a piece of cake. It's normal to make mistakes. Not speaking fluent English isn't synonymous with ignorance. If a gringo babbles one Spanish word in Colombia, he's a hero. We're proud that he spoke one word, but some Americans get upset if you don't speak English well.

When I looked around, I felt empty and regretted my decisions. I asked God for explanations. Were you wrong? Did you forget me? I often asked if I had misbehaved to deserve this. I was sad. My eyes were red with heavy tears. I cried so much that I felt I was going to bleed out. I calmed down and remembered free will. I had made my choice. It was my fault.

I felt guilty for that decision and for easily deluding myself. I blamed loneliness and promises made. Maybe that man felt lonelier than me when he made promises. Perhaps in the midst of his selfish desires, he forgot that he should treat her in the same way that he conquered her, with sweetness. I wanted a magic wand so this wouldn't happen to other women. The government needs to make laws to protect immigrant women who come here to marry. If you're going to bring Latin American women here, respect them and offer love, affection, humor, and joy. Don't humiliate, hurt, or touch them with the petal of a flower.

Every American who sees an immigrant should look at him humanely and understand that everyone has a mission or a cross to carry and dreams. They're not going to steal anything, so leave the inappropriate jealousy. Getting here wasn't easy. It would be good to not be seen as usurpers or thieves. We've shed many tears of blood and have paid the price.

Many ask, if it's difficult, why are we here? Why don't we leave?

Because America offers opportunities and security for everyone.

Thanks to my husband's patience, to my teacher Leah Hamann for inviting me to write. I love writing. I dream of writing books and making movies. God bless you, the USA, and my son, Juan Jose Arcila, my inspiration. I love him to infinity and beyond.

Nelsy Bruns is 55 and originally from Colombia.

From Casablanca to Minnesota

SAMIRA ABDOUNI, RICHFIELD, MN

After fourteen months of waiting and patience, my U.S. visa finally in hand, passing by different steps, I finished by getting the interview appointment in the Moroccan consulate of U.S. in Casablanca. It was a long journey with a lot of stress and hope to join my husband and to live as a normal family with our child.

I got my visa in February 2021, the flight planned in May to keep everything right in Morocco during my absence, but our flight was canceled twice due to COVID so we changed it to April. It was so hard to leave the country, the family, and my original world. The change was not easy but when I thought that we would be with my husband, the ideas changed and everything became clearer and easier.

The day of flight, I didn't sleep. I was excited, scared, taking the airplane for the first time. Something huge for me and my three-year-old son. We had one stop in Washington for twelve hours, spent in the airport. We arrived in Minnesota after twenty hours from Morocco. It's the start of our new life. After more than three years, we are finally together, a small family which is going to live each moment in a different way, sharing happiness, sadness, dreams, and stability.

Minnesota is a totally different world for us. We were surprised by the nature, which is just amazing, the lakes, the parks everywhere. We spent a real moment of fun in spring and summer. We went to the beach, we did barbecue outside, did a lot of activities such as walking, playing tennis, bicycling, shopping, going to different restaurants... and the weather was good. It was a perfect beginning of a new life for our family.

In September, my son started going to preschool. It's a new and good experience for him. He loves it, he made friends, learned a lot, and that made a huge change in his personality. Then in October, we joined family school. It is a good opportunity for me to develop my English and my contacts, and have an idea of what's going on outside my small world in the U.S.

Parenting and ESL classes are so helpful to improve and reach my dream which is go to college to continue my studies in computing. I believe that the best is yet to come, just work hard, be patient.

Samira Abdouni is 29 and originally from Morocco.

Gobbledygook

ACHALA CHAM, STILLWATER, MN

When I arrived at the airport in America, all I heard was gobbledygook. It sounded like something I was never going to learn. That was twenty-seven years ago, now I can speak and understand that gobbledygook.

Achala Cham is 45 and originally from Sudan.

A Life in a New Country

ANONYMOUS, LAKEVILLE, MN

In 2006, I decided to move to the U.S. It was a difficult decision that took me away from my beloved family and friends. I remember it was very hard to be in the new country and not know the language, but I knew it would positively change my family and my life. Therefore, I needed to learn the language, so I started to take ESL (English as a Second Language) class.

After a few months of studying, I was able to get my driver's license. During that period, I struggled to find a job that I enjoyed. It took me two years to find a stable job that was not for a temp agency. Everything was so new in my new home. I missed my country a lot! Being away from my country, family, and friends was tough for me. It took me a while to make new friends and adapt to the new country. After having some friends, a job, and speaking some English, my life became a lot easier. On the plus side, I was able to visit my county three years later.

I sometimes have to look back to all those memories when I face challenges in life to help me with self-motivation. I was able to overcome a large obstacle then and I am able to overcome the next obstacle that life gives me.

Today I am really proud of my decision and I feel very fortunate to call the "land of opportunity" my home. This place has offered many opportunities for me and my family. I truly believe that in order to be successful, we must have courage, determination, and work hard to reach our goals.

Thanks to Allah

HASAN GELATOR, ST. PAUL, MN

I was born in Hawassa City in Ethiopia. I have a big family of four brothers and four sisters. I finished tenth grade and went to Adama Science and Technology University to study construction. After that, I worked in construction.

I arrived in America on March 28, 2018. Everything was new and so difficult. However, my older brother lives here, so he helped me. I worked at Benihana from July 2018 to April 2021. Now I work as a school bus driver. Thanks to Allah for everything.

Hasan Gelator is 31 and originally from Ethiopia.

My Childhood Experiences

DAH MOO PAW, ST. PAUL, MN

When I was a child, I really loved to go to school. I was so excited to want to go to school. But the problem is I have to pay if I go to school. But when I was in my country, it was hard to find money and it was also hard to find a job. But my mom tries to find me money to go to school, because she says school is important to us. So then we make money, because of my mom, so I can go to school. On my first day of school, I was happy because I love school. I want to go to school in the morning like 8 a.m. then come back at 2 p.m. Sometimes they didn't give us lunch. I just have to wait until I get home and eat. They don't have activities or sports. I was so bored that the teacher only talked and we studied. I hated when we had a test. If we didn't pass, the teacher hit us with a ruler or made us clean the bathroom. I don't like school in my country much, because teachers treat students like that, so I don't like it.

Also I don't want to live in Thailand because it is hard to find a job. Then I hear some people talk about coming to the USA. I am so interested, because I want to start a better life and live a good life with my family. Then in 2015, I came to the USA. I am happy to live here because I can learn languages and also there is free school I don't have to pay for. I really love living in the USA but the thing I don't like is the snow.

Dah Moo Paw is 21 and originally from Burma.

My Life and Coming to America

HEI LER HTOO, ST. PAUL, MN

My name is Hei Ler Htoo, I'm from Thailand. Thailand is one of the most beautiful places in my life. I love to live there but my family doesn't have everything they need. Difficult to find a job. My family works hard to get money so we can go to school. In Thailand, if you go to school you have to pay money.

Coming to America is one of my biggest dreams. At first, my family didn't like America at all. After four or five years, they finally changed their minds, and we decided to come. I arrived in 2016. I came with my mother, father, my sister, and one of my youngest brothers. The rest of the siblings stay in Thailand because they have family there. My first year in the U.S. is really difficult. My sister and I went to school without a jacket or boots. At that time there was a lot of snow and it was my first time seeing snow. My sister and I missed our bus a few times. My first year in school was really difficult for me, I went to school without knowing English. I don't know how to speak English, not even one word. Hard to make a friend, food tastes so weird.

Then after a few years in the U.S., I tried to make a friend, and I tried a lot of different foods. Now I have a lot of friends and I love all American food. My favorite food is steak, pizza, and pasta. I graduated in 2021 from Humboldt Senior High School. After I graduated I decided to come to the Hubbs Center for Lifelong Learning. The Hubbs Center is for adults and it was the best school in St. Paul. This school is for everyone and free. The teacher is nice, making friends with people who are older than me is so respectful. Coming to the Hubbs Center is one of the best ideas, even though it takes a lot of time, I know it is worth it.

Hei Ler Htoo is 18 and originally from Burma.

Happy in the USA

SABLEWORK MENTESNOT, ST. PAUL, MN

I was born in Merawi city in Ethiopia in June 1995. I have four sisters and two brothers. My father is seventy years old and my mother is sixty-two. Both of them are fun. They go to church every day in the morning and the afternoon. So, our life is good.

I came to the USA on October 4, 2021. I live in a St. Paul apartment with my husband and our one-year-old child. Minnesota is better than Ethiopia because it has many lakes and the people smile a lot. When I finish English classes at the Hubbs Center for Lifelong Learning, I plan to go to college to study nursing.

Sablework Mentesnot is 27 and originally from Ethiopia.

My Life Story

NANG BAWK, ST. PAUL, MN

I was born in the village Sin Lum in Myanmar. My village is on the mountain, very high. I lived there until I passed the high school final examination. I moved to Myitkyina city. I went to Teacher Training School for one year and worked eleven years. When I was sixteen years old, my country had a civil war. Some people left the village for a better life. At that time, I had another job. I worked ten years. I came to my husband. He lived in Jade Land City. I lived with him for thirty years. I had three children. My husband died in 2012.

So my son called me and I came to the USA on September 17, 2018. I lived with my elder son's family. They have three children. Every day, I take care of them. They speak the English language. At first, I didn't understand, but now I understand a little because I learn English at Neighborhood House. I am thankful for the USA government and staff. Now I am learning English. English is very difficult for me, but I try to listen, to speak, to read English. English is very important for me.

When the children grow up and graduate and get a good job, I will be happy and satisfied. I hope my future will be good.

Nang Bawk is 74 and originally from Myanmar.

Coming to the United States

AALIYAH SEID, MAPLE GROVE, MN

On July 13, 2013, my family and I moved to the United States. We had to leave our country for many reasons. It took us a while to adapt because its all different food, schools, culture, and celebrations. We came to the U.S. because we wanted a new life. My mom went through many things that I never thought would happen, but thank God now we are here in the United States for a better future. It was worth spending a few days of darkness to get here, but also not everything is easy in this country. You have to earn a living. It does not matter that one is an immigrant.

We are all worth the same no matter what country we are in. You always have to do it. My biggest dream is to be completely healthy so I can live my life fully, work, and be independent. I want to graduate from college to give back just a little of all that life has given me.

Aaliyah Seid is 23 and originally from Saudi Arabia.

Coming to America

ANONYMOUS, MINNEAPOLIS, MN

I was born in Somalia. When I got older, I moved to the U.S. and started a new life in a new country and lived a different lifestyle. I got a job, car, and apartment, simple things. Some things were different, like the weather, because I had never even heard about snow ever before. So some things were difficult to get used to. But I think it was a huge success.

My Story

MEKA DAMTE, BURNSVILLE, MN

My name is Meka. I live in Burnsville, Minnesota. I have a husband. I have a son. I first lived in Ethiopia. I was a student when I lived in Ethiopia. Then I went to Dubai as a worker. The house I worked in was very busy. I had no rest. I worked for more than seven years, then I came to the United States with my boss. I did not want to return to Dubai.

Now, thank God my husband will help me a lot. Thank you very much. I am very happy. I could not speak English. I am learning a lot now. I am making a difference. Thank God first. Then I thank my teacher so much for helping me. Praise be to Allah, and may the Creator of all the worlds protect us.

Meka Damte is 31 and originally from Ethiopia.

Moving to Minnesota

ANISA USMAN, LAKEVILLE, MN

Moving to Minnesota in the wintertime was challenging because of the cold weather and snow. Finding warm clothes for the weather and walking on the snow was very difficult. Transportation in the winter was not easy because of all the weather conditions, which made it hard to find a job. I was new to the English language and it was confusing which made it difficult to communicate with people.

Although moving to Minnesota in the winter was challenging in the beginning, eventually I got used to it. I improved my English, made kind friends, and found a job to support myself. Minnesota is a nice place to live and I love it here.

Anisa Usman is 42 and originally from Ethiopia.

My Trip to the U.S.

FATOUMATA DIAKITE, BROOKLYN CENTER, MN

My name is Fatoumata, I was born in Guinea, a country of West Africa. On December 25, 2017, I met my husband in Conakry, Guinea. It was so great and lovely to talk about the process of getting married.

Next, he went and saw my family and my parents agreed with our marriage, and then my husband returned to the U.S. for processing of my visa application. After he got to America, one month later we started the process. We are thankful to God for his help. I was very worried about finding the visa because people said that an American visa is not easy to get. That time, I became very slim. But I'm grateful for my husband who didn't give up despite spending a lot of money. Second, I went to Senegal for my interview in April 2019. I spent one month there. On May 2, I passed the interview, and May 7, I got the visa and the same day I returned to Guinea.

On May 17, 2019, my religious marriage was done, and then I came to the U.S. on May 25, 2019. I remembered that day my family was with me in the airport, they were crying and I was too. Once in America, I got my first pregnancy and it wasn't easy for me because I was new. I didn't understand anything in English. It was hard to speak with people. But my husband brought me to the Adult Education Center in Columbia High School where I learned English, and now I manage in English. In all of this, I say the biggest thanks to the lion who is my lovely husband, for his bravery. Finally, I've two beautiful princesses. My husband and I live in peace and harmony with our children thanks to God.

Fatoumata Diakite is 21 and originally from Guinea.

My Life and My Family

LAY MOH, ST. PAUL, MN

My name is Lay Moh. I am Karen. I was born in Burma and I grew up in Thailand. I lived in Thailand around twenty-two years. Every day, I went to school and I studied with my friends and I felt happy. I like all my teachers. In 2012, I graduated from high school. When I finished high school, I became a teacher to teach the students at school. I taught at school one year and I studied nursing two years. On September 30, 2014, I married. Now I have one daughter and one son.

On July 24, 2019, I have to come to USA with my family. When I arrived in the USA, the first thing I saw was many people and many cars and many buildings and beautiful snow. I felt very happy. On October 25, 2019, I went to school at Roseville Adult Learning Center for five months, excited and happy to see my new teachers and new students. Sometimes I felt sad, because I can't speak English very well but I tried to speak, write, and read every day. On September 24, 2021, I went to Open Door Learning Center in Arlington Hills.

Lay Moh is 29 and originally from Thailand.

My First Month in the USA

ESMERALDA MEJIA, ST. PAUL, MN

My sister was feeling sick, and my daughter was also sick when we arrived in Anoka. We lived there only a week. My friend called me to come to St. Paul. Because my family was sick in Honduras, I didn't call my mom. She was in the hospital with my sister for one month. Every day, my daughter cried because she missed our family.

In the USA, everything is different from my country, especially the language. For example, one day at a gas station, I bought one card and said put fifty dollars on the card. But the cashier did not understand me. He said fifteen dollars. So I am so sad. I took the card and the fifteen dollars.

Esmeralda Mejia is 32 and originally from Honduras.

Arriving in Minnesota

EMEBET TEGEGN, ST. PAUL, MN

My husband and I won the Diversity Immigrant Visa program lottery in Ethiopia and got to come to America. I had one son at that time. I felt like I was going to a different planet and would never see my family again. When we got to America, it was winter. We thought that America would be like heaven, but that couldn't be farther from the truth.

While America is a great country, it isn't heaven. The culture was very different, there was a language barrier, the weather was different. After nine months, we finally got a job. My husband got a car, but I took the bus to go to work. The first time I went to work, my husband told me to never take rides from anyone, no matter what. The first day, I got help taking the bus. The second day, I took the wrong bus. As time went on, more and more people got off the bus. I was confused because I still wasn't at my stop. I told the bus driver I was going to the airport. He said I was on the wrong bus. I told him I would take another bus and he directed me on which one to take. It was extremely snowy and windy that day. I got off the bus and could barely walk.

I waited for more than one hour. My fingers and ears were freezing. I really thought I was going to die. No one bothered to help. Back home, if anyone saw you outside in the rain, they would tell you to come in. I decided that I would ask for a ride. I waved my hand for the next taxi that came by. He stopped for me and I got in the car. I saw that he was Habesha Ethiopian, like me. I started crying and told him what happened. He took me to the airport. I asked the driver how much for the ride and he told me don't worry about it.

Even once I arrived at the airport, I couldn't find my store. I didn't know where to go since it was only my second day. Eventually, I found my store, and once I saw my manager, I started crying. It was 9 a.m., even though my shift started at 5 a.m. I'll never ever forget this for the rest of my life.

Emebet Tegegn is 45 and originally from Ethiopia.

First Day in the United States

TALISO OSMAN, WAITE PARK, MN

When I came to America, I was tired because the flight took a long time. Some volunteers waited for me at the airport. I saw the volunteers and I cried because I was very tired. They hugged me. After I came to the house, I was happy and grateful that I could sleep in a safe place!

Taliso Osman is 32 and originally from Somalia.

My Mother's Journey

SHUKRI MOHAMUD, MINNEAPOLIS, MN

My mom's name is Ibado. She is sixty-three years old. She was born in Somalia, and was one of fourteen children. The kids looked after the animals and the farm. They didn't go to school.

When my mom was fifteen, she moved to Mogadishu. Here, she went to school. At eighteen, she got married to my dad. They had eleven children, but only seven kids grew up. My parents had a food shop and the kids all helped out. Unfortunately, my dad died when I was nine years old.

My mom had the shop until we left Somalia. In 2006, there was war between the Somali government and a terrorist group. We went to a refugee camp. There was no water, no hospital, no beds, and nothing except for what we brought. We lived there for five months and then went back to the city.

My mom opened her shop again and we went to school when it was safe.We stayed in Somalia for four more years and then we moved to Kenya. At this point, I was eighteen. Somalia was unsafe again with war, so we left.

We went to a refugee camp that was aided by the UN. Got a house, water, food, blankets, and more. We lived in Kenya for four years. Mostly, we stayed home. We didn't like it there. Sometimes people got sick from the mosquitos. It was malaria. I had a cousin who died in Kenya. She was only twelve years old.

The UN asked the United States if they would take refugees. When the United States allowed refugees to come, my mom asked if our family could go. We waited two years until we could leave. When it was our turn, all the adults and teenagers were interviewed by the UN. After the UN was done, we had two more rounds of interviews with people from the United States. We waited a year between the interviews from the United Nations and the United States.

It was about two more years before we actually left Kenya and went to the United States. There was my mom, brother, two sisters, two kids, and me. We landed in New York, but I thought we could've been in China. We saw so many different kinds of people. We stayed one night in a New York hotel and then went to Pennsylvania.

Shukri Mohamud is 28 and originally from Somalia.

My Journey to the USA

LIIA LAPSHIN, ROSEMOUNT, MN

My life was good in my home country. I lived in a beautiful village in Transcarpatia, Ukraine. I was a student in the medical university and had a clear plan for my future, but it all changed.

I came to the USA in April 2021. It was a happy and difficult journey at the same time. I came here because my fiancé was living in the USA. It was terrible when we were living in different places in the world, so I was happy to be together with my loving fiancé. While I was happy about moving near my fiancé, my family, friends, and plans for the future stayed in Ukraine.

The technical aspect of my journey was easy, but emotionally it was difficult. My journey to the USA was my first trip on a plane. I was scared and had no idea about traveling by plane. I was alone and had to be brave. In total, my trip lasted nineteen hours. I was tired and exhausted, but the journey wasn't as scary as I thought. I arrived in Minnesota on April 25 at 10:30 p.m. I was so happy to see my fiancé and hug him.

Now, I live in the USA. Of course, I miss my parents, brother, sister, and my friends. But I realize that now my family is here, it's me and my husband.

Liia Lapshin is 23 and originally from Ukraine.

My Life

JOSE GUERRA, ST. PAUL, MN

My life in Mexico. I was very happy, because in Mexico are my friends Daisy, Sergio, and Renato. I miss you guys.

My dog, Bear. This dog is very, very beautiful!!! My black cat, OMG only my life, he stayed in Mexico City.

But my new life in the USA is very good, for now l have a new job. This work is very good!!! New history in this city.

Maybe new friends, need more time for my new life in the USA.

Jose Guerra is 25 and originally from Mexico.

My Story

PAH KYAT, ST. PAUL, MN

I would like to tell you about my life. I was born in Burma and my family still lives there. I have two brothers and two sisters. When the war started in my country, I was separated from my parents and moved with my grandma to a refugee camp in Thailand. While I lived there, I went to school, but didn't graduate. I studied different subjects such as English, Burmese, and my main language, Karen. When I was nineteen years old, the United States government welcomed Thailand refugees to immigrate to the United States of America. I told my grandmother and aunt I wanted to go to the U.S. and they said you can if you want, so I registered to go.

I arrived in St. Paul in August 2012. I went to an office that taught me how to use electricity safely. They also taught me how to count money and the different kinds of bills and coins. My caseworker helped me with many things. He helped me buy money orders for my rent. He told me to see a doctor for a check-up to see how good my health was. I really appreciate him.

I like the St. Paul community. There are a lot of fun places in Minnesota, such as the Minnesota Zoo, Como Zoo, the Minnesota State Fair, the Mall of America, and the Maplewood Mall. I also like to fish and hunt. I usually go hunting when it is small game season. I only hunt for squirrels.

Someday, I want my sisters and brothers to come here to live. When I talk to them, they say they want to live here like me because my country has a civil war and there are not enough jobs. They also told me they like snow and fall because they are beautiful.

I love St. Paul, Minnesota because there is help for our community and our education. I like my school and teacher because she helps us write. All Hubbs Center for Lifelong Learning teachers, all people in the United States and government, I appreciate you for welcoming me to your country and school. I have a good life in your country. I am married, have three children, work as a roofer, go to school four nights a week, and go to the gym three times a week. I expect a good future here. Thank you!

Pah Kyat is 29 and originally from Burma.

Hard Work and Dedication

RIGOBERTO PONCE JR., DETROIT LAKES, MN

Twelve years ago, I was brought to the U.S. for the second time with the purpose of a good life. I was born in California in 1994. My mother took me to her home in Mexico when I was one. My single mother worked hard and wanted the best for us. I became independent at eight years old by taking care of my youngest brother and household chores. Jahir knew he was loved and he didn't need to be sad without his father.

One Sunday, my mother took us to eat at our favorite restaurant. She said, "*Hijo, nos vamos ahir para los Estados Unidos la semana que viene.*" I was sad about leaving my childhood friends, my school, and most importantly my *abuelos*; they always taught me good manners and to stay educated.

We lived in Phoenix for a year. I had the worst days of my life going to school. I was in front of the class, not knowing English at all, getting introduced to the other students. Seven months later, we moved to California and lived with my uncle for a year. Then we moved to my mother's boyfriend's house. Jose treated us well. He said to always be a humble person. Do not get attached to material things; they come and go. Weeks later, he got killed. After his funeral, his sisters wanted everything that belonged to him: house, cars, even furniture. Mother didn't want to deal with it, so she gave them everything.

Mother found a job and a house to rent. Our new journey started from there. I learned a lot in middle school, where I got involved in after-school activities. In high school, I got involved in alcohol and other harmful drugs. I didn't care about my education so I dropped out in eleventh grade.

My daughter was born when I was nineteen. I always had a job but needed my education to get a better career. I made a wrong decision that changed my life. Here I am in jail.

All year I've been trying to change my life, so I decided to get my diploma. I'm working hard on reading, writing, and learning new skills. It's never too late to get our lives back on track. We all have the potential to do more than we expect. With dedication and hard work and faith, everything is possible in this beautiful life.

Rigoberto Ponce Jr. is 25 and originally from South Central, CA.

A New Chance at Life

ANONYMOUS, LAKEVILLE, MN

January 20 was the first day I set foot in the United States. That day was a long day for me since I applied for political asylum. They needed to ask me many questions and review all my information. The interviews lasted almost the whole day. I was very tired and sleepy. Some of the immigration officers were very bad. Eventually, the officer told me that he would return the next day to continue with the procedures. It was quite hard.

The next day, the officer who interviewed me the night before arrived and told me that they would take me to a detention center. There, a judge would decide if I stayed in the United States or returned to Mexico.

I spent more than a month in that detention center. There, I met many women from different countries. They all had different situations of how they had arrived in the United States. There were many sad cases. Some women shared they had lost a friend on their way to the U.S. There were women who had been waiting for more than seven months in the detention center without seeing their relatives or children. We slept in cold rooms. I thank God that where I was was not as bad as some of the other detention centers. I am thankful I was able to meet many strong women.

The days that I spent waiting for my immigration papers helped me to see that we are all human beings and that we all deserve a new chance at life. That's why I want to tell a little part of what I experienced when I arrived in this country. I'm glad that you are reading this piece of history. We all deserve that opportunity to share our stories. God bless the good people in all countries.

Coming to America

OLGA L., ROSEMOUNT, MN

I was born and married in Russia. My parents and brothers and sisters came to America in 2002, but my husband, children, and I came in 2006.

It was a long, hard, and difficult process. At that time, I had five small children. A lot of documents needed to be completed. The trip to the U.S. was long and hard. The car ride to Moscow from my hometown, Rostov-on-Don, is about 1,000 kilometers. From there, we changed planes four times.

It was hard, but we made it to Minnesota. We really like our new place of residence.

Olga L. is 47 and originally from Russia.

My Story

CESAR A. GELABERT, BROOKLYN CENTER, MN

My name is Cesar. I'm from Nagua, Dominican Republic. In 2005, I wanted to come to the USA for new opportunities. In the Dominican, I worked many hours every day with very little pay. The first year in Minnesota was challenging, because I spoke very little English.

I found a job that helped me learn about the country and make some money. The culture here is also very different from my country. A friend helped me get a job. My first job was working with Mexicans, who only spoke Spanish, but I wanted to learn more English. In 2014, I started taking English classes at Brooklyn Center Adult Basic Education Center. It has helped me so much, and there are many students from all over the world.

I'm grateful to God for getting me where I am today. Thanks to some friends who helped me. It was not impossible, but it wasn't easy. There is a phrase that says, "Wanting is power." You have a lot of power when you really want something. You can make it happen!

Cesar A. Gelabert is 44 and originally from the Dominican Republic.

I Love Minnesota

PEDRO FUENTES, ST. PAUL, MN

When I was in El Salvador, I lived with my family. We went to church together. I had a welding and electricity job. At the end of the year, my family and I went to the beach in the city.

In 2018, I flew to view the United States. When I got here I did not want to work ever again, but eventually I started working as a painter. I like sports a lot. I love soccer. I love this place a lot, too.

Pedro Fuentes is 27 and originally from El Salvador.

My Life in Minnesota

ANONYMOUS, APPLE VALLEY, MN

I came to Minnesota in 2002. At that time, I was very nervous because everything was new. I saw things I never saw before in my country. The weather is very cold in winter and the days are so short. The summer days are longer with more daylight. The fall is very beautiful, with changing, colorful leaves. The spring has very nice weather. Everywhere in Minnesota there are blooms with beautiful color. During my first year in Minnesota, I had a very difficult time learning how to drive and learning English. After a few years, my English improved and I can communicate better with others now.

I am very happy with my life now. I have a small family. My husband is still working and my son is in high school now. I have a better job; I work a part-time job that is not very hard for me and I have more free time for my family. Now I'm very content with my life.

My Family's Travels to the United States

VAN DANG, BROOKLYN CENTER, MN

I'd be happy to share my story about when I moved to the U.S. I came to the U.S. in 2014 with all my family members and with my hope for a better life. The first year, I felt confused about the language, culture, and weather… Because it was totally different from my life in the south of Viet Nam. I have a new life in a new country. I was so worried all the time that I could not sleep well. I lost five pounds in a month.

However, I believe hard work will help me achieve my goals. The first thing I did was find work and learn English. In the U.S., education is very important. I need to know how to speak and listen to English to help me find a good job. I really appreciate the U.S. because there are so many opportunities here for my family and me. My sons are going to college and they will get a good job next year. My husband has a job at an electric company in the U.S. even though he just speaks Vietnamese.

About myself, I dream about finishing school and someday getting my GED and a new job which I like. So I go to school every Monday and Wednesday and I often practice English when I have free time. I hope that I will be more confident when communicating.

I have many reasons for loving the U.S. I want to live here. I always tell my sons to think about their friends and relatives who live in their country. They do not have enough meals or many opportunities like in the U.S. As an immigrant, I hope that you will improve your English language and be available to learn new things every day and most importantly, never give up. Thank you to all the teachers that have been teaching us with their whole hearts.

Van Dang is 53 and originally from Viet Nam.

Coming to America

FATUMA OSMAN, MINNEAPOLIS, MN

When I came to America, I came first to Nashville. My life was so difficult. I was so all alone. I didn't have any relatives or friends. After five months, I started working in a Tyson chicken plant. A few months later, I moved to Shelbyville because the plant was there. I could not live in Nashville anymore because it was one hour to drive. When I moved to Shelbyville, my house was near my job. I could not get other jobs because I didn't know how to drive. I could not drive because I did not have a license. I tried first to get a permit. I was going to the DMV every other week. I went there ten times because I didn't know how to speak English. I didn't know how to read. It was so difficult.

Finally, I got a permit. I tried to learn how to drive after that. I worked hard at my job at FedEx. I carried heavy boxes. I also worked at Under Armour. I had two jobs. I tried my best. I worked every day. I needed money to help my family back in Kenya. I paid school fees for my sisters and my daughter. I succeeded in helping my family. My long-term goal is to be a business lady. I would love to have a business doing interior design.

Fatuma Osman is 38 and originally from Somalia.

Leaving and Emigrating

IBTIHAJ AL ZUBAIDI, COLUMBIA HEIGHTS, MN

We left Iraq; me, my husband, and my three kids, because of the wars and their suffering. We settled in the United Arab Emirates (UAE) for nearly twenty years. My kids completed their university studies in the UAE. Later, we immigrated to America without my husband because he was working as an engineer in the UAE, so he didn't get a visa.

The beginning in America was good for my kids because they studied English well in the UAE, but it was not good for me. First, there was the difficulty of language and also the separation from my husband. A year after my arrival, I joined the adult school. This helped me to learn the language somewhat so that I could understand others. I am still studying and got a job. Now, all my affairs have improved, and I am still waiting for my husband to come.

Ibtihaj Al Zubaidi is 61 and originally from Iraq.

Coming to America

FARIDA IBRAHIM, NEW HOPE, MN

When I was a child, I didn't know about the U.S. When I grew up and went to school, I heard my teacher talk about World War I and World War II. The Americans and Germans were fighting. Year after year, my mom told us that we had a lot of cousins in the United States. In 1999, they came to visit us in Ethiopia. They told us many stories about living in the U.S. Some were good, and some were bad. They told us that the United States is a big country, and it has a lot of people living there.

These are the positive things they told us. You have the chance to learn a new language. You can go to a great school. You have freedom. You can buy a nice house, and you can get a good job. It's a good place to raise your children. If you're a disabled person, the government will help you. But these are some of the bad things they told us. Children don't listen to their parents, because they listen to their friends. Some children join gangs and become out of control. When children become eighteen years old, they're considered adults so they don't think their parents' ideas are good.

When I came to the U.S., I saw that all the things my cousins told us were true and even more. There is so much opportunity here in the United States, so a person can become whatever they dream to be. I love America!

Farida Ibrahim is 34 and originally from Ethiopia.

The Bad Month

SHAMSO MOHAMED, MINNEAPOLIS, MN

I was sad because my family was far away. I was in America and my husband and my two daughters were in Kenya. I married my husband in 2003. At that time, I was staying in Kenya. My daughter was born in 2004. Another daughter was born in 2005. My son Mohammed was born in 2008. I came to the U.S. in 2009. I came alone with my son. He was two months old. My husband and two daughters stayed in Kenya. My brother sponsored me to come to the United States with my baby. I became a U.S. citizen in 2015. When I became a citizen, I went back to Kenya in 2015. My husband was driving a taxi in Kenya and his mother was taking care of the daughters. Then I stayed three months with my husband and children.

I came back to the United States and I have a little baby boy who was born after I visited Kenya. I started the process of getting my husband and children to the U.S. They were approved in 2017. But just after I got the application approved for the visa, the president of the U.S. said no immigrant can come to the U.S. from Somalia. I wanted happiness but the president said those words and then I felt sad. That was a bad month. But finally my lawyer helped me and talked to Senator Amy Klobuchar. She said, "Don't worry. I will talk to Kenya," and when she talked to Kenya, they sent the visa, and they brought my children and husband over to the U.S., which gave me the happiness that I always hoped for. I went to the airport along with my two sons and saw my husband. When I saw him, I felt happy. When I saw my two daughters, I felt so happy that I cried and they cried too. Now I live a happy life with all my children and husband.

Shamso Mohamed is 40 and originally from Somalia.

Journey to the U.S.

RICHARD AYEWONOU, COON RAPIDS, MN

Coming to America has been a big achievement for me. I never dreamed of coming to the U.S. because of my background, but God has blessed me. All my life has been challenging. I never grew up with my parents. They were too young when I was born. Both of them were students. They did not have what it takes to take care of a child. But my grandfather took the responsibility to take care of me. Unfortunately, he died two years after I was born. Then they took me to my great-grandmother, to a village in another country called Benin. And my parents lived in Togo where I was born. I did not see my father until I turned eight. I didn't even recognize him when I saw him for the first time. He came to the village where I lived and he returned the same day. After that, it took another ten years before I saw him again. For my mom, on the other hand, I first saw her when I was about twenty years old.

I didn't have anyone to put me in school until I reached the age of twelve. That is why I wasn't able to finish high school. Thanks to God that my dad won a Diversity Immigrant Visa program lottery. And he decided to bring me to the U.S. I don't know how my life would be without me coming to the United States. Being here, I have the opportunity to work and go to school. I have been blessed by many. I am so grateful for the United States. I came to the conclusion that it doesn't matter where you were born, how you were born or your background, God can bless anyone he chooses. I thank my family and all my teachers who brought me this far.

Richard Ayewonou is 30 and originally from Togo.

When I Came to the USA

SHENG LOR CHANG, MAPLEWOOD, MN

I came by myself. I saw many different people. I was very worried because I don't know how to speak English but I came to Minnesota and I was very happy. The first person I saw when I left the gate was my husband. I was very happy to see him. When we came home, I saw my grandma and grandpa at home, waiting for me. Finally, we had dinner together.

Sheng Lor Chang is 31 and originally from Laos.

My First Impression of the U.S.

LEONEL HERNANDEZ, ST. PAUL, MN

My name is Leonel Hernandez. My first impression of the U.S. was that the the streets are very clean

And I can ride the bus without fear, but here, it is very expensive to ride the bus.

Here in Minnesota, it's very cold and there are many buildings.

I feel happy because I saw my dad after eight years, I have the opportunity to know the snow, and

I am happy because I have my mother and my father together.

The people here are very polite. For example, when I ride a bicycle, the people give me the right of way in their cars.

Leonel Hernandez is 25 and originally from El Salvador.

I'm Coming Home!

FADUMO ABIKAR, BLOOMINGTON, MN

Hi, my name is Fadumo and I left my hometown (Africa). My first experience in America was bad. It was also really cold. In my hometown, it rarely rains and never snows. I thought I was never gonna last a day and just considered going back to Africa. After I got a job, that's when things started to go uphill for me. Now I live in a house with five adorable kids.

Fadumo Abikar is 46 and originally from Somalia.

When I Came to America

KHADRA WARSAME, MINNEAPOLIS, MN

I came to America from Somalia on January 22, 2020. It was very cold and snow was everywhere. I had not seen ice before because my country does not have ice. After I had been here for a month and a half, I started studying English at a school in Hopkins. I had a good teacher. Her name is Jill. She helped me to understand things about America very well. She taught our whole class how to take the bus. Also, she taught us about American holidays because she knew that I was new to this country.

I did not have a car and I did not know how to drive. My husband worked full-time, so nobody helped me when I needed to go somewhere. One day, I decided that I have to get a driver's permit, but at that time there was Covid-19 and everywhere the offices were closed. They said to make an appointment. I started learning and reading the permit book but it was very hard. There were times that I felt that I would never get my permit. Finally, I had success and I passed because it was very important to me to get a license. If I didn't have a license, I couldn't drive where I wanted to go. Now I can go to my job and get groceries without someone giving me a ride.

Khadra Warsame is 27 and originally from Somalia.

Minnesota

HERIBERTO CORTEZ RAMIREZ, WEST ST. PAUL, MN

When I arrived in Minnesota in April, it was cold and sunny. The snow had melted, making the ground soft and muddy. In Minnesota, I can see the four seasons. I like autumn because I can see different colors of leaves and trees in the cities' landscape. In the winter, it is colder when it is windy, but in January it is even more cold. The lakes are frozen and the cars can go on the lake for fishing. Spring is different every year. Some years are rainy and muddy, and some years are sunny and not very cold. I like the seasons.

Heriberto Cortez Ramirez is 42 and originally from Mexico.

Crossing the Border

ANONYMOUS, ROSEMOUNT, MN

I was five years old when I came to the USA. When I was five, my parents wanted to give me a better life in the U.S. They packed what they could carry which included a minimal amount of clothing. We couldn't even take food for our journey.

We walked day and night for three or four days. We only ate once, which was cold chicken. From what I remember, we not only did not eat much, but we had to drink dirty water. Thankfully, we made it alive. We arrived in the U.S. with no money and had to live with one of my older brothers in a little apartment. Even though things were tight, my parents manged to give me a good life. I was too young to understand at first, but now that I am older, I am thankful for what my parents did. Their courage has given me a good life. I went through a lot, but I have made it this far and will live a happy life.

What I Brought with Me

EDUANY RIVERA, MINNESOTA

I came to the Unites States in July of 2019 with my son. I packed documents, my clothes, and clothes for my son. I left behind my family and all of my things. It was hard because we did not know how to speak English. It was difficult to adapt to another lifestyle.

Eduany Rivera lives in Minnesota.

Moments of Resilience

Featured Author

Thiet Thi Tran

DETROIT LAKES, MN

I am Tran Thi-Thiet, but my nickname is Linda Tran. I was born in Vĩnh Long, Vietnam in 1982. I graduated high school and started working in business after school. I was introduced to my husband through his uncle, and we married in 2011. We lived apart for several years, until I moved to Minnesota to be with him in 2015. I am the only person in my family to move to the United States, but some of my husband's family live near us. I studied very hard and became a U.S. citizen in 2019. I work very hard, and I sometimes miss my family very much. However, I am happy to go to school and study English. I love my teachers and the friends I've made through school.

Thiet Thi Tran's Citizenship Story

When I first came to Minnesota, I felt so worried, because l spoke a different language and everything was new for me. Before I applied for citizenship, I went to school to learn English and things for citizenship.

I had my interview for citizenship on December 9, 2018, in Duluth, Minnesota. It was a very difficult drive that took four hours. When I arrived, I waited for thirty minutes. Then the man who interviewed me came in and I was afraid of him because he talked fast and spoke quietly. I asked him to please speak slowly, but he just looked at me with an unhappy face. I failed the interview because I didn't understand enough English. I went home and I was sad for a long time.

After about four months, I went back to school. Then I went back for another interview. When I arrived, I realized the interview was going to be with the same man! I was so worried because the man spoke very fast and quiet again. I tried very hard, and I passed! I was so happy!! When I called my parents in Vietnam, they were so happy, too.

It had been three years since I had seen my family, so I decided to take a trip to Vietnam while I was waiting for the oath-taking ceremony. I arrived at my father's home on February 6, 2019. I called my friend in the U.S. because she was checking my mail. She read a letter to me that said the oath-taking ceremony for my citizenship would be on March 3, 2019. I wouldn't be back by then, so asked my friend to go to the office and explain. Luckily, they moved my appointment to April 4, 2019.

When I was visiting Vietnam, I made sure I went during the Lunar New Year. The Lunar New Year is very important. We were very happy and smiled a lot. I went shopping with my family. We saw flowers, peach blossoms, and apricot blossoms. We went to a fireworks show and watched people dance in lion costumes in the street. We also went to the pagodas to pray. I loved eating candy, coconut, and vegetables. The next day, we slept a lot, then visited my grandma and my aunt. We brought gifts, money, kisses, and hugs for everyone. It was a great party!

Thiet Thi Tran is 39 and originally from Vietnam.

My New Life in America

HAWI JARSO, ST. PAUL, MN

When I arrived in the USA my life was very bad, but now it is very good. Some of the things I was lacking during the bad time was a lack of food, shelter, job, the English language, and comfort in this Minnesota weather.

I had to put all of my energy into getting into a better place. Unfortunately, I could not find a job that enabled me to pay all of my bills, so I continued to take ESL classes and work part-time jobs. There was a period of time when I had to go to work at 3 a.m. by bus. That was my life every day, in winter as well as summer, until I passed my driving test. My life was a long bumpy road.

After fighting for my life for so long, I finally learned English, found a better job, became a citizen, bought a house, and brought my family here from Oromia. Also, I am a mother of a nine-year-old child. I am so proud of my life in the USA. America, my child, and my teachers have taught me so much about myself. I am achieving all of my goals.

Moreover, I am taking classes with wonderful teachers and working to get further along in my education, so I can go to college for a Bachelor's of Science in Biology at the University of Minnesota. Ultimately, I would like to work with animals, maybe even be a veterinarian.

Hawi Jarso is 37 and originally from Oromia.

Black Ice Is Very Dangerous

OMAR DIRIYE, MINNEAPOLIS, MN

My name is Omar Diriye. I am from Somalia. I came from Malta to London.

After London, I went to New York. Next, I went to Alaska. In Alaska, I rode in a car to my new apartment. I saw black ice. When I walked to my apartment, I fell on the ice. I hurt my head.

Omar Diriye is 33 and originally from Somalia.

My Challenge

FERTUN ALI, WAITE PARK, MN

When I was married, it was difficult to get pregnant. After two years, I went to the hospital. After that, I told the doctor everything about my life. My doctor wrote a prescription and he said, "take one a day." After one year, I went to another hospital. He said, "Change your food. Eat vegetables, fish, and eggs." I want to go back another time to know about my health. Having children is important to me.

Fertun Ali is 32 and originally from Ethiopia

My Biggest Challenge

SUMAYA M., ROSEMOUNT, MN

My biggest challenge since coming to America has been getting used to the cold weather in Minnesota. I come from a country that has hot weather throughout the year. When I first came to America, it was February 2012, the worst of the bitter cold months. It was very challenging getting used to the cold weather. I didn't like going out or driving in it. It was a nightmare for me!

As the years went by though, I became used to it. Now, I am able to drive in the snow. And even though I still hate the cold months, I go where I want to go, and do the things I want to do. My body didn't like the change in the weather from warm, hot weather to freezing winters in Minnesota, but I have now adapted to it, and I don't get bothered by the cold weather.

Sumaya M. is 30 and originally from Somalia.

A Single Mother Navigating the World

RUKIYA SAMATAR, MINNEAPOLIS, MN

I came to Minnesota from Ethiopia seventeen years ago. I came with my five children and it was very interesting for me because I came when it was first snowing. I had never seen snow before in my life and it was also cold. I bought a winter jacket and boots and now I love wintertime.

My children and I struggled a lot, but we are grateful for everything we have. It was hard to learn a new language and go to work in a new country. You have to learn everything all over again. I used to go to school part-time, but I had to quit because I needed work. Today, I am focusing on school to learn more about English. My children are grown and are in college. I am also a grandma today. I am proud of my life and everything I have.

Rukiya Samatar is 52 and originally from Somalia..

Persuasive Writing

TIGIST MESFIN, WORTHINGTON, MN

How and why to eat breakfast.

Breakfast is important. Breakfast is important for life forever! Eating breakfast in the morning is important. Breakfast makes the stomach feel happy. It is necessary and healthy. It is important for human beings. Breakfast is the most important meal of the day.

Tigist Mesfin is 47 and originally from Ethiopia..

Difficulties of My Life

PI LA MU, ST. PAUL, MN

My name is Pi La Mu. I was born in Myanmar. I grew up in a small village in the countryside. I had a big family, but my parents were destitute. Most of the time, we didn't have enough food for the whole family. But when I was born, my parents were wealthy until I was five.

It all started when my younger brother was born, and a war started. Enemies flew over with jets, dropped bombs, and took a lot of prisoners. At that time, I didn't have a comfortable place to sleep, and I couldn't stay with my father either. During the war, an enemy shot my father, my house was burned, and all my treasures were stolen. At the same time, my mother also started having heart problems. After that, I had a difficult time living in the world and felt sorrowful in my life.

After I saw what my parents were going through, I took full responsibility to finish the harvest every year with my parents until I moved to a refugee camp. I lived a couple years in the refugee camp for studies. During the time I was studying in camp, I had a comfortable place to sleep and study. I lived in the camp until I moved to the U.S.

When I first immigrated to a new country, I hoped to earn money to support my parents and make them happy. But at that time I had the option to choose between a job or school. I had a difficult decision to make. I chose a job because I wanted to pull my parents out of a destitute place. When I got a job, I had difficulty doing things like talking to.strangers and wanting to go somewhere. But now, thankfully, I don't have difficulty living and going everywhere. I live better than before. But I regret losing my mother.

Pi La Mu is 36 and originally from Myanmar.

Life in a New Country

JUAN CARLOS ARIZA, MINNESOTA

Minnesota is the first place I lived in the U.S. The most important things I had to learn were English and the lifestyle of the USA.

When I first arrived here, I went to garage sales, usually people said things to me but I couldn't understand them and I only said yes. This was funny for me because I didn't know what they said to me. Another time, a police officer stopped me, but I didn't do anything wrong.

Juan Carlos Ariza is originally from Mexico.

Six Years Living in the USA

MICHELLE PINEDA, COLUMBIA HEIGHTS, MN

When I came to the United States I was a young teenager. I lived in Texas for two months at a shelter house, then finally came to Minnesota just a few days before my birthday. I was excited because at that time, it was snowing. I have never seen snow before, but at the same time I didn't like the cold weather. Cold is a big no for me.

Also it took me some time to adapt myself to this country because everything is so different from my country. Weather, food, the people, animals, traffic, everything is different! From the first day I came here to now, I still can't adapt. Sometimes I just want to go back to my country but here I have more opportunities for me and my son. So I'll stay here for a few more years.

Michelle Pineda is 19 and originally from Honduras.

Untitled

MI KIM, MAPLEWOOD, MN

I play golf with great zeal, though I still yearn for a better player to square down in golf. I wonder if I can go next year to South Korea. I feel stress when there is something I want to do and I can't and it keeps being postponed, plus my kids give me stress. When I get a good score playing golf, I get satisfaction. After a stressful day, I will hike or ride my bike then go to bed. I feel pity for my daughter who had a large dog for only a week and she took him hiking and he ran off, and for four or five days, she could not find it, but she did find him.

Mi Kim is 57 and originally from South Korea.

Trapped in a Trap House

MOLLY KRUEGER, ST. CLOUD, MN

I walked in "free" from out there

Smoked with fiends who never shared theirs

Moments turn to hours -no showers-

Hours to days and days to nights -no toilet paper-

Trapped in a Trap House!

Overdose after overdose, CPR, and Narcan just another vice

No safe room in sight -only mice-

Trapped in a Trap House!

I know the passage in

Yet it is not clear

Where is the "rabbit hole" so I can make it out of here?!

Trapped in a Trap House!

Everyone is a thief, a liar, a pervert for hire!

Yet we are moms, dads, sons, and daughters, Godsons but

Everyone's a liar

We have an army behind us yet we stand alone

Where is the way out of here?

No one has shown

I am trapped in a trap house, I just want to go home

I want to make things right!

I used to be a good wife

I just want to go home and make life right

This isn't supposed to be my life.

Molly Krueger is originally from Foley, MN.

How to Be a Good Person

JIEHUA LIN, BROOKLYN PARK, MN

Everyone has a specific character, some of them are positive, some of them are indifferent, and some of them are enthusiastic. Some of them are humble and some of them are honest. Because we have different upbringings, environments, cultures, and backgrounds, we are varied human beings, but everyone wants to be a good person. First we should have a kind heart. If we are able to help someone who needs it, we won't hesitate to do it. We have an idiom in China: "The donor's rose hand has a lingering fragrance."

Many entrepreneurs are rich and generous. They establish nonprofit institutions to help someone who needs help, like medical help and student scholarships. I think they are good people. Their lives are valuable and worthy.

Second, if we want to be good people, we should be honest and loyal. We live in a big community, we should be honest with our friends and coworkers. It is a good way to maintain great relationships. Even in the family, the spouses should be loyal to each other. It is a good way to protect kids growing up. Lots of kids are hurt by their parents' divorce. If we want to be good people, we should change some bad habits to adjust the relationship to keep the family harmony.

Everyone has a different view about being a good person. I think integrity and kindness are basic to being a good person. If you are a successful businessman or movie star, you can donate the money to society or a poor country. Even if we are ordinary people, we are still able to help someone. We can be a volunteer to serve the community.

Jiehua Lin is 40 and originally from China.

My First Big Challenge in the U.S.

SERGIO CENTENO, ST. PAUL, MN

I was born in Costa Rica. I lived in a little house on the mountain. I often went to the city to study and work. On November 8, 2020, I moved to the USA. When I arrived in this country I saw snow for the first time. I traveled to Duluth and Wisconsin which are so beautiful. I plan to travel to New York but first I need to study English, my biggest challenge.

Sergio Centeno is 23 and originally from Costa Rica.

The Cold Weather

QATRA ISSE, APPLE VALLEY, MN

The first day I saw snow was December 2003, at the airport when I arrived in the United States. I went outside so I could touch it. The snow felt so soft and watery. It was so pretty but it was so cold. I was surprised it was so cold. I was not prepared for that cold weather. At that moment, I did not have warm clothes.

I didn't think I could live here. I wanted to go back home. As it turns it out, I have lived here for eighteen years. Minnesota has become my home where I belong. Now, I have a beautiful family who grew up in the cold weather and love it so much!

Qatra Isse is 38 and originally from Somalia.

Not Hearing

TOBEY NGUYEN, ROSEMOUNT, MN

Not hearing has made my life very difficult. I was born prematurely in Vietnam. When I was four years old, I felt itchy inside my ears and could not hear my parents talk. When my dad brought me to the hospital to check my ears, they found that my left ear is deeper than my right. The doctor put headphones on me and told me to raise my hand if I heard a beep loudly. The next month, my mom and I went back to the hospital and I got two hearing aids. When I went to school, classmates talked loudly, and played together but I couldn't. My mom hired a tutor to teach me to study and to listen. I wished I could hear and talk like they could. I hardly talked to my family and friends because the hearing aids were so quiet.

When I was ten years old, my expensive hearing aids broke. I couldn't hear TV with Vietnamese subtitles. I seldom studied because it was too difficult to hear and understand. I came to America with my parents. I went to high school but I spoke little English and didn't have hearing aids. Then, my dad brought me to hospital and I got new hearing aids. I had free hearing aids and a microphone to use in high school. A doctor said I could get free cochlear implant surgery when I was eighteen years old. If I waited until after twenty-one years old, I would need to pay a lot of money for it. I was confused about surgery in my ears, so I didn't agree to it because it was scary. I was scared about the surgery but my parents convinced me to do it. When the surgery was done, I couldn't sleep for four or five days. When the pain was finally gone in my left ear, I got a new cochlear implant.

Now, my left implant works well but the hearing aids aren't balanced. I would like to get an implant for my right ear next year and to have free insurance for both cochlear implants. I hope both are balanced hearing in the future. Masks make it even more difficult to understand people. I currently use a transcription app on my phone to read what people say. Although I rarely talk, the app helps me to understand.

Tobey Nguyen is 21 and originally from Vietnam.

Persuasive Writing

JACOBO LOPEZ, WORTHINGTON, MN

I care about raising my children. When we go to the store, I caution my children how I buy food. We buy food because it is important for the family. Because in the future they'll live strong and healthy.

Jacobo Lopez is 36 and originally from Guatamela.

To Be UnQuiet

KELLI STAPLES, MINNEAPOLIS, MN

Healing is a major process

For the better

We think about putting bandaids over our bodies

We do not have to be clever

It happens in more than one way

It can happen in our mind or we can pick ourself up physically

To heal ourself

To Be unQuiet

Kelli Staples is 25 and originally from Cass Lake, MN.

My Many Challenges When I Came to the USA

KAILA TRAN, BROOKLYN PARK, MN

I was born in Vietnam. In my country I only spoke Vietnamese, and I spent twenty-five years of my life in my country with Vietnamese culture. In 1997, I finished my bachelor's degree in four years. I worked in the government for a year as an accountant. In 1998, I married and came to the USA. On my first day in Minnesota, I saw snow in the sky and everywhere in the street. I knew I faced a lot of challenges, and I would start everything over again.

My first challenge was not speaking English. I had little time to learn English in my country, but when I came here and I talked, nobody could understand me. I was embarrassed when I met people. My second challenge was the weather. In my country, all year long it is the same weather. It's hot! But in Minnesota, it's very cold! When I came to Minnesota in March, the weather was still cold. I just stayed inside my house. My third challenge was not having my driver's license. In my country, I just rode motorcycles, and now I need to learn how to drive a car. Anytime I need to go somewhere, I have to wait for my husband to take me. It's not comfortable. My fourth challenge was that I can't work the same job as in my country. My first job was assembly at an electronics company, and I was shocked!

All my challenges made me feel like I had a mouth, but I can't talk. I had feet, but I can't walk. So I educated myself, never gave up and now I feel like the USA is my home country. I am very grateful to the United States for giving me a wonderful family. Thank you teacher (Gary) for helping me learn more English. Thank you everyone for being in my life.

Kaila Tran is 47 and originally from Vietnam.

The Biggest Challenge of My Life

EMILIANO REYNOSO LEMUS, MINNESOTA

I am used to change, I lived in four different states in my country, always making new friends.

This time it's a little different, because I came to a place so far away.

This way of speaking is different from mine, and that is the biggest challenge I have right now.

Emiliano Reynoso Lemus is originally from Mexico.

Growing Up in a Bad Neighborhood

EH KAW SAY, ST. PAUL, MN

My name is Eh Kaw Say. I came to the United States in 2015. Something I remember is that when I got here, the first thing I wanted to do was to see the snow and play with it. I was living on the East Side in St. Paul and that was when I learned that life in the USA is not easy. Also, I learned that all the things that I thought before I came here were entirely different than what I imagined.

I grew up in a bad neighborhood. One day

I was moving to a new place. I got a lot of new friends. Sometimes in this crazy city, people shot and murdered each other. One time, I got robbed by three men by University Avenue right after the school bus dropped me off.

My life on the East Side was crazy. I saw a lot of things, you know, drugs and more. My friends were like "Try this, try that," you know, and I joined a gang. They did bad things that were crazy and you know, two of the biggest gangs had like a war in 2019. It was the worst year of my life. Two of my bros died by shooting. That's how I learned that people go too deep.

That's why my family moved to Willmar to start a new life. I learned that people always have a choice—to choose good or evil. I learned from my mistakes and I tried to make better decisions and choices. I was driving in South Dakota at that time and there was a tornado and my car was lifted off the road. Everything was dark. That's when I started to feel like I needed help from God. I started praying and the sky lightened up in only the place that I was gonna go. That's how I learned that God is the greatest.

Eh Kaw Say is 18 and originally from Thailand.

My Life-Changing Move

AYAN ISSE, APPLE VALLEY, MN

I'm originally from Somalia but came to the United States from Kenya in 2011. My move to the United States was difficult. When I arrived, the weather was colder than I was used to in Africa. I didn't know how to dress for the weather and didn't have the right clothing anyway. Also, I wasn't used to the weather changing so often, like it does here.

I needed a lot of help when I was first here. Every time I wanted to go shopping, I needed to ask for help. I couldn't get to places that I wanted to go because I couldn't drive. Even if I could drive, I didn't know where to go or how to get there.

Finding a job was another challenge. It is hard to find a job if you don't know English and don't have transportation, so I decided to go school to learn English.

After two years of struggling, I became homesick so I went back to Africa. When I returned to the U.S., everything became easier. My husband was back home in Kenya so I sent him a visa. He is with me right now and we have three beautiful kids. My husband works and I am a housewife and student.

Ayan Isse is 35 and originally from Somalia.

My Life

ABSHIRO MUHUMED, ST. PAUL, MN

I was born in Somalia on March 11. Somalia is in East Africa. I moved to a Kenya refugee camp with my family because of the civil war in Somalia. I have a big, very nice family. I have two sisters and three brothers. My parents still live in the refugee camp. When I was young I went to a very small, but fun school.

I came to America on November 13, 2014. At first it was very difficult. Now, I go to English classes at the Hubbs Center for Lifelong Learning. I start a new job tomorrow at Walmart. Life is not as difficult now.

Abshiro Muhumed is 40 and originally from Somalia.

Memories

JEREMIAH BAUER, BAYPORT, MN

I woke up today feeling like a fawn lost in the woods. Searching inside of my mind, realizing how big, dark, and lonely this world really is. Looking for memories, as this will help me feel better throughout the day. Sometimes lost as a blind squirrel searching for a nut, and it's difficult to find my way.

As the day grows old like the leaves on the trees change colors, I realize what is most important in this life, like the blood flowing through my veins. Remember the good memories as I get older. People and things fade and all I have left is myself. Like a fish in the river lets out one last air bubble as he fades as well.

Jeremiah Bauer is 36 and originally from Owatonna, MN.

My Challenge with Postpartum Depression

ANONYMOUS, BURNSVILLE, MN

After I gave birth to my third baby, I had postpartum depression. At that time I cried a lot, didn't like chatting with anyone, and just trapped myself in a room most of the time. Maybe it was because of COVID-19 and being stuck at home every day! In addition to the pandemic, I didn't get any breaks from caring for my baby.

One day, I went to see the doctor and told her that I had postpartum depression! The doctor just chatted with me. After my first appointment, she often called me just to check in and talk for a while. After my husband understood my condition, he spent more time with me. He also told me to do things that I enjoy, like going to school.

Slowly, the worst days passed. I'm so lucky for all the people who helped me!

Persuasive Writing

MARCH MOO, WORTHINGTON, MN

Why should I send my kids to school?

School is very important for my kids to get an education and to build their knowledge. In the future of their life, to be proud of themselves, to get a better job, and make good money. Also, I will be proud to be their mom.

March Moo is 33 and originally from Myanmar.

My Lost Friend

HODAN ABDULLE, EAGAN, MN

Asli was the best friend I ever met in my life.

Asli and I grew up in the same place in Somalia.

She was a self-confident person.

She was polite and pleasant.

Asli had a positive attitude.

She was kind to all people.

She told her friends funny stories.

People liked the way she expressed herself.

Asli and I sewed every day. We never argued.

I haven't seen her for twenty years.

In Somalia, we didn't use phones.

She wasn't a close family member so I had no one to ask about her.

Someone said she went to Europe.

I wish I could find her.

Asli is a nice person and I miss her alot

Hodan Abdulle is 40 and originally from Somalia..

Persuasive Writing

MUE TAH, WORTHINGTON, MN

Playground.

Playground is a good place and safe for the children. Playground has many fun things to play with. Children are very excited when they see the playground.

At the playground, children can play with their friends. They are sliding, swinging, walking around, and playing together. They play for fun, but they get a good exercise. They become stronger, physically fit, and healthy. If you want your kids healthy and stronger, take them to the playground.

Playground is very important for the children. All children love the playground.

Mue Tah is 48 and originally from Myanmar.

My First Day at a New School

NAME MO, ST. PAUL, MN

I will always remember my first day at school. I woke up early in the morning at 5 a.m. I waited for the bus at 6:10 a.m. and the bus came around 6:15 or 6:20 a.m. I get to school around 6:45 a.m. and go to eat breakfast. My school's name is Elsik High School. At that time, I was seventeen years old.

When I arrived, the school building was huge. I did not know where my classroom was. There were a lot of other students in the school. This school had 4,000 or 5,000 students. I saw someone I thought looked like a Karenni boy from my country. I had never spoken to him and never saw him before, but I was happy to see him. I called him and he came toward me with a smile on his face. Now, he knows me and talks to me. He asked me, "What grade are you now?" And I said, "I am in ninth grade." He told the teacher, "She is a new student and she doesn't know her classroom." Teacher said, "Follow me," and I followed her. She is so good. She tells me everything about the school.

I am going to school every day because I am happy to see my teacher and my friends.

Name Mo is 21 and originally from Thailand.

Persuasive Writing

RUTH BROWN, WORTHINGTON, MN

Filling your life with love.

In this world we need to live with love. Love, it is an emotion, feeling. With love we experience a joyful connection with everything! Life, family, even with the community where we live.

Fill our life with love. It makes us do positive things, and not think of doing bad things. We must continue looking for where to live in peace. Where our children can live happily. We can pretend that we are love, but if we do not feel it, we will not be in peace.

Take your time to do what makes you happy. Life teaches us to take advantage of time, time teaches us to give more value to life, and to fill ourselves with love.

Ruth Brown is 36 and originally from Mexico.

What I Am Thankful For

HAWA TRAWALLY, MINNETONKA, MN

I am thankful for my health and my family—for everything. I am thankful for being here today, even though these were difficult years for many people. Some people lost their jobs, and some people had Covid, and some people died from Covid. But I am thankful for my family and friends, for being healthy, even though these were stressful years for my mother in Africa. She lost her job and had Covid too, but every day I am thankful to Allah for making my mother feel healthy.

For me, every hour is great. And I feel gratitude in my heart each time I meet someone and look at his/her smile.

Hawa Trawally is 22 and originally from Guinea.

Terrible Days in My Life

ELENA PARUNINA, NEW HOPE, MN

This story happened in February 2014. I had examination days at the university. That day, I successfully passed the test on the architecture of civil buildings, and in the evening my sister and I went to the theater to watch a performance. That February day was very warm and sunny. It seemed that it was supposed to be a great and successful day for me, but I had felt apathetic since the morning, as if a stone was in my heart.

As usual, in the evening before bedtime, my sister and I called our mother, but she did not answer our calls that night. We began to worry, because my mother lived alone in another city. We tried to call her again the next morning, but my mother still did not answer. My sister decided to ask her boyfriend to take her to our mother in his car. The trip took four hours. I didn't go because I had a lecture and exam that day.

When they arrived, Mom did not open the door and my sister's boyfriend had to break the door down. When they entered, they saw Mom lying on her bed. They couldn't wake her up and immediately called an ambulance. When the ambulance arrived, they brought her back into consciousness and took her to the hospital. The doctor said that our mother had had a stroke. She was just fifty years old. When my sister called me and told me everything, I was attending a lecture at the university.

I felt so terrible about this news. There was a feeling inside of me like a bomb that was going to explode. I did not want to show my feelings to the other students, so I left the classroom without the permission of the teacher. He shouted at me that I was uncultured and not responsible, but I could not answer him. I cried all the way out of the university. I was very afraid for my mother's life, because strokes took the lives of my grandparents.

The next day, I went to my mother's city. She was conscious and felt better. But she did not remember anything that had happened to her. After five days, she was discharged from the hospital. Fortunately, Mom has fully recovered and is trying to lead a healthy life. But my sister decided to move to Mom's city to live near her so she won't be alone anymore.

Elena Parunina is 26 and originally from Russia.

When I Needed Help

JEYLANI ABDULLE, ST. CLOUD, MN

I need help when I need to do something I can't do by myself. I would like to talk about a little story that happened to me. A long time ago, I was flying to another country and I didn't have a ride to go to the airport. I was concerned about how I needed to get a ride to the airport. I definitely needed help at that time. Finally I missed the flight.

Jeylani Abdulle is 34 and originally from Somalia.

My Mental Health Way

VALENTINA ORTIZ, MINNEAPOLIS, MN

Let's talk about the elephant in the room. This "elephant" is very difficult, and it is depression. I think depression is like something on your back. You can't get rid of it; it is like a heavy, loaded backpack. I know this because I experienced depression, and I want to share my experience.

When I first came to the USA, in the beginning, I was really focused on finding a job, locating a place to live, and completing all the other necessities for staying alive. However, even though I settled into U.S. life nicely, I didn't feel well enough to enjoy it. On some days, I didn't even feel like getting out of bed. I realized I was experiencing depression. This caused a lot of problems in my day-to-day life, so I brainstormed for ways to feel better.

To solve this problem, I decided to find a hobby, and I worked on self-care. Now, two years later, I feel good about everything in my life here. These days, I still make time to relax and focus on myself. Experiencing depression pushed me to take my mental health seriously. This is my experience, but if you feel you are in a depression like I was, please get help and take care of yourself.

Valentina Ortiz is 24 and originally from Mexico.

Persuasive Writing

STARRY HTOO, WORTHINGTON, MN

The bullying makes me feel badly. Because, I never saw it in my life before. When I came here my son told me, "Mom, in my school my friends hurt me." I told him you do bad thing to them? He told me, "I didn't do anything to them." I told him, tell your teacher and your teacher will take care for this.

Starry Htoo is 29 and originally from Myanmar.

An Unforgettable and Sad Day

ANONYMOUS, LAKEVILLE, MN

I'm from Chihuahua, Mexico. I have lived in Minnesota since 2015. We are a family of five. We always travel to Mexico for the holidays to see family and friends. We were there for Christmas 2019. We were having a good time and everything was good. We got together the next morning to have leftover food and were having a good time.

January 1 is where it all started. We were at my mom's, and my husband went to see his grandmother at her house because that morning she was sick. He took my seventeen-month-old son with him. After a few minutes, I received a call from him telling me that an accident had occurred.

My heart started going fast. I was so scared. Everything went so fast, I saw my son vomiting and crying so hard, I held him in my arms, and we drove to the hospital. We almost lost him. He was hospitalized for four days there, but after an upper endoscopy, the doctor told us that it was something serious. Since he was born in the United States, he recommended we move his treatment here. We drove to El Paso, Texas to a children's hospital. He was there for another ten days. My mother-in-law had given him motor degreaser by accident, so his esophagus burned. The doctors had to place a nasogastric tube for him to be able to eat.

That was scary because everything was so new to us, and we didn't know what God had prepared for us. I had to travel to Minnesota with my son on an airplane for the first time. Thank God my sister traveled with me. My husband had to travel by car with our two other children.

Now my son has a gastronomic tube (g-tube) and sometimes is able to eat by mouth. We are almost two years into treatment. We don't know what God has in store for us. The future is unknown but I'm grateful that we still have our son with us. He is a happy boy. I keep praying for him to recover completely and have a normal life with his eating.

Since that day we haven't seen our family and haven't traveled to Mexico. I hope we can do it one day again. January 1, 2020: the saddest and most unforgettable day of my life.

Persuasive Writing

ANN IBRAHIM, WORTHINGTON, MN

Healthy food is very important to people. It makes them more healthy and fit and they can do their daily activities easier. When your body is healthy, that protects you from many diseases.

Ann Ibrahim is 35 and originally from Sudan.

The Civil War of Somalia

IFRAH WARSAME, ST. PAUL, MN

When my country started a civil war, I left my home in the capital. I lost my family. I saw people running, so I followed them, even though I did not know them. I asked them why everyone was running. They said they were running because of the gunshots. They told me to run far away. I ran to a barn on a farm in Afgoye. When I was sleeping, I heard gunshots above me. At night they stopped.

I saw my relatives in a car. I got in with them. After we had driven a little bit, the war started again. They shot at us and killed two of my relatives. Both of them fell on us. After that, we went to a place called Kismayo and I saw all of my family there. When everybody saw me they were shocked. They had been thinking for a month or more that I was dead. My dad was so surprised and happy I was alive, he could not stop hugging me.

Ifrah Warsame is 43 and originally from Somalia.

When I Moved to Minnesota

MUMINA KOCHI, ST. PAUL, MN

My name is Mumina. When I moved to Minnesota, I got very confused because I didn't know any person, or where to go shopping, where to go to adult school. I felt very confused. One day, I go outside to the park. The park is near my home. I walk to the park. When I walk, I see one woman. I asked, "Do you know where I go to do adult learning?" She said, "Yes," and showed me. I said, "Thank you for showing me." She said, "You too." The adult learning center is near my home. It took me nine months to find it. When I go to the adult learning center, I feel happy.

Mumina Kochi is 48 and originally from Ethiopia.

Persuasive Writing

MU AYE, WORTHINGTON, MN

Stop Germs.

Why do I write about stopping germs? Because every day I teach my kids how to do it.

It is important that everyone know about how to stop germs. Germs are things that can make you sick. Germs can get in your body when you breathe. Germs can get in our mouth from our fingers too. Germs are tiny things we can't see. Wash your hands with soap and water to get germs off. We wash our hands before we eat and after we go to the bathroom.

Germs can get in our body when we get a cut in our skin. We wash our hands after we play outside, touch animals, catch our sneezes, use tissues when we sneeze, and throw it into the trash. We wash our hands after we do something, touch something, catch something. We wash our hands any time when we are done

Mu Aye is 36 and originally from Myanmar.

From Guatemala to America

OSVALDO MARTIN CHAVEZ, ST. PAUL, MN

I lived with my family in Guatemala. I have three brothers and two sisters. I went to school through ninth grade in my country. I wanted to go to college but my family doesn't have money and there are no jobs in my country.

I didn't have a job in my country and I wanted to work. So I came to America to work and make money. I live with friends. I do not speak English well enough, so I go to school at the Hubbs Center for Lifelong Learning. I hope to go to college after I get my GED. In my free time, I go to the gym.

Osvaldo Martin Chavez is 25 and originally from Guatemala.

Daily Work

HALIMA DUALEH, MINNEAPOLIS, MN

I write every day about my daily work. I wake up every day at 5:10 a.m. with my children and husband, to perform *Wudu*, washing to prepare to pray. We pray together. After praying, we eat breakfast before heading to different schools, and I drive all three of my children. After that, I drive to school where I work, and it's a very difficult job. I work at a preschool. It is a very busy job that starts at 8 a.m. and ends at 2 p.m. I am a teacher of fourteen three to five-year-olds. Following work, I pick up my children.

I enjoy learning, but it is difficult for me to find time to do so. I'm looking for a teacher and a student who are both active. I'd like to gather some advice from teachers and students who are as busy as I am. I want to learn well but still want to have time to be a good mother, worker, and housewife. It is difficult to achieve your goals when you are a mother, a worker, a student, and a housewife, but I'll get it one day.

Halima Dualeh is 45 and originally from Somalia.

Persuasive Writing

MI MI, WORTHINGTON, MN

Being flexible in life can help with a lot of things. It can be the extent to which a person can cope with changes. Thinking about problems and tasks in a creative way. Mental flexibility can help with accepting change, living values, and taking risks. It can come with positives and respectfulness by you or others.

Mi Mi is 33 and originally from Myanmar.

Leaving Home

YASIRIE SUAREZ, ST. CLOUD, MN

I needed help when I decided to leave my home in Puerto Rico. First, I needed a home to live in during the first month in Minnesota. Next, I needed a job and a place to learn English. I finally found the help I needed because my best friend offered to let me stay at her house. She took me to the employment agencies and adult school and now, four months later, I have a job, car, and English class.

Yasirie Suarez is 38 and originally from Puerto Rico.

A New Life in the Land of Opportunities

MARIA SANCHEZ, BROOKLYN CENTER, MN

I was born, studied, and lived a long time in Michoacán, México. My country has beautiful landscapes and delicious food. When I was a child, I thought it was the best place in the world. My opinion changed when I finished studying my career and I realized that my country was not so perfect.

One day, my husband and I talked about traveling to the United States and starting a life there. Three reasons pushed us to make the trip. The first reason was insecurity in our country. My country was a secure place to live, work, and visit, but this situation changed when the robberies, kidnappings, and deaths increased considerably. The news was always talking about those topics. The second was gender discrimination that is frequent in Mexico, because many people have the idea that a man can do more things than a woman or other people think the woman must stay home and should not work. Those ideas make it difficult for a woman to get a job even after studying. The third reason was the economy. The salaries in my country are low, so people face a difficult situation because you get a little money and the things that you need are very expensive. The solution would be getting more money, but that is impossible because the legally established minimum wage is very low.

I came to live in Minnesota in 2020. When I arrived here, I was scared because it was a big change: another language, another culture, and I had never driven before. With the passage of time, I achieved many things: learning to drive and getting my driver's license. Shortly after that, my baby was born. During this time, I decided to learn English, so I started going to English school. When I finish learning this language, I hope to achieve my other goals, which are to obtain my GED, become a citizen, and get a job as a legal assistant.

Finally, I can say Minnesota is a place full of opportunities to improve your life.

Maria Sanchez is 27 and originally from Mexico.

Competition

FOZIYA JARA, ST. PAUL, MN

The teacher tells us about the competition and he said, "I only pick five students, two girls and three boys." First, we practiced for the competition with my group. Then we went to the podium and we did our speech. We tried to talk as clearly as possible. The other groups from other schools talked too. Then the finale would come and so we practiced on each other.

Second, we stood and practiced with each other. There were lots of people and friends. We stood and then we talked. The announcer said, "The finale has come!" We got ready and stood at the podium. The group got together and planned. Our teacher said, "We have to win this! We have to make it up to the podium and show our strengths." And then we had confidence after what he said. We took the podium and talked. When we were in the bus, we were so afraid because we were in a different city we did not know about.

At the finale, the announcer told us to stand at the podium. Then we were ready for competition with each other. The announcer said to us, "Whoever wins the competition, they will get the trophy." Then the teacher said, "Don't be afraid, be strong." Then my group said "Don't worry Mr. Ali, we will win." The announcer counted the number one to three because we are going speak in front of people. We started the competition and when we were done, the announcer said "I am going to tell you which groups is going to win." He said, "One, two, three, Mr. Ali's group is the winner!" We were so happy because we won and made it.

Foziya Jara is 22 and originally from Ethiopia.

Challenge in the New Place

SPI PAW, ST. PAUL, MN

On July 22, 2019, I moved to America by flight. I crossed Thailand, China, and California, countries with lots of language barriers. It was my first time travelling by flight, so I was so excited and scared of people at the same time.

Once, when I lived in California, I was so thirsty to drink water but I had no idea how to ask for it. On the way, people asked me, "How are you?" And I didn't know how to reply. When I reached Spokane, Washington, I saw a beautiful place of nice things, and it is a wonderful place I never saw before. I also struggled with many things. Since I had no job, no car, I didn't know how to buy food. When we were going to the shop, I didn't know how to ask in English. It was very hard for me and

I'm too shy to ask a question. I also struggled in church since I didn't know anyone. Some people asked me, "Can you sing?" I said, "No!" I'm so shy. When people look to me and they start talking, I think they are talking about me. Everyone around me spoke to each other only in English, so it was an unforgettable moment of my life. When I had a job, I didn't know people. They taught me and asked me many questions.

Above all things, when I look back on the other side, there are people around me who truly care for me and explained every little thing to me. I didn't know because I didn't understand what they were saying to me. Step by step, I understand a little and I know my boss and my line leader, they are both truly kind. They are teaching me and explaining things to me every time, as well as clarifying every little thing that I'm supposed to know.

Now, I have more confidence about myself. When I traveled by flight for the second time, I felt the difference because it was quite amazing. Now I have a job and I have a lot of friends. They love me and help me to come to the school. They are kind and support me when I need help. I'm very happy to see new places and new things to change my life.

Spi Paw is 24 and originally from Thailand.

Advice

LYDIA ALEJANDRA SANDOVAL, FOREST LAKE, MN

In a world where you can be anything, be valorous.

Lydia Alejandra Sandoval is 32 and originally from Maplewood, MN.

AKH in Minnesota

AISHA HUSSEIN, FRIDLEY, MN

First, when I left my mom's house on January 20, 2012, all my family was upset and cried. No one liked me leaving the country. One of my brothers and I went to the next city where we stayed for twenty-four hours. Then the second day, my brother came back to my mom, but I was ready to go to Kenya. I had three other brothers in Kenya.

Then, I was traveling with other people. We arrived after twenty hours, and we got a hotel. Then, we got some information about the borders, and we heard about fighting. We decided to stay until they cooled down, but there was not enough water. Also it was hot, and I had never seen anything like that. However, after seven days, we were ready to go and we traveled again for twenty-four hours.

Finally we arrived. I met one of my brothers and his wife. I was so happy to have them and they got a new baby boy after three days. They were so excited to have us here almost at the same time. My brother was a shopkeeper and his wife stayed home with the baby to take a break. I wanted to go outside, but I didn't know the Kenyan language. Then, I started to ask my sister-in-law for each word and I decided to go to school to learn Swahili and English.

When my brother and I met the school leader, he told us to pay for it every month. But I didn't have any money. I chose to move to another city because it was cheaper. My brother's family and I went there. We met our two brothers and were happy again. And after one month, I started to teach the Quran to young kids and then I got money. But it was so hot and dry.

However, I started going to school. But after two months, I wouldn't go everyday because it was so hot and dry. Also, it was so far away. Finally, I attended adult school, but not as much. Anyway, it was close to me. I kept going and going and my husband came to Kenya. He met me and then he came back to the U.S. and he sent me a visa. It took twelve months. Then, I came to America. Thank you to God and my husband.

Aisha Hussein is 30 and originally from Ethiopia.

Persuasive Writing

MARLENY ESQUIVEL, WORTHINGTON, MN

Why should you do exercise?

Exercise is good for your body and soul because you feel more free and helps with your memory and brain function, and protects against many chronic diseases. It lowers blood pressure and improves heart health, improves your quality of sleep, and reduces anxiety and depression. It combats cancer and related fatigue. That is why you should exercise regularly.

Marleny Esquivel is 32 and originally from Guatemala.

From Tanzania to Woodbury

DORICA MBILIMA, WOODBURY, MN

In 2003, I was married in my home country of Tanzania and moved to the United States to start a family with my husband who was already living in Minnesota.

In 2018, we decided to return to our country to give our children an opportunity to live there and get to know our extended family.

I returned to the United States on July 4, 2019 and interviewed for a position with Robert Half, an accounting firm. I was hired as a traveling accountant. During this time, I was feeling off… not quite right. At the clinic, they thought I was having a panic attack. The next month, I had a stroke.

My sister-in-law took me to Hennepin County Medical Center. They put a stent in my head to open up the vein that carries blood to the brain. I was struggling with my speech and cognition—I didn't know the date, who the president was, or my children's birthdays. My husband wanted me to get a second opinion at the Mayo Clinic.

The doctors at Mayo realized I had Moyamoya disease, a rare blood vessel disorder in which the carotid artery in the skull becomes blocked or narrowed.

I was at Mayo for six days, undergoing all sorts of tests. My husband had to translate everything the doctors said into Swahili for it to make sense to me. They realized the stent I had in my head had collapsed. I was scheduled to have two brain surgeries.

My first surgery was at the beginning of Covid. I was lucky to have an assistant doctor who knew Moyamoya disease well. Very few people could be near me, but my pastor and my brother's pastor came to pray for me and for the doctors. That first surgery took eight hours, and the medical staff were texting my husband throughout. The doctors and the prayers were successful! The next month, I had the second surgery.

My healing journey started with speech therapy and physical therapy. I use an app on my phone called Constant Therapy. I attend the Robbinsdale school district's stroke and brain injury recovery class, which has helped me so much.

My dream of moving to Texas was crushed because insurance is not good there. I don't know if I will get my accounting skills back. I go to Mayo for follow-ups. My healing journey is not over, but I have made so much progress!

Dorica Mbilima is 43 and originally from Tanzania.

Persuasive Writing

MARLEN HERNANDEZ, WORTHINGTON, MN

Eating breakfast is important for our health. Our stomach needs food in the morning. This helps our organs to be well. This keeps us from getting sick. But there are different types of people who can't eat breakfast. Some for work, other for diets, others for some disease, or they don't want to because they feel full.

Marlen Hernandez is 45 and originally from Guatemala.

The Pandemic and Distance Learning

NADIA MOHAMED, FRIDLEY, MN

During the COVID-19 pandemic, my children's school learning has changed to be online, and I remember everything was a challenge for me. First, I have to be an expert about how to use a computer and online classes to support my kids, and there were connection problems at that time, because all students had to attend at the same time. I was a bit nervous and I was not sure if we did things correctly or not. Sometimes I had to go out while they were online, but all teachers were helpful and patient because not all students took the online studies seriously.

But this experience makes me more professional and has given me skills on computers and programs. I think learning these skills will make me write more stories about myself, like writing diaries about my daily life and stories about my past. This experience will also help me solve some of the problems that are listed above.

Nadia Mohamed is 48 and originally from Yemen.

Childhood Autobiography in Myanmar

PAW TER HSA HTOO, ST. PAUL, MN

Myanmar was the country I was born in. This country is controlled by the Burmese military. There are seven states in this country, Mon State, Kachin State, Shan State, Chin State, Karen State, Karenni State, and Arakan State. We are different nationalities, so we have different languages and cultures.

I was born in Karen State, in a small town called Papu. I lived there for three days and my parents moved to the mountain village to escape their life of war. At that time, the Burmese were fighting with Karen. The Burmese soldiers destroyed the villages, arrested people, put them in jail, and killed people.

When I was five years old, I started to go to school in my small village. My parents encouraged me to go to school to become a good leader in my future life. There are not many students going to school. They did not know how much the education was for their future, and their parents were not interested in the education. Also parents did not have enough money to support their children for teacher salary and school uniforms. Every day, I am happy in my school with my friends. School started at 8:30 a.m. and finished at 3:30 p.m., Monday to Friday. When I came home after school, my mother started cooking and I helped my mom to take care of my sister and play with her.

Six years later, the Burmese came close to my village and they started to shoot mortars into my village. Then the villagers ran to the safe place in the jungle. At night, the Burmese soldiers burned my village and rice paddy. It was a bad time, we couldn't go anywhere to find food. Many families got malaria and diarrhea, and many people passed away. I felt very sad when I saw some of my friends die.

My parents tried to get out of this place to move to a refugee camp in Thailand. One year later, we arrived in a refugee camp. I saw many of our Karen people come to the refugee camp like my family. I asked my parents, "Is it a safe place for us?" And they said, "Yes." Now we have food. It is supported by NGOs and UNHCR. They gave shelter supplies to build our own house. I went back to school again in the refugee camp.

Paw Ter Hsa Htoo is 50 and originally from Kawthoolei (Karen State).

Persuasive Writing

MAY HTOO, WORTHINGTON, MN

Wonderful Summer.

I very much like the summer because when I'm going out to the river, I go fishing and I see many nature things. So I can relax my body and also I can breathe the fresh air. I forget everything, all my depression. The fresh air, summer is making me happy.

May Htoo is 36 and originally from Myanmar.

A Challenge I Had with My Friend

SEMIRA JARA, ST. PAUL, MN

My friend's name is Caltu. She lives in Ethiopia. She is twenty years old. She is at least five feet, seven inches. She has brown hair, and has brown eyes. Before, she went to school, but now she has a husband and son.

When Caltu and I were together in my country, we were friends since we were children. Caltu is my best friend that I had in my heart. We did not go to school that much because we were so lazy and did not want to study school.

One day, Caltu and one of the girls had a fight because some girls were touching her clothes. Then, I disrespected Caltu for the first time. I said to

Caltu, "Next time, please do not say anything bad to people," and she said, "Sorry, Semira, I know you like to respect people more than me." I said to her, "It's okay, people make mistakes and you do too." Caltu told me, "Why are you so nice to everyone?" "Sometime people are different from each other," I answered.

Caltu and I swam in the river together every day. Caltu sometimes wants to challenge me. She wants to challenge me to play a game. The game she wants to challenge me with is the rock game. How we play that game is we get to dig the floor and look for the rock, and put the rock in the place that we dig in. When we start that game, Caltu wins because she knows how to play that game more than I do. When she wins the game, I get to bring something for her like candy, chocolate, or chocolate chip cookies.

The last day of Caltu and I. One day I found out that I was coming to the United States so I had to leave the city where me and Caltu lived and move from Addis Ababa. Before I left Caltu, I went to the store and bought food and some matching clothes. After that, we hung out together and had fun playing games and having parties. The day I had to leave had come. I had to say goodbye because I knew I would not see her for a long time, so we both said goodbye and went our own separate ways. Caltu is my best friend that I have in my life.

Semira Jara is 20 and originally from Ethiopia.

Me and My One Coach

MUHAMMED BATI, ST. PAUL, MN

My coach got me mad when l was fourteen years old. He said to me in front of my friend, "You will never win. Maybe you can run for fun." I was not doing anything wrong, but he said that to me.

First, the problem is some people come there from the federal government and they ask our team, how was running going? How was the program? l tell the truth, and others do too, we tell them we have some problems, no shoes and other things like jackets, shorts, and sweats.

One guy is mean and tells the coach. After they're gone, wow, they're mad and Coach says we'll talk. They think the main person who did a bad thing is me.

That day passes, and after one month, the federal government send us shiny shoes, jackets, and other clothes. The morning after our training, we go to the office because it is the day to get the shoes and clothes. When l get there, the one coach says, "You are not on our team and these shoes and clothes are not for you." "What do you mean?" I ask. He is just silent and he gives the other athletes a lot of things, clothes, jacket, brand new, but for others and for me, zero. I feel sad because l need it. l do not have that kind of shoes and clothes. He says again to me, "You can go home."

Every athlete is there. I say, "It is okay. I can buy these things, but just give these to some other athletes. They cannot buy it, you hear me?" I tell him, "I swear, you hear me coach? You will read my name on the top of the world poster. This is the beginning, it is not my end." He says, "That is just a dream. It is not easy to get on top of the world." l feel a little emotional and l say, "l swear, if you go to every block, you will see my poster and name. Goodbye, my friend."

My friends are shocked, but l will reach my goal. l left and never went back there. Even when l feel tired when I'm training, l think about that day. Always, l push myself forward because l promise myself. l do not know the day, but may Allah help me to reach my goal. Always l hope.

Muhammed Bati is 22 and originally from Ethiopia.

About My Life

SALMA KHUSHAL, RICHFIELD, MN

I'm living in Minnesota. When I was in Afghanistan, I was very happy. I lived near my family. My mom, dad, brothers, and sisters all love me and helped me, but I had some problems. I didn't have my freedom.

In 2016, we came to the U.S. l was happy that now I have my freedom. I can go to the school. I can drive a car. Life is full of challenges, ups and downs. In the U.S., I have my freedom but I wasn't understanding the people and culture. That was a big challenge for me, but I never gave up. Five years ago, I tried too hard to understand the language and people. Now I can understand the language. Now my life in the U.S. with my husband and my three beautiful daughters is very good.

I'm happy, but I miss my mom, dad, sisters, and brothers. The situation in Afghanistan is very bad. My family is not safe there. They don't have enough food. I'm very worried about my family.

Salma Khushal is 25 and originally from Afghanistan.

Persuasive Writing

MELISSA FLORES, WORTHINGTON, MN

Recycle and take care of the environment.

For a long time we have listened about the contamination, garbage in the ocean, and the changes in the weather. Today we have ways to recycle, but not all people recycle. Maybe it is not a big deal for many people, but it's very important to recycle and take care of the environment. I think the government could have a law for taking care our environment and decreasing the garbage. All people in the whole world, we have to take care and teach our children to take care of the environment too.

Melissa Flores is 39 and originally from the United States.

Being an Immigrant Parent

ANDREA ORTEGA, EDEN PRAIRIE, MN

When my kids were in school in my home country, I liked being involved with their education. I believed that I was being a good mom. I used to say, "I have everything that I have dreamed of achieving in my life." All those things changed three years ago.

The first day here, I opened my eyes and everything was different. I felt like I had lost everything. I was devastated. When my children started school, we did not understand how school works in this country.

I could not help my kids with their homework because my English skills were so low. I was very frustrated; I missed my old life in Ecuador. I could not explain my thoughts and understand others. Many times I closed my eyes; I imagined I was dreaming.

These three years have been hard. We participate and work less. Some people would say that we are shy or impolite, but we are not. It is just the language limitation.

My fourteen-year-old child had some trouble in a class. He said that his teacher spoke very fast, and he could not understand well.

I would like the school to be more involved with immigrant students and parents. For example, they should understand why an immigrant student takes a cell phone in class to easier and faster translate words. The good strategies that I learned in my country to educate my kids, many of them are not useful here. Someone said you should not change your identity as an Ecuadorian, but that person never belonged to two cultures. I cannot keep my entire culture. At the beginning, I tried to be like I was in Ecuador, but it did not work.

I thought that I needed to rebuild my identity, considering the two cultures. Some traditions and lifestyles of my country, I have been trying to do at a medium level. It has helped me to feel a little happier.

As a speaker of English as a second language, first I think in Spanish, which means I think two times. After translating Spanish to English, many times it does not make sense in English. Finally, it is very important for me to feel welcome in a friendly environment. So I can feel confident to interact.

I am here! I am part of this land. I want to do many things; I just need help to learn.

Andrea Ortega is 34 and originally from Ecuador.

Civil War

ABDULLAHI OSMAN, ST. CLOUD, MN

When the civil war was happening in Somalia in 1991, I was young. It was a Sunday morning when someone knocked on our door. When I opened the door, I saw a gunman who beat me with the gun, killed my mom and dad and hurt my brother. At that time, I felt sad. The people of my neighborhood were shocked and came together. They said, "What can we do?" Our children and old men and women were scared. Finally, I got to the U.S. and I forgot everything that happened. Now I am working and all my children are going to school. We are happy now.

Abdullahi Osman is 45 and originally from Somalia.

Coming to America

ANONYMOUS, ST. PAUL, MN

Everything was hard when I came to America. There are six people in my family. I lost my dad when I was a kid. I came to the USA by marriage on October 16, 2016. People could not understand me because of my accent. Also, the weather is hard, because it is so different than my country. On my first day at work, I cried because I had not done that kind of job before.

Now, everything is good. I have become familiar with jobs in America and I got a better job. I am attending an English class to improve my English so I can get a GED.

How to Save Money

YAN JUAN, BROOKLYN PARK, MN

I come from China. I came to the USA in 1992. At that time I was a teenager. I worked in a company. The company paid workers twelve dollars an hour. I worked eight hours a day, Monday to Friday. The company paid me every two weeks by check, and I deposited my check into my bank. I saved some of my money in the bank.

After I was married, I worked in a company for four years. I already saved my money in the bank at that time. In 1997, my family opened Panda Garden Buffet. At the time the store opened, the store was very busy. I was a cashier. Every month, I made more money. Then as I saved my money, I opened a certificate of deposit (CD) in my bank, and I put my money in CDs that had more interest. I didn't use too much money.

I saved my money in my bank, and when I had more money, I opened another CD. I always care about my money. I remember that I opened my CD in 2008. At that time the economy was very low. Nobody had money to buy houses at that time. I closed my bank CDs; I took all my money and I bought three houses with a one-time payment with my sister. We had three houses to rent for more than $4,500 each month, my money was growing faster than I could put it in my bank; people paid the rent. My houses were rented for more than ten years. I got my money. Last year the house prices were raised so high. I sold two houses: one house sold for more than $280,000, the other house sold for more than $290,000. I got more money than I had ever gotten from working at any job before. Now I still rent one house for $1,800 each month. I was so lucky, I can always make more money than before.

In the future, I want my son and my daughter to have their own house, but now my children are saving their money. My children finished at the University of Minnesota and they don't have student loans. They are both very happy, they have their jobs now. I hope I have good luck and will save my money more than before.

Yan Juan is 50 and originally from China.

Life Teaches a New Lesson

REETA WILSON, MINNETONKA, MN

After school, I joined college. The first time I left my family, I stayed in a hostel. I was very excited and happy to stay with friends. For the first few days, I enjoyed it, but after that, I missed my family. The first weekend, my mom came to visit me, and when I saw her, I couldn't control my feelings and I started crying. She also felt bad. I said to her, "I don't want to stay here because the food is not good, the bathroom is not clean, and I'm not studying here."

She comforted me and left. After that, my dad wrote a letter to me. He said, "Studies are important to you and your future. I wish for you to finish your graduation." I love my dad, so I listened to his words. I studied there for three years. In that time, I learned a lot of things. I met a lot of people. Each person is different. Some people are kind, some are not nice. I learned how to handle them. I helped some students with disabilities. Now I feel happy about that. One of my friends couldn't walk without support; she always made jokes and kept the people around her happy. She studied well. After college, we didn't have any contact. Still I remember her.

I realized later a lot of students studied there. If you want to study, only focus on it and don't think about anything else.

Reeta Wilson is 42 and originally from India.

A Time I Needed Help

FATHI IBRAHIM, ST. CLOUD, MN

A time I needed help was when I lost my apartment lease form. I didn't have an extra form, so I went to the office to tell the manager that I lost my lease form, but he could not understand what I was talking about. I was a little confused. I went back to my house to find someone to help me. I went to my neighbor to ask if they could help me. My neighbor called the office to tell them what I needed. The manager sent the lease form in the mail. That was the time I needed help.

Fathi Ibrahim is 23 and originally from Kenya.

My First Experience in Minnesota

AMADOU SOW, BROOKLYN CENTER, MN

I came to Minnesota on January 20. I was so excited, but the first thing I was very surprised to see was a lot of snow because I had never seen snow. I stayed with my host family for three months, and they were so nice to me. The second step I did was to look for a job, but my uncle told me I had to wait for my social security before I found a job.

At the time, I didn't speak or understand English and I was worried about how I could get a job. I was planning to save money to rent my own place. I have a family back home, and I have to send them money too, and my wife was pregnant. I was tired of staying at home as it was very lonely when everyone left. I was not used to being alone, and it was cold and I didn't know where to go.

The day I started the work, I was so happy. It was a bakery company. The first day, they taught us and the work was really difficult, but the first day was good after I worked. I was worried about how to get back home. I asked some of my coworkers, but my English was really bad. When they saw my address they asked me to follow them. I had difficulty going to work because I had to take two buses. It was very hard at the beginning because sometimes you have to wait thirty or forty-five minutes before the bus arrives and it was really cold!

When you arrive at a new place, it is very hard to familiarize yourself with the systems, but if you focus on improving yourself, you will be satisfied at the end. For me, I learned many things here, like you don't have to speak very good English to get a job because the people are so understanding.

For the first year, it was very difficult for me, but now, *alhamdulillah*, I have a job I like. I have my car and I study to improve my English. Next year, I will start my community college degree in pre-engineering, and I have the possibility to help my family back home. At the end of my story, I will say never give up, keep going and one day you will see a good result.

Amadou Sow is 27 and originally from Guinea-Conakry.

From My Culture and Traditions

Featured Author

Rochelle M. Anderson

MINNETONKA, MN

I have lived in Minnesota my entire life, in St. Louis Park and in Minnetonka, and attended St. Olaf College and the University of Minnesota Law School. I have owned a poodle since age twelve, and I like to travel, go camping in the Rockies, and see movies, plays, the Twins, and the original *Star Trek*. My favorite things are my two daughters and two granddaughters.

In 2007, I had a horrible stroke and almost died. Since the stroke, I have had aphasia. Aphasia means I have trouble talking, reading, and understanding speech. My right side is broken and I have trouble walking and using my right hand. Dictation and Kindle have both improved my life. My husband has helped me down this new path.

Robbinsdale Area Schools has a class for brain injury and stroke survivors. My favorite activity is reading short stories and listening to them at the same time. With Robbinsdale class and my teacher, I am getting better. As I have improved, I have written blogs, short stories, and entries for Journeys. For two years, I have been in a poetry group for people with aphasia and brain injury and we will soon have a chapbook published. Finally, at Crop Art in the Minnesota State Fair, for the last six years, I have submitted works with an aphasia theme.

Of course, I still love canoeing and keep looking for loons.

1969

Woodstock, Neil Armstrong walking on the moon, *Sesame Street*, *Abbey Road*, hair, bell bottom jeans, pot-laced brownies, Vietnam. I was ten years old.

After school, we had two free hours before dinner. Our parents were working so we would go to each other's houses, sometimes grandparents were there. All the houses looked the same on the outside. They were all built in the 1950s. But inside, everything was different. The houses were very small. I could never understand how the parents had one room, the grandparents had another, and the five or six kids all stayed in the other small bedroom. Somehow it all worked.

I never knew why grandparents were staying in these tiny houses. What had happened in their lives? I became busier and didn't visit my friends' houses much anymore. As an adult, I wished I had learned more about them when I was ten years old. This was 1969, twenty-five years after World War II. Many of the grandparents couldn't speak English, many wore strange clothes, cooked odd food, and went to different worship services.

One of my friend's parents and grandparents were Japanese-American citizens and they had been in an internment camp. I didn't even know what that meant. I met her grandparents, but we never talked much. Her dad even was a U.S. soldier in WWII. After the war, he moved to Minnesota, went to college, and became an engineer. All I remember is that he bowled once weekly at Southtown and my friend and I shopped.

Another of my friends' grandmothers had a tattoo on her arm that meant she was in Auschwitz during the Holocaust in German-occupied Poland. I think I knew a little bit about this from Hogan's Heroes but really didn't learn more until high school. My friend's dad was in the concentration camp, and in the U.S. he joined the Navy, and later he had a boat on Lake Minnetonka and wore skippers' clothes.

I think many people our age heard stories in their own family, but some didn't want to listen, and grandparents didn't always want to talk about the horrible things that happened to them. I wish I had been mature enough to ask about their lives when I was ten years old.

Houses were the same outside, but very different inside. 1969 changed my life forever.

Rochelle M. Anderson is 62 and originally from St. Louis Park, MN.

I Was

RENU NAVAWIBUN, ST. PAUL, MN

I did eat eggs.
I did not like to read books.
I liked drinking beer.
I disliked singing.
I was ugly.
I was not pretty.
I loved music.
I hated people who talked too loudly.
I could cook.
I could not eat mangos.
I wanted to work.
I did not want to walk.
I was.

Renu Navawibun is 33 and originally from Thailand.

Why I Am a Gardener

ANONYMOUS, BURNSVILLE, MN

Plants are very important beings on the face of the earth, since they are the carriers of our nutrition and are beautiful throughout the world. Therefore, they must be protected and cared for because the trees give us shade and help purify the air.

Somali Independence Day

HABIBO OSMAN, ST. CLOUD, MN

I am from Somalia. Somalia has a big celebration on July 1. All Somali people wear blue and white dresses. They paint their faces with stars. They sing and dance for three days. They make all different foods like rice, goat meat, camel meat, pasta, corn, beans, and sambusas. Then they eat together with their fingers.

Habibo Osman is 33 and originally from Somalia.

I Was

IFRAH AHMED NUR, ST. PAUL, MN

I did like to play with kids.
I didn't like dancing.
I liked taking care of my parents.
I disliked yelling at people.
I was a happy person.
I was not paying attention to everything.
I loved my parents.
I hated dishwashing.
I could finish my high school.
I could not get away from a civil war in my country.
I did not want to have children.
I wanted to go abroad.
I was.

Ifrah Ahmed Nur is 40 and originally from Somalia.

My Family Is Successful

SAFIYA MAHAMED, MINNEAPOLIS, MN

My mother was happy when she had her children come in the home and work together inside. We did jobs like cleaning and cooking. We cooked rice, meat, and chicken. Also we made orange juice and tea. She was happy and excited when we finished work. She wanted to show her children she was happy. She hugged and kissed us, and she smiled. We got together and talked with my mom. She would give advice. She said, "When you want to do something, always talk together and ask for some ideas. Always help the other one. If you work together always, our family can succeed."

When I was older, I wanted to start a business, so I talked to my older brother Yacqob. I said, "I want to start a business in the city. What do you think?" My brother said, "Starting a business is very good. I will help you." He gave me some money.He said, "First two months, we will work together, me and you." I opened a restaurant. I cooked a lot of different foods. I made meat, rice, chicken, sambusas, and donuts called *mandazi*. These foods I learned from my mom. After three months, I had enough money to start another business or to give to my mom. I gave it to my mother and my father. They were excited for me. In America, a person who wants to start a business can go to a bank or maybe the government for money. In Somalia, if you don't have enough money to open a business, you get help from your family. I like the Somali way because the money is not a loan with interest. It is sometimes a gift.

Safiya Mahamed is 46 and originally from Somalia.

Technology Woes

ERIN MCDONALD, MINNEAPOLIS, MN

FaceTime, Clever, Zoom, SeeSaw.
Portal, Group Chat, Newsela.

Naviance, PowerPoint, Twitter, DMs.
iMessage, Skype meetings, Microsoft Teams.

Metaverse, Gigawatts, Google Meet.
Bleep, Blorp, Gleep, Glop, LMNOP.

TBH, IRL, SMH.
WTF, FML, IMO!

ICYMI:
I miss paper.

Erin McDonald is 48 and originally from Hopkins, MN.

My Country

OSCAR CABRERA, WEST ST. PAUL, MN

I'm from Mexico. It is a country located in the southern part of North America. Everyone speaks Spanish there. It is sunny, but I like it a lot. The most important foods are lamb barbecue, tacos carnitas, tamales, and posole. The beautiful places in my country are the beaches in Acapulco, Cancún, Puerto Vallarta, and Mazatlán. I like the beaches and the food. I don't like the corruption and the presidents.

My first weeks in the U.S. were bad because I did not know how to order food. Sometimes it was funny when I ordered food in Spanish.

Oscar Cabrera is originally from Mexico.

The Beautiful Farms of Thailand

PWINT AYE, MAPLEWOOD, MN

The most beautiful places in my country of Thailand are the farms. My language is Karen. In the language of Burmese, a farm is called *ladsamar*. The farms are located outside in the country.

I visited the farms while I was living in the refugee camp Mae La where I lived with my grandmother, sisters, little brother, and my cousin. My grandmother died in 2013 in the Mae La refugee camp. My mother and father were working on a farm. My mother and father grew bananas, mangos, coconuts, and many flowers. There were also chickens.

When I go back to the farm, I will take my family here in Minnesota, my husband, my daughter, and my son. From Thailand, I will bring along my mother, That Aye, my father, Nae Lo, and my little brother and little sister.

The farms are beautiful places in Thailand because there are many green trees and I hear many sounds in the morning. There, I will see my family members, such as my aunties, uncles, and many cousins. I will also go to see my old friends.

Seeing my family is my favorite thing about the farm. I have not been to Thailand in a year. I plan to go to a Thailand refugee camp where my husband and I will get married. When you marry, you give food to people and offerings to Buddha.

In Thailand, I hear the sound of many birds and the waterfall that is at my house. The air feels very good.

Pwint Aye is 28 and originally from Thailand.

My Country

SEMHAR PAULOS, MINNESOTA

I'm from Eritrea, in East Africa. In my country, everyone speaks Tigrinya. Some people also speak other languages, like Tiagra. One important holiday is Easter. One of the most beautiful places in my country is Massawa. I like the people in my country, but I don't like the economy.

Semhar Paulos is originally from Eritrea.

Celebration in My Town; A Day Back in My Town

YANELY, MINNESOTA

When I was a child, I saw how my family started to get ready for the coming celebration in my town. Everybody was so excited, and for almost a month, my family was preparing. They needed to make sufficient food for everyone because anyone is welcome to be part of this celebration. The head staff person, who is called mayordomo, starts making new candles and flowers from wax. This celebration starts in the first month of the year and continues for twenty-eight days.

On the first day of the celebration, everything is ready. The mayordomo's family and friends come to the house around 8 p.m. to start the parade. Lots of people bring buckets of flowers. On this day, the parade is accompanied by groups of people called *tecuanes* who are dressed in different types of costumes. Aztecs and Chinelos are part of the parade too. Other *tecuanes*, called *viejitos*, are part of the parade too. *Viejitos* are *tecuanes* with old man costumes. The mayordomos even get a musician group. Minutes before the parade starts, the candles are lit and stay on all the way to the church.

For these twenty-eight days of celebration, many people come to sell things in town. Sometimes, I saw people from Asia come to the town. Rides are one of the biggest attractions. Before and after the parade in the center of the town, called a plaza, there is live music every night.

In this celebration there are two important dates: the 24th and the 25th. On these dates the *tecuanes,* Aztecs, Chinelos, and other groups dance for almost the whole day. The dance is considered like a prayer. After the twenty-eight days of celebration, life in the town goes back to normal and people start counting the days until next year.

This is one of my favorite things that I miss. I am so grateful to my husband who made possible the return to my town. When we finally almost landed at the airport, my heart was pumping too fast. I was so happy to see my family and friends again. Unfortunately, my grandma got so sick at the time I was in the town. We stayed in the city all the time and didn't do what we had planned to do. After a week, my grandma passed away.

At least I saw her again and she met my kids and husband.

Yanely is 32 and originally from Mexico.

My Beautiful Mexico

ELIZABETH ESTRADA, RICHFIELD, MN

In México, everything is different from Minnesota.

I love México. I like it because it is not as cold as here and it does not snow. The celebrations are different and very beautiful. December 12 is a day that is celebrated as a big day because it is the day of The Lady of Guadalupe. In my town, a group of people go on a pilgrimage by bicycle to the Basilica of Guadalupe, which is in México City. They leave around 5 a.m. and arrive in México City around 7 p.m.

On December 24, the birth of the child Jesus is celebrated. You get a bag of fruit with animal cookies and sweet candies, which in my town are called *colacion.*

We have very beautiful traditions where the family gets together to celebrate the New Year. They build castles and bulls out of fireworks. They run the firework bulls around the center of my town and burn them where they celebrate something big.

On the last Friday of October, the traditional Orange Fair is celebrated. People buy things to offer their faithful deceased. They sell plates, mats, waxes, copal, and clay comal. They have mechanical games such as the Wheel of Fortune, the Dragon Ride, Bumper Cars, and many more.

I miss my family the most, since I have been away from them for fifteen years. I also miss eating warm bread coming out of the brick oven, cooked with wood and the tortillas cooked in the clay comal with wood. I hope to return some day not too far away to enjoy all those beautiful traditions.

Elizabeth Estrada is 34 and originally from Mexico.

My Favorite Holiday

ANONYMOUS, MINNEAPOLIS, MN

My favorite holiday is Ramadan. Ramadan is the month where Muslims all around the world fast. Ramadan is a holy month when God forgives the past sins of those who observe fasting, prayer, and a faithful intention. During this month, Muslims give money to the poor and help anyone who is in need.

Ramadan comes only once a year, so we Muslims try to do our very best to please our Lord. In this month, families and communities come together and break their fast, which I really enjoy. We Muslims fast during this month to please our God and to be thankful for things that we take for granted, like water. When I fast for the whole day and it is time to break my fast, everything tastes so good. When you fast, it cleans the body of toxins and forces cells into processes that are not usually stimulated when a steady stream of fuel from food is always present.

Communities come together and pray Tarawih, which is also called Ramadan night prayer. The Tarawih is a lot longer than our regular daily prayers. Sometimes we fast for twenty-nine or thirty days in Ramadan.

After Ramadan is over, our first holiday is called Eid al-Fitr, where children get money from elders. In the morning, the whole community comes together and prays together. Later, parents take their kids to playgrounds. Kids have fun while the elders talk with each other.

The Origin of the Cañaris

MARITHZA RIVERA, MINNEAPOLIS, MN

The Cañaris were an ethnic group that lived in the current provinces of Azuay and Cañar. It is believed that their name is related to the idea of believing they are descendants of the snake and the macaw, two figures that have important relevance in the worldview of this people and modern Ecuador.

According to legend, in those lands the goddess Pachamama sent a flood that covered even the top of the highest mountain. Everything was destroyed in its path and only two brothers survived, having barely managed to reach a summit that was not yet covered with water. They hoped that at some point the water level would drop, and they decided to wait there.

But the water did not go down, and they had no humanly possible way to get food, so in a matter of days they began to faint. But fortunately, and just when they were about to die of hunger, the brothers discovered a cave in which there was food. They returned the next day and food appeared again, as if by magic.

They didn't understand what was happening, until one day they realized that two women in the shape of macaws were the ones who left food there daily. With the beauty of their feathers and their feminine silhouette, each macaw fell in love with each brother Cañari, whose love was reciprocated. Each one formed different families and had many children. From these new descendants were born those who would be the first settlers of Cañar called Los Cañaris.

Marithza Rivera is 24 and originally from Ecuador.

Social Security

AZZA SARHAN, BROOKLYN PARK, MN

The purpose of this article is to highlight the difference between the social security system in the U.S. and the social security system in Egypt. First the age, workers in the U.S. are qualified for full social security benefits at the age of sixty-six. In Egypt, on the other hand, the social security age is set to sixty years old. Additionally, in Egypt, early retirement with full benefits is available for workers who meet certain conditions.

Second, the social security amount. When comparing the social security payouts in the U.S. and Egypt with the cost of living in each country, Egypt is paying much higher amounts than the U.S. Third, the annual payout increase. The social security percent increase in the U.S. is very low in comparison to the inflation rate from one year to another. The social security annual increase in Egypt could reach fifteen percent each year.

The conclusion of this comparison leads to one result which is that the Egyptian social security system is much better than that of the U.S. The one question that remains is where Egypt is getting the funding to secure such a system?

Azza Sarhan is 57 and originally from Egypt.

A Sticky, Tasty Traditional Food

ABDI HASSAN, MINNEAPOLIS, MN

"Delicious!" That is what I say when I eat the most important food in Somali culture. This traditional Somali dish is called *soor* and almost all Somalis eat it. It is a common dish made of cornmeal that is mixed with butter and milk. This dinner is often offered at get-togethers such as family reunions, visits from friends, and parties, but it is also eaten every day in some households. It is cooked to be very sticky, and if you throw it at a wall, it will stick! It is traditionally eaten with the hands or a wooden spoon. In my family, we eat it often with vegetables and meat. This tasty food is in every Somali home, and it is enjoyed by many people in my culture. I recommend you try it.

Abdi Hassan is 45 and originally from Somalia.

My Country

PATRICIA AGUAYO, MINNESOTA

My country is Ecuador, which is in South America. People speak Spanish there. In Ecuador there is rain, winter, summer, and beautiful beaches. The important foods are: *hornado*, *mote*, and shrimp ceviche.

Some things I don't like about my country are economic instability, unemployment, and insecurity.

Some of the beautiful places in my country are the Presidential House, the House of Culture, and the Museo del Hombre. I love the beaches, mountains, and diversity in nature. I can visit both the beaches and the mountains in one day.

Patricia Aguayo is originally from Ecuador.

My Culture and My Life

SIAD NUR, ST. PAUL, MN

My name is Siad Nur. I was born in Somalia and lived as a refugee in Asmara, the capital city of Eritrea, for eight years. My culture has many farmers. We cultivate fields and raise camels and goats. We have mangos and grapes. In my culture, we eat rice, cereal, and meat. Goat and camel are favorite meats for us.

I have been in the United States for five years. I am married and have eight children. The oldest child is eighteen and the youngest is one. I drive a school bus. I also attend English Language Learning classes at the Hubbs Center for Lifelong Learning. My goal is to study mechanics when I go to college.

Siad Nur is 42 and originally from Somalia.

The Mid-Autumn Festival

FENGLIANG CHEN, LAKEVILLE, MN

The Mid-Autumn Festival is one of the most important Chinese festivals. It is celebrated on the fifteenth day of the eighth lunar calendar every year. A couple days before the festival, everyone in the family will help to make the house clean and beautiful. Lanterns will be hung in front of the doors.

In the evening, there will be a big family dinner. People who work far away from their homes will try to come back home if they can. After dinner, people will light lanterns, which are usually red and round. Children will play with their own toy lanterns for fun.

At night, the moon is usually round and bright. People can enjoy the moon and eat moon-cakes, which are the special food for this festival. They can also eat fruits, and drink tea. They talk about each other and look forward to the future together.

Fengliang Chen is 40 and originally from China.

A Lie or Strategy Move?

NATALIYA KRUPATHKYKH, MAPLE GROVE, MN

My favorite holiday is March 8 — International Women's Day. On this day men congratulate their mothers, wives, daughters, sisters, and girlfriends.

This holiday reminds me about our happiest time in my country. My husband brought gifts for me and my daughters on this day. Also, he has never forgotten about his mother and sisters. But I like this holiday because I have a son who always tries to follow the same track as my husband. He liked to make surprises. It made me happy, but not because I am a selfish person who loves attention.

More importantly, I thought about my son's future family. This tradition went on until one day that I remember distinctly. My husband and my daughter were in the USA. My son and I were in Ukraine, waiting for visas.

My son was a student at university, had a part-time job, and had a girlfriend. I bought food to celebrate the holiday with my son, but he called me and said that he would have a party with his girlfriend. I felt alone that evening. I said to myself, "My son has grown up already." But, I didn't want good traditions to leave my family. Next day my friend called me. She shared with me how her husband and two sons congratulated her.

Then my friend asked me if my son had congratulated me. I said, "Yes, of course." I started to describe how big the bouquet of roses was. My son was in the next room. I thought that he was sleeping after the midnight party. An hour later he came in my room and said that he had heard my lie. I replied, "Never mind, my dear. This lie hasn't harmed anyone. I just didn't want to disappoint my friend."

He saw a slight sadness in my eyes. An hour later my son brought flowers and chocolate. He said, "Sorry I forgot about you. I didn't know that this holiday was important to you." I thanked him.

I said to myself, "This incident is important for you, my dear son, for your future family." Since that time, he has never forgotten to congratulate me. Also, on this holiday his wife and daughter get generous gifts.

Some will say it is a lie. Some will say it was a strategy move. I agree. But the result is good.

Nataliya Krupathkykh is 62 and originally from Ukraine.

Peace Poem

CARMELO SOLARTE, ST. PAUL, MN

Peace is like God.

Peace is feeling happy every day.

Peace is being calm.

Carmelo Solarte is originally from Venezuela.

Mogadishu

HAWO RAGE, ST. PAUL, MN

The most beautiful place in the world is my sweet home country of Somalia, specifically the city of Mogadishu. It is where I was born and grew up, and where I saw a lot of things. There are two big, beautiful oceans, the Indian Ocean and the Atlantic Ocean. These two oceans surround the city. People go fishing, swimming, boating, and some people just like to go and stay for a vacation. There are many farms where the farmers grow fresh and organic foods such as corn, bananas, mangos, and other fruits and vegetables. There are neem trees around the city. This is a beautiful place.

Somalia has three rivers surrounding it: the Juba River, the Shabelle River, and the Ganaane River. These rivers are used by the farmers for water. People also swim in the rivers, and in the country, they will wash their clothing in the river. Animals also can drink from them. The rivers are thirty kilometers from the city.

The city is a place of many cultures. We have the same religion, and it is a happy place where there are museums, bigger markets than other places in Somalia, and government housing. There are big schools and a university where anyone who graduated high school and passes the state test can go to. It is a very hard test and I passed it. That was fifteen years ago!

Hawo Rage is 32 and originally from Somalia.

I Was

DAISY GUADALUPE HERRERA SANCHEZ, WOODBURY, MN

I did jump.

I did not eat vegetables.

I liked playing.

I disliked washing dishes.

I was helpful with my grandmother.

I was not healthy.

I loved making cookies with my mom.

I hated people who hurt my feelings.

I could dance.

I could not like school.

I wanted to travel to Disney.

I did not want to grow up so fast.

I was.

Daisy Guadalupe Herrera Sanchez is 40 and originally from Mexico.

My New Year

VORANAN SOMSANUK, LAKEVILLE, MN

The time goes so fast. The seasons pass again and again. The holiday is coming. Many people are planning to start a new thing or move on to a better one, but I think the most important part of the New Year is that we can spend time together with family.

My New Year is April 13–15 of every year. People who work far from home prepare to return home and get ready to spend time with family. Because some people can only see their family once a year, it's a good time to be together on the New Year. Many families wake up early to make food and bring it to a temple. Buddhism is the religion that most people in my country practice.

After visiting the temple, people are ready to celebrate in a traditional way with water. In Thai, New Year is called Songkran. People grab their own buckets or water guns and fill them up with water and splash each other. It feels fresh and a little wet. In some cities, they play with water all day and all night. In small towns, they only play during the daytime and nighttime.

Many Thai people make a lot of food for the New Year. They also spend time sharing about the past and planning what to do in the new year. We have one more thing to do before the New Year celebration is over. Younger people show their respect to elderly people in their families. They ask for forgiveness and the older people give blessings for good luck and good health. Now it's time to say goodbye and go back to work and move on in the New Year.

Voranan Somsanuk is 31 and originally from Thailand.

My Favorite Holiday

NANCY CALDERON, COLUMBIA HEIGHTS, MN

There are many different holidays in my country but my favorites are Carnaval and Holy Week. I am from Ecuador, and I am from the city of Loja. In Loja, we have two types of holidays, the most special for us is Holy Week and Carnaval. For Holy Week, we meet with the whole neighborhood to pray. We start on Monday and end on Easter Sunday. On Good Friday, we pray all day and fast. On Saturday we go to the river and share many kinds of food together. The last day is Easter Sunday. On Easter Sunday, we put on our best new clothes and we all celebrate Easter together in the neighborhood.

For Carnaval, we celebrate it differently. These days we celebrate by eating food and sweet dessert, and dancing to music. We celebrate it with our whole family together and it's the best time to share with grandparents, uncles, and cousins. Since there are so many people together, things can get a little crazy. Part of this celebration is throwing things at each other. People throw eggs, ketchup, flour, mustard, and water with flowers in it. For many Lojanos, it is a lot of fun, but for some, not so much. For me it is very fun and I enjoyed it a lot. In conclusion, I hope I have taught you how important Holy Week and Carnaval are to me. These two holidays are incredible holidays that always bring a smile to my face.

Nancy Calderon is 41 and originally from Ecuador.

I Was

JAZMIN NAVARRO GARCIA, ST. PAUL, MN

I did sleep with my teddy.

I did not hug strong.

I liked sleeping at night.

I disliked cleaning my bed.

I was happy with my teddy.

I was not comfortable on the pillow.

I loved my teddy as my friend.

I hated my brother mocking me.

I could have more teddys.

I could not buy more.

I wanted to have money.

I did not want to sleep alone.

I was.

Jazmin Navarro Garcia is 31 and originally from Mexico.

Celebration

TRANG PHAM, ST. CLOUD, MN

In my country, a big celebration is during the Lunar New Year. The Lunar New Year is January of the lunar calendar. We celebrate for three days. On those days, young people make a good wish to old people. Then the old people give a gift to young people, like lucky money. During those three days, we wear new clothes and eat good foods like cake made from sticky rice and mung beans, bitter melon soup, and crunchy peanut candy. We also don't have to work on that day.

Trang Pham is 49 and originally from Viet Nam.

Insadong

YOONMI YOU BARFUSS, MAHTOMEDI, MN

For me, Insadong is the most beautiful and fun place to see in Seoul, Korea. It is the place where I lived in Korea and I spent a lot of time there. I always enjoyed being there and seeing the cultural art museums as well as the art fairs that were in the streets. This is the best place to satisfy all your senses. You will enjoy the traditional buildings in which both past and present co-exist in harmony, with the old Korean style having been carefully restored.

My favorite season to visit Insadong is the spring. There are cherry blossoms on the trees on either side of the street. When these trees are blooming, it is amazingly beautiful and it smells so good. This is why it is a favorite of many dating couples. There are also great traditional tea houses, restaurants, street food, galleries, and fine art pieces you can buy.

Yoonmi You Barfuss is 46 and originally from South Korea.

Giving Is a World Culture

ANONYMOUS, ST. PAUL, MN

Giving and supporting those in need, or just helping each other, is an ancient world culture. As far as I know, sharing started based on religion. I am from East Africa. Ethiopia, as a society, has a culture of giving food to needy people (individuals or families). On the other hand, there is a culture called Debo. Debo is helping someone in your area that needs assistance with things he or she can't accomplish by themselves. That includes building a house, farming, weeding, collecting the harvest, and so on. For the Debo, everyone who participates, brings his or her tools, skills, and works together. The person who called for Debo is responsible for preparing adequate food and drink for the crowd.

There are organizations that work to support families in need. Most organizations work near big cities. Of course, the greatest need is in the cities or on the outskirts of the cities. After I arrived in North America, I recognized the giving and receiving culture is widely used in this society. There are a lot of resources to help everyone stand on his or her feet. For example, there are churches that give used and new items to the person who cannot afford such items by themselves. These churches can work in two different ways. They can receive donations from their members, then individuals and/or organizations pass items to a person who is in need. Another way churches support the community is through the monetary support of charitable institutions. For instance, Habitat for Humanity is an organization that participates in building houses for people in need. Everyone can participate in this kind of organization. Donations can range from spare change, a little building material, or a full house. Not only that, there is an opportunity to contribute your skills, time, and money to fulfill what needs to be done. Even if those are two different ways to help our communities, engaging in this type of kindness persuaded me to conclude that sharing is a world culture.

The River Termos's Nature Is Contemplated

SONIA LOPEZ, MAPLEWOOD, MN

The most beautiful place in my country of El Salvador is Termos del Río. In English, this translates into River Thermos, and it is located in La Libertad. I visited Termos del Río in June of this year. When I go to see this place of beauty again, I will take with me my granddaughter, Adrianna, who is eight years old.

In 2017, all my family went to see the river. It is beautiful because it is a cool place and if you are cold there is a natural hot water pool. That is why it is called River Thermos. The water is so clear. If you go there you will see horse and carriage tours of the pools, a pool of artificial waves, a cable car, and many more kinds of entertainment and restaurants. I hear the birds sing, the sound of trees moved by the wind, the hot water springs, children playing, and music. Being at Termos del Río, I feel relaxed and happy, because I'm with the rest of my family, my nieces and nephews.

Sonia Lopez is 54 and originally from El Salvador.

Irecha

HANA BORENA, MAPLEWOOD, MN

My name is Hana and I come from Ethiopia. One thing I like about my country is Irecha, a week-long Thanksgiving celebration in the spring. I like this holiday because all Oromo people from across the country and the world come together to celebrate the passing of the harsh winter and to thank God for the good harvest and a nice summer. We celebrate by wearing our cultural clothing, dancing, and having a feast of many foods. There is a lot of drinking of a honey drink, which we call *bokaa*. Most of all, my favorite thing about this holiday is the fact that there is a vast amount of dialects, religions, and dance, but we are one under the name Oromo.

Hana Borena is 39 and originally from Ethiopia.

There Are Differences between Ethiopian and U.S. Cultures

ANONYMOUS, MINNEAPOLIS, MN

I have seen a lot of differences between Ethiopia, where I come from, and U.S. culture. The way people interact and weather are all different.

One of the differences is in the way people interact. For example, people in the U.S. look at you when you talk to them. Eye contact is very important in U.S., but it is not the same in Ethiopia. Most people in the U.S are simply smiling. In Ethiopia, people don't smile at people they do not know.

Both Ethiopia and Minnesota have four

seasons, but they are very different. In summer, Ethiopia is cool and rainy, while Minnesota is hot and sunny. In fall, Ethiopia is cooler and windy, while Minnesota is colder and trees drop the leaves. In winter, Ethiopia is cooler but there is no snow, while in Minnesota, a lot of snow comes. In spring, Ethiopia has some rain and is warmer, and it is the same in Minnesota.

How an ID Bracelet Helped Solve a Fifty-Four-Year-Old Mystery

CHRISTELLE BAISSAT, MINNETONKA, MN

Antoine de Saint-Exupéry had a hectic life. Born in June 1900, he was a successful author, an intrepid aviator, and a warrior. He was born in France and traveled the world, flying to North Africa and South America. He moved to New York in 1940, after the fall of France during World War II. He wrote several novels based on his flying experiences. His novel *The Little Prince* was first published in 1943 in New York and Paris. It is the fourth best selling book in the world after the Bible. In 1943, he went back to France to fight against the Germans as a military reconnaissance pilot. On July 31, 1944, he took off for a mission from Corsica and never came back. His death remained a mystery for fifty-four years, fueled by the craziest theories. Some people assumed that he committed suicide, others that he was still alive.

In 1998, a fisherman from Marseille, Jean Claude Bianco, saw something sparkling in his net. He took a closer look; it was an ID bracelet. After wiping it off, he could read Saint-Exupéry's name. What an amazing surprise for him! He knew all about Saint-Exupéry's disappearance and couldn't believe what he had found. When his discovery became public, some people even accused him to be a con artist, claiming that the chain was a fake. Some experts examined the engraved inscriptions (Saint-Exupéry's and his wife's names and the address of his editor) before certifying it was authentic. This bracelet was a gift from his spouse, Consuelo. A local archeologist, Luc Vanrell, began a treasure hunt to locate Saint-Exupéry's plane based on the place where the chain was found. It took him two years to finally spot Saint-Exupéry's plane wreck off the coast of Marseille.

What was even more remarkable was that Luc Vanrell, with the help of passionate volunteers, was able to find out who the German pilot was who shot down Saint-Exupéry's plane and interviewed him in 2008. His name was Horst Rippert. Rippert remembered that day and was full of regret. He had read all Saint-Exupéry's books in his youth and admired him. He said that if he had known what he was doing, he never would have done it.

Christelle Baissat is 48 and originally from France.

My Culture

KAO LOR, BROOKLYN PARK, MN

Culture shows many things; who you are and where you are from. I'm Hmong. The Hmong have diversity in themselves. Hmong don't have a country or an official language, and we have a beautiful culture.

I grew up in Laos. One thing in my culture is called "Call spirit," in Hmong it is called "*Hu plig*." It means to make you feel good about something that happened to you. In Hmong culture we do it in the New Year, when we are scared about something, or for marriage. Every year, Hmong families call spirits during the New Year.

There are two steps to call a spirit. First, we prepare eggs, incense, rice, and chickens. We put them out in front of the door and call everyone's spirit to come back and welcome the New Year. We say "Today is good. Tonight is a good night. I call my family; I call everyone who went somewhere; I call you to come back home." Then we kill the chickens and boil eggs. We boil the chicken, but we don't cut off any part.

Second, when everything is ready, we put it back outside and call again. After, we bring the chicken in to make soup or other dishes. If you eat the egg, that means your spirit will come back to your body and bring happiness.

In marriage, we also call spirits, but it is different because it means welcoming a new daughter-in-law. At this time, we kill a pet or cow and invite other family and friends to join. We prepare white string, eggs, chicken, and rice. An elder in the family comes to call a spirit, "Today is a good day. We are welcoming our daughter-in-law. We are very happy. If her spirit has gone somewhere, please come back home." Then family and friends celebrate.

In calling spirits, sometimes we go somewhere if we are scared of something. In Hmong culture, we have to call spirits to make you feel comforted and happy. We prepare in a way similar to how we call spirit in the New Year and in marriage.

Calling spirit is the most beautiful part of my culture. I love to join because it is a festival in my culture and it has been on my mind since I was a child. Every year I can't wait to eat an egg and welcome my spirit.

I am proud to be Hmong.

Kao Lor is 24 and originally from Laos.

First Gathering Season

TABASHISH OGITCHIDA, WHITE EARTH, MN

There I was, enjoying a pleasant mid-August eve admiring my garden in the fortieth revolution of life as an Anishinaabe *enin* (man). I was yet to join the legions of teams of *mahnomen* gatherers. A gathering team consists of two people: a "knocker" and a "poler." The knocker sits low in a seat of the canoe and uses two two-foot cedar sticks called knockers to gently bend the wild rice stalks into the hull of the canoe and knocks the heads of the rice, freeing the ripened grains into the canoe's bottom. The poler's duty is to stand upright in the back of the canoe, employing a twenty-foot wooden pole, which is fitted with a duckbill device on one end that expands upon contact with the muddy shallow bottom of the lake, propelling the team forward into untouched patches of *mahnomen*.

In Anishinaabemowiin (Indigenous language), *mahnomen* means "food that grows on water." In English, it refers to the edible marine grass known as wild rice that cultivates in the muddy shallows of lakes of the central Midwestern region of Turtle Island (America). This is the only ecosystem in the world where this natural food source can be found on Mama Aakii (Mother Earth).

A well-recognized, well-worn work truck comes chugging into my driveway, disrupting the peace of my otherwise quiet, uneventful evening. It was my neighbor Chakka. Chakka is a nickname I call my lifelong friend and neighbor. I wondered what he was doing pulling into my yard so late into his evening; it was 6:30 p.m. I asked Chakka what he was doing running around the neighborhood all hours of the night. Chakka replied, "Wanna go ricing? I'm looking for a poler." My mouth went dry and a wave of nervousness came over me. A voice in my head screamed, "Go proclaim your birthright!" Another whispered, "He's a 300-plus pound ricing veteran with thirty-plus seasons under his belt and you've never been out on the rice beds!" I looked to the West and calmly said, "What lake and when you wanna head out *niij* (friend)?"

In my first season we gathered over 1,500 pounds of *mahnomen*, collectively. Our best take of rice was 540 pounds in a single day. We could've easily hit 600 pounds, but I figure Ol' Chakka didn't want to see a rookie ricer hit the 600 pound club in his first season gathering. "Aho...."

Tabashish Ogitchida is 45 and originally from White Earth Nation.

The Culture in Minnesota

NGA TRUONG, SAVAGE, MN

If anyone asks me where the most beautiful culture is, I will not hesitate to answer that it is in Minnesota. Perhaps this is what surprised me the most when coming to this state.

The culture of Minnesota touches me with its friendliness and politeness. Every smile, greeting, and considerate gesture towards others fills me with gratitude, even though the actions may be small. Men, even if they are old, are still willing to let others go before them.

Another aspect of culture that I appreciate is Thanksgiving Day. It has filled me with deep gratitude for relationships. The holiday made me feel that everything that exists around me is a gift that life has given me, most recently the gift of teachers.

Finally, the education here is highly valued. The education system, with the support of the government, has helped me a lot. In addition, dedicated teachers motivate me to work hard to learn, so I can improve my life.

Although I miss my hometown very much, I still love and will forever love Minnesota.

Nga Truong is 41 and originally from Viet Nam.

Eid Celebration in My Country

HALI ABDI, ST. CLOUD, MN

It is important for all Muslims to celebrate Eid. This is our tradition in my family. My sisters and my children invite friends and neighbors. It is such a fun day. We eat very special food because, for Muslims, it is a happy day. We wear new clothes and all eat food together. This celebration is very good. I love it! I would like to someday get together with all my family.

Hali Abdi is 45 and originally from Somalia.

My Lovely Job

NENETTE KABONGO, BLAINE, MN

I decided to do this job when my mom passed away in 2004. Doctors didn't want to treat her because we didn't have money and the next day my mom passed. That situation hurt me so much, so from that day, I told myself that all my life I will be helping others.

Helping is something that makes me happy as it looks like putting light in someone's life. As a nurse assistant, we deal with different illnesses, like dementia. Someone who has dementia, you cannot change them, but you need to put yourself in their place in their world of thinking in the past. Helping is the best thing or gift you can give.

Nenette Kabongo is 31 and originally from the Democratic Republic of the Congo.

Mexico

DOLORES VAZQUEZ, MINNESOTA

I am from Mexico, which is in Latin America (Central and South America). People speak Spanish in my country. The important foods are barbacoa, tacos, pozole, and menudo.

In Mexico, there are beaches, ancient pyramids, and a historical center. All of Mexico is very, very beautiful.

Dolores Vazquez is originally from Mexico.

Bhutan

POOJA BISWA, MAPLEWOOD, MN

I believe that the most beautiful place in the world is Bhutan. Bhutan is a Buddhist kingdom. It is a peaceful, small country with mountains and hills, in the Himalayas, on the eastern edge of Asia. The population is 771,612. Bhutan is ruled by a king. The king's name is Jigme Namgyel Wangchuck. People who live in Bhutan wear the national dress as it is part of their culture. The *gho* is for men and a *kira* is for women. The national language is Dzongkha and Thimphu is the capital city. In the high Himalayas, a peak such as Jomolhari, which is 7,326 meters high, is a popular trekking destination.

Paro Taktsang Monastery, also known as Tiger's Nest, clings to a cliff above Paro Valley. It is a small and peaceful country. In Bhutan, many *Gumbas* (monasteries) are located there, such as Paro Taktsang Talo Monastery, Druk Wangyel Monastery, et cetera. Bhutan is known for its natural beauty, forest conservation, gross national product, happiness, great culture, and heritage. The Bhutanese are known for living in harmony with the environment. Tashichho Dzong is one of the most beautiful tourist places in Bhutan. There are many mountains and trees.

I was born in Bhutan in 1993. My father is in the army, and through his job, I spent my whole childhood in Bhutan. I have seen lots of things in the place of my birth, such as Tshang where the world's largest Buddha statue is. I lived in the Haa

Valley and have gone to Thimphu, Paraencies, Punakha, and Phuentsholing. The currencies of Bhutan is the Ngutnrum and Indian Rupee. China and India border Bhutan. The national food is *ema ditshi* which is one of my favorites. *Emi* means chili and *ditshi* means cheese. Bhutanese people eat a lot of chiles, and the farmers who grow them earn a good living from their production.

Every Bhutanese person dries their chiles on the roof of their house and every house has a dragon design on it. The dragon is in the Bhutanese flag and it is called the Druk. A typical western-style house in Bhutan is two stories high with a large airy attic that is used for storage. So many *dzongs* are there such as Tashichho Dzong, Drukgyel Dzong, and Lhuentse Dzong. This is a place where every year many tourists visit.

Pooja Biswa is 26 and originally from Nepal.

How to Prepare an Altar for the Day of the Dead

RENEE HOLGUIN, MAPLE GROVE, MN

Step 1:

First, you have to collect photos from your dear ones who passed away. It's really important for the altar; it's like the base of everything. You can also make the altar stairs with any kind of box. Then you have to add seven stairs. Every stair means a different side or perspective for the souls. For example, the first stair means heaven and the second one means hell. The seven stairs represent a whole trial for the soul.

Step 2:

The second step is making the favorite food of your beloved ones who passed away. Maybe they're hungry and want to eat or they are thirsty from the walk they made between the underworld and the living earth.

Side note: In popular Mexican folklore, they have the belief that the dead people's souls visit the loved ones on the night of November 2 and then they go back to the underworld.

Step 3:

In the third step, you have to add Mexican marigold or *cempazuchitl* flowers. These fragrances are said to attract souls to the altar. Their bright and cheerful color also celebrates life instead of feeling bitter about death.

Step 4:

Next, add candles to the altar. It will help the souls to see the light and return home.

Step 5:

This step is optional, but you can also prepare or make your altar in a graveyard and visit the person who passed away. In Mexico, it's typical to celebrate the Day of the Dead in a graveyard and bring the souls a mariachi band, just like a party!

Step 6:

Last, but not least, you can add dead bread to the altar. Don't worry, it is normal bread, but it has a different form.

Renee Holguin is 26 and originally from Mexico.

My Country

JOSE ALBERTO RODRIGUEZ, MAPLEWOOD, MN

I am from Honduras, which is in Central America. People there speak Spanish, and some people speak Garifuna.

The weather is very hot and uncomfortable.

One of the important foods in my country is *baleadas*.

Some of the important holidays are Independence Day, Christmas, and New Years.

Some beautiful places are Lake de Yojoa and Aguas Termales.

I don't like the weather in Honduras, and it's very dangerous.

But it has beautiful places and beautiful people.

Jose Alberto Rodriguez is originally from Honduras.

The Most Beautiful Place in Mexico

MINERVA AYALA, LANDFALL, MN

The most beautiful place in my country of Mexico is the Piramides de Xochicalco. In English, this translates into Pyramid of Xochicalco. This place is located in the state of Morelos. When I go there I take with me my camera and many bottles of water as it is very hot and you get very thirsty. It is beautiful because of the great stone construction and the images made of stone. The main attraction is the statue of Quetzalcóatl which means "feathered serpent."

My favorite thing about Xochicalco are the pyramids. They are very high and when you are up there you can see everything that is below you. There are many pyramids and they are different sizes. You will hear birds, the conversations of people talking about the history of the construction of the place. The site is hot, calm, and quiet. Being in such a place, I feel peace. The pyramids are beautiful, they are:

Big
Handsome
Strong
Peaceful
History.

Minerva Ayala is 31 and originally from Mexico.

Difficult Situation in My Country

BET SI PAW, ST. PAUL, MN

My name is Bet Si. I was born in 1991 in Karen State in Burma. Burma is located in Southeast Asia. It was a military dictatorship at that time. Some people lived in the city and some, like me, lived in villages surrounded by the mountains. Most of the villagers were farmers who grew crops to support their families. If we needed something for our home, such as blankets, salts, and some snacks, we would travel for one or two days to the nearest town. Most of the time, we consumed the food that came from our farms. For example, if we wanted to eat fish, we caught it in the river. Some food came from the farms and some from the jungle. My family farmed and grew crops such as rice, vegetables, and fruits. We had an ordinary life in the village. All villagers collaborated and shared food with each other. I was very young at that time, so I don't remember many things, but my grandparents and parents talk about their experiences when they lived in the village. Their lives were very peaceful at that time.

When I turned five years old, I had to move to another place because my village was caught in a civil war. I couldn't live in my village anymore so my family and I left the village and moved to a different place. We had to move to many different places over the ten years that followed. Finally, my family decided to move to the Thailand refugee camp to save our lives. When we lived in the camp, we got donations from UNHCR (United Nations High Commissioner for Refugees), which gave us food and shelter to survive. Also we got some education in camp. For example, I could attend high school. I thanked a lot of organizations who helped us when we were refugees. After we lived in camp for twelve years, we got the opportunity to migrate to the United States. This is my story.

Bet Si Paw is 30 and originally from Burma.

My Hometown Matagalpa - Nicaragua, C. A.

CARMEN ROA MAIRENA, GOLDEN VALLEY, MN

The city of Matagalpa, where I was born and grew up, is beautiful, surrounded by green hills, mountains, and rivers. It has nice weather. Matagalpa is in the north central part of Nicaragua and was settled by Mayan natives.

In 1852, Germans settled in Matagalpa with the purpose of cultivating 200 acres of land per person, which were granted by the government. They were required to promote the cultivation, processing, and marketing of coffee. Over time, these settlers built farms, established towns, and increased the wealth of Matagalpa and Nicaragua.

The Matagalpa natives learned to work beside the foreign people and made the city one of the most prosperous and important cities of Nicaragua.

Matagalpa's people are friendly, kind, and hard workers, with their faith, principles, and family values; most of them are Catholic. The Matagalpinos like to smile, are sociable, and have a good sense of humor. During the national celebration they usually dress up with national costumes. The official language is Spanish.

Among the Matagalpinos are many writers, musicians, composers, and painters. One of them is poet Rubén Darío, who was born in 1867 in Metapa. On May 26, 1920, this town was named "City of Rubén Darío" to honor the memory of the poet who gave glory to Nicaragua.

Matagalpa also has several institutions of higher learning, including universities and libraries accessible to students of the surrounding areas. Matagalpa has a rich history, good international commerce, good roads and communication, and educated people.

In 1962, I was teaching math in a high school when President John F. Kennedy came to promote the Alliance for Progress. Part of this program was to improve education through better teacher training. My supervisor asked me to work in the program.

I had the honor of working in my city in one of the most prestigious institutions of education in Nicaragua, the Instituto Nacional Eliseo Picado. I worked successfully with high school students and others in the program. Teaching those students was one of the best experiences of my life. I enjoyed helping many of them become good professionals and good citizens.

When I went back to my country a few years ago, I met with some of my students, and it was good to know that they continued to study in the university and were doing good things for the community.

Carmen Roa Mairena is 84 and originally from Nicaragua.

Myself: Working on the Farm

MARTIN CELIS ALVAREZ, FRIDLEY, MN

Hello my name is Martin. When I was was young, ten years old, I had to help my dad on the farm to work on harvesting the limes, oranges, bananas, and cane. Also I had to help him to keep the grass short, so I cut the grass with the machete or hoe to not leave the grass growing up. Also, we planted beans and corn, so I helped my dad to work on the farm and at the same time I went to the elementary school. I went to the farm in the mornings and I went to school in the afternoons.

Also we had two horses and one donkey and we took care of them. It was not easy and sad because I had to work on the farm and go to school at the same time, and I didn't have time to spend with my friends and play with them because I was so busy. Sometimes I went fishing to get fish and shark.

Martin Celis Alvarez is 37 and originally from Mexico

The Most Beautiful Place in El Salvador

MARIA ISABEL AGUILIAR, ST. PAUL, MN

The most beautiful place in the world in my country of El Salvador is the town of Chalatenango. The town is in Central America. I hope to go there in a few years. It is beautiful because my people are there and there is my food and the places are creative. I will go there to see my family, friends, and different places. My favorite thing in El Salvador is the fruits, mangos, pineapples, tangerines, and oranges. You will hear birds and music and the air is fresh.

Maria Isabel Aguiliar is 34 and originally from El Salvador.

Close-Knit Connections

Featured Author

Muniba Mohammed

CRYSTAL, MN

My name is Muniba Mohammed, and I am from Ethiopia. I was born in 1992 in a small town called Aweday. My parents have eight kids, I am the sixth, and I have five sisters and two brothers. I had many unforgettable moments when I was young and to help me remember, people have photo albums full of pictures that capture the best moments of our lives. Some of these moments signify the passage of time, vacations, and other events that are important to me. Growing up, I spent a lot of time with my brother. We would play together and even went to the same class together. In 2010, I got married to my lovely husband and two years later, came to the United States. 2012 was a sad year for me because it was the moment that I had to leave my family in Ethiopia. It was a very painful time, and I especially miss my brother. However, thanks to technology, I can see him every day. Currently, I am enjoying family life and am attending Robbinsdale School District's Adult Academic Program/Early Childhood Family Education. Lastly, I can't wait for my daughter to read this letter at some point in the future.

To My Daughter

Today you are three years old. I want to tell you about some of the developments and characteristics I see in you at this time. These are very typical for your age. You are growing and learning so much, and I am happy to watch you develop.

To my dearest daughter, as you grow older, I want you to fly out like a free bird and go forth and pursue all your dreams. Live life to the fullest and make sure that your happiness is second to none. While you are at it, just remember that every time you need a hug or a place to call your own, I am always here.

I am so lucky to have you as my daughter. You make me happy when you are sharing and taking turns with your friends. I am happy to watch you grow and learn. I can't believe you are already three years old but still you're my little baby. You are so strong, and you can tell the difference between things. You are smart because you know the alphabet and how to count numbers. You are also so strong and can stand on a line with one foot and jump high. I like the way you play with your siblings and share your ideas with them. You are good at listening and paying attention when we are talking.

You may grow up from being a cute little girl to a beautiful young woman, but you will forever be the person you have always been. My dearest daughter, just watching you smile makes me realize how beautiful my life is. Your love is a gift that I open every day. No matter where you go in life or who you grow up to be, I will always be right there standing behind you and encouraging you to live your dreams.

It is important to me to help you grow and develop, so I will do many things to help with your development. I will also do everything that will help you at school. I know you're growing, and you can do everything on your own, but mamma is always by your side.

Muniba Mohammed is 29 and originally from Ethiopia.

My Story

SU SU CLAY, FULDA, MN

My name is Su Su Clay and I'm twenty-five years old. I was born in Karen State in Myanmar. I have one brother and two sisters.

When I was five years old, I moved to a Thailand refugee camp. The reason that I had to move to Thailand is because Myanmar had a civil war in Karen State. I grew up in the refugee camp and I studied there for fourteen years. Thailand is better than my own country even though I had to live inside the camp.

One day I had an opportunity to come to America and I thought how lucky I am! America has equal opportunities for everyone.

I got married last summer. I work at Maple Lawn Senior Care in Fulda, Minnesota, and I attend ESL class. My life is good in Fulda and there are many kind people around me.

Su Su Clay is 25 and originally from Burma.

My Grandmother in American Samoa

MALILA FLORES, OAKDALE, MN

My grandmother didn't have her own house in American Samoa. She lived with all fourteen of us! My parents, my seven siblings, Lis who was kind, Tia who was always eager to help. There was also Alma who was a father figure to everyone, and Moe who was the rebellious one, followed by Kasa who was always causing trouble. My sister Jo was the sociable one, spending time with her friends. Tui was the spoiled baby of the family, my aunties Sala, who was the oldest, and Ola, plus my cousins Lome and Vali and I. I came before Tui.

It was a blue house with a metal roof where we shared only one bathroom, a kitchen, living room, and two bedrooms. We lived on an island so we were not inside much, only to sleep. There was also a big separate open house with no walls, only a roof for village meetings. The house was really close to the beach, about a three-minute walk. From sunrise to dusk, my house was always noisy with the sounds of everyone yelling at each other.

I do not really remember much about my grandmother but what I do remember is that she shared stories about our Samoa culture, that one male in the entire family had to represent our family in the village meetings or gatherings and that person is called *matai*. *Taupou* is a woman that represents the entire family for village gatherings and dancing. I also remember that she would cook nice food. I remember she was slim, five feet tall with grayish black hair and she always had a smile on her face. She did speak English but it was not perfect, mostly she spoke Samoan. In July 1990, my grandmother, Faalevela, passed away on the island of Tau Manua when I was about four years old.

Malila Flores is 35 and originally from American Samoa.

My Best Friend

MUHAMMAD KHAN, ST. CLOUD, MN

There are many important people in my life, but Mr. Karim is my best friend in my whole life. I have known him for forty years. He is a teacher. He was my neighbor since school time. He is a helpful person. He has a great personality, we share texts and videos with each other, and we talk on the phone nearly daily. He helps me, whenever I become sad. He is also a religious person. He helps the poor. He is good with his neighbors. He is a humble person so I like him, and I consider him my best friend.

Muhammad Khan is 54 and originally from Pakistan.

My Journey to America

DEEQO ABSHIR, MINNEAPOLIS, MN

I was born in Mogadishu, Somalia in 1993. In my family, there were three children—two boys and one girl, me. One day my mother died. Our family was very sad. After that, my father and his family and my mother's family came together to decide a future life for me and my brothers. My father's family agreed to take the two boys. I was to go with my grandmother. I was just three years old at that time.

When I was about twelve years old, I asked my grandmother, "Where is my mother?" She told me, "Your mother is not here." My grandmother asked me, "If your mother was here, what would you be doing?" I told her that I would go with my mother. She said to me, "If I tell you the truth, don't be angry with me." I said okay. She said, "Your mother died and you have two brothers." I said, "Wow, where are they?" She said that they were in the city. I really wanted to see my brothers, so my grandmother and I went to the city to meet my grandfather and one of my brothers. My grandfather told me that only one brother was there. The other one is out of the country. He lives in Australia now. My grandfather said that we would contact him on the phone. He said to him, "Your sister is here, come and talk to her. He said that he loves you so much!"

After that I went to Uganda for eight years and then I came to the United States. I still haven't seen my one brother. I hope to someday.

Deeqo Abshir is 28 and originally from Somalia.

My Favorite Rocks

BECKY GARCIA, MINNEAPOLIS, MN

My rock collecting started many years ago. I would walk along the railroad tracks looking for interesting rocks. I decided on certain rocks and started to paint them with fingernail polish as lady bugs. My family got them for presents.

As more people learned that I liked rocks, they'd bring me a rock from their travels to add to my collection. Here is a list of the cool rocks I've collected so far:

India, 2014 – Dad and stepmom Gwen.

Arizona, 2015 – My sister Amy brought me a carved owl.

Burma and Southeast Asia, 2016 – Stepmom Gwen; one rock is a carved frog.

Jericho, Israel, 2016 – Stepmom Gwen.

Hot Springs, CA, 2016 – Mom.

Jamaica, 2016 & 2018 – Housekeeper Cherie.

Italy, 2018 – My sister Carrie was at a yoga conference.

Duluth, MN, 2020 – April from Hennepin County Services.

Emily, MN, 2021 – A rock from my cousin Glen's cabin.

Minneapolis, MN, 2021 – A carved turtle rock bought for twenty-five cents from a garage sale.

I like to collect rocks because they are fascinating. They come in different shapes, colors, textures, sizes, and ages. I enjoy just looking at them and appreciating their differences.

Becky Garcia is 45 and originally from St. Paul, MN.

Healthy Life for My Family

HEATHER HERNANDEZ, BURNSVILLE, MN

Keeping health to my family is really
important for me, because I know
this helps my sons grow tall and
strong.

I try to give good food, like
vegetables and fruits, water, milk, yogurt,
and cereal.

Every morning Diego and Santiago,
they drink milk. I do the lunch for
Diego and usually I put fruit in.

When I cook the dinner I
try to cook one or two vegetables
in it. I need to be very creative
because my little son does not
like to eat vegetables, then I need
to mash the vegetables and cook
funny food.

I do an octopus with a sausage
or sometimes, I involve my kids

cooking with me.

All of this makes me feel like a good
mom and happy. Because I know
that my kids are healthy and
have good nutrition.

Another way to help my family
be healthy is to be sure that
they drink water every day.

Also my children do exercise,
they play on the playground, and
Diego practices soccer every Sunday.
All my family goes to see Diego play,
I love these moments, because we can
share time and enjoy!

Finally Diego and Santiago sleep for
ten to twelve hours per day.

I try to do all of this for myself too
and to be a good example for my kids.
But usually this is very difficult for me,
because I come back from my work at
midnight.

Heather Hernandez is 28 and originally from Mexico.

My Friend's Success

PATENGDA VUETHORTONGBRONG, MINNEAPOLIS, MN

My friend, Douya, is a successful person for four reasons. First, she graduated from college. Because of her diploma, she now has a good job. Secondly, she owns a house and a car. Her house is very big and beautiful, and her car is shiny and new. Thirdly, she also has a house that she rents to people. This allows her to have extra money. Finally, she also has a happy family. She has one child she adores. In conclusion, Douya is a successful person because she has everything she dreams about.

Patengda Vuethortongbrong is 23 and originally from Laos.

My Grandmother's House in Liberia

PATIENCE LIFE GARYEAZON, MN

My grandmother Anna has a beautiful home in Monrovia, Liberia. There are four rooms in it and a beautiful pink bathroom and a yellow kitchen. My grandmother's house is full of wonderful things, such as pictures of her parents and beautiful flowers. She and my grandfather, along with some of their grandchildren all live together. My grandmother loves to cook and clean every day. Sometimes she cooks on Sundays and invites people from church to come over. Her favorite place in her house is the kitchen where she loves to bake bread: banana, rice, and cornbreads. In my grandmother's house, she has many church hats and we are not allowed to touch her church hats.

Patience Life Garyeazon is 24 and originally from Liberia.

My Feline Miracle

ROSA PIZANO GALVAN, MINNEAPOLIS, MN

What the love and company of a pet can achieve in the life of a family. About eight months ago, my oldest daughter adopted a cat. The cat was only three weeks old. She was so small that my daughter fed her with a spoon. Well, she had always wanted a pet. One day, when I returned from work, I was surprised that there was a kitten in the living room.

So now we had one more member in the family. My three children were very happy with this cat. Her father and I never wanted to adopt a pet, because I always thought it was an extra job for me to take care of a pet.

Two of my children had suffered from anxiety.

They took therapy for two years, and the treatment helped them. They have succeeded in school. But they still occasionally have some relapses. What I have been noticing in these months is that it has helped them a lot with their mood. They are very calm and their fears and anger have been disappearing. And all this has happened since the cat came into our lives. This cat has been the best therapy for them.

I hope that my story can help other people who are experiencing something similar to what I have lived.

Rosa Pizano Galvan is 43 and originally from Mexico.

An Important Person

NHIA VUE, ST. PAUL, MN

I have a big family. I have three brothers and three sisters. My three sisters are older than my three brothers. I am the youngest one in the family. My mother and father are so busy working in the field. My older sister her name is Youa Vue. She must stay home to take care of me and go to school. She has been there for me for most of my childhood. She put me behind her back. She is very important to me.

When I was baby, she took care of me. I could say she is my second mother. I did not know that until I was three years old. My mother told me she was the one taking care of me when I was just one month old until I was three years old. Therefore, I know she is taking care of me. She is very friendly with me and buys all things that I want. She buys me a pretty dress and make-up, then takes a picture.

My sister has black hair and brown eyes and has a beautiful body. She is five feet and four inches tall. She is quiet and a soft-spoken person. She likes to eat chicken and noodles soup. She's interested in sewing Hmong clothes and reads books. She is not interested in soccer. She married on the December 2007 New Year, when I was five years old. I missed her so much, and I cried a lot during her wedding. After that, my sister moved out of the city. I did not see my sister since 2008 until I was fifteen years old. I get to see my sister again when I come to the United States. Now she has three baby boys. During that time, I felt sad because it will be so long until I will get to see her again. I plan to save more money, and in 2023, I will go see her in Laos.

Nhia Vue is 19 and originally from Laos.

A Good Life

REYNA NUNEZ JAIMES, ST. PAUL, MN

I am from Zihuatanejo, Mexico. I came to the United States on May 14, 2005. I have three daughters and three sons. We moved here for better jobs and a good future for our family.

My first job is childcare for my children. One of our sons has epilepsy, so I need to help him get to the swimming pool for exercise. I am also a homemaker.

This state has nice weather. We have a good life in this country.

Reyna Nunez Jaimes is 53 and originally from Mexico.

When My Daughter Was Born

ANONYMOUS, ST. CLOUD, MN

When my daughter was born, she smiled.

Outside, there was a moon.

I felt so good like a mattress.

I named you Nejat because I liked the name.

You looked like me.

Life Is Short

AZZA ELSHABRAWI, COLUMBIA HEIGHTS, MN

When I won the American immigration program, I was very happy. So I left my family and my job and came to America with my husband and two daughters. While I was traveling, I did not hug my father and mother, and I told them when I come back, I will hug you a lot. My father died a year later, and then I realized that life is too short. When I gave birth to my third daughter, I didn't waste time being without them. We must do the things that make us happy in their time and not postpone them. We don't know if we or our loved ones will be there tomorrow.

Azza Elshabrawi is 33 and originally from Egypt.

My Best Gift

EDGAR GUTIERREZ, MINNESOTA

The best gift I ever received is my niece, daughter to my sister. I think she was a gift of God. This was four years ago. Because five months before, my mother passed away and my niece was born.

Edgar Gutierrez is originally from Guatemala.

My Family

VO DIEM, RICHFIELD, MN

I am Vietnamese.

In Vietnam I have eight siblings, two brothers, and six sisters. I am the first sister.

My country has many rivers and rice fields. I love my country.

I went to Minnesota two years ago. I live in Minnesota now. I live with my daughter, and her family has a husband and two children.

I like it at home, but I do not like outside because it's cold.

I like to care for my grandchildren.

I like cooking Vietnamese food, like rice, pho, and spring rolls.

I like game puzzles.

December 9 is my granddaughter's birthday. My family and I will hold a party to celebrate her birthday. We will make a cake. I knit her a pink hat, a seven-color scarf, and pink mittens.

I wake up at 3 a.m., meditate, and do yoga exercises. I prepare for a new day.

Thank you for listening to my story.

Vo Diem is 67 and originally from Vietnam.

When I Was Born

ANONYMOUS, ST. CLOUD, MN

When I was born, it was a long time ago.

My mother was young like a flower.
My father was nice.

I was my mother's first child.

I was born in the land of Somalia
where the land is good.

My father was a farmer man
and I was a healthy baby.

When I was born, Allah said you're alive.
Everything is good. I made you.

I saw mom through my brown eyes.

Important Person

LAH MOO, ST. PAUL, MN

Back in Burma, it was hard for my parents to provide for us due to the Burmese military. If they see anyone go out, they captured them and even killed them. Even though life was hard, my parents tried their best. Even though the enemy were around, my dad always sneaked out at nighttime to bring food.

One day, the Burmese military attacked our small village and destroyed our home and we had to run for our life. My mom carried me, and my dad carried my brother. The Burmese military chased after us. Some of the villagers got shot and died.

We spent weeks in the jungle. Even though we were hungry and cold, we couldn't build a fire because the enemies were around us. We had to eat fruits to survive. One night, it was raining hard and we couldn't find any shelter. My dad covered me under his arm all through the night.

It took us one month to get to the Thailand border. The Thai soldiers helped us and took us to the refugee camp.

In the refugee camp, life was hard too. But it wasn't hard like in Burma. After six years, I started to go to school and make friends. Sometimes I went to the river with my friends and when I went back home, my mom hit me because she was worried about me.

After I turned thirteen, I told my parents to apply to come to the USA. My parents agreed. After four years of waiting, the U.S. finally called us. I was so happy.

I came to America in 2013. After arriving, life was much easier. I ate many good foods. My parents had to work to provide food and pay rent. After a few months, I started school and learned English. After five years, I met my boyfriend. After one year, we decided to have a baby.

In 2020, my baby was born. After a week, my whole family got COVID-19. My dad passed away due to COVID-19. He was the person who protected me all the time. I cried for a week. My boyfriend stayed right beside me. I still miss my dad.

I decided to go back to school and learn more English and my boyfriend is taking care of me. I am living my life happily with him and my son.

Lah Moo is 24 and originally from Burma.

Shared Pain

CRAIG HANDELAND, MINNEAPOLIS, MN

Mom,

My pain was yours...

All my life I hurt like you...

Only I was weak and you were strong...

Your strength strengthened me...

It built me up and got me through...

It made me a strong man...

You taught me how to love and feel for others...

All my life I felt for you...

Son,

My pain was yours...

All my life I hurt like you...

At the end, when I was weak, your strength strengthened me...

I could feel you and you could feel me...

You saved me, you healed me...

I felt for you...

Now, I feel with you...

It's time we save and heal you...

We're not through...

I love you.

Love, Mom

1962–2020

Craig Handeland is 39 and originally from Minneapolis, MN.

My Mother the Lion

MADELYN AGUILAR, MINNEAPOLIS, MN

One of the most important people in my life is my mom. She is the bravest individual I have ever known. She was born in a farm-like environment where there was a lack of both income and emotional understanding. She told me that for weeks, her family ate only beans. Buying a piece of meat was hardly ever a choice, and when they did, they celebrated.

When she was a teenager, she was lent to an uncle who mistreated her and gave her responsibilities that would steal her dreams and childhood. Every time my mom tells me her story, I sense resentment and pain.

She told me that at that time in her life she would have to get up early to make a fire and prepare tortillas by hand so that my uncles could eat some of them and sell the rest. She was not allowed to go to school like her cousins did. Rather, she had the responsibilities of a grown-up. His family had no morning chores. She would hand-wash their clothes and her own.

She kept moving forward, staying busy and enduring the present. When she was around twenty, she was able to do what her mother suggested: become certified as a dressmaker. She worked long hours at a textile factory, sometimes staying overnight.

She met the man who made my mom pregnant and left. Raising a baby, however, gave her faith in herself. My older brother, her son, was the light in her eyes, and he kept her moving on even though she didn't have the love of a husband.

She never lost her own true spirit. She cared for my brother, me, and others as well. Every time I would go through emotional distress, she was there when there was no one else.

One time over a year ago, my day felt different; everything felt lonely and gray. I was sitting on the living room couch, weeping. I saw no light inside my soul. She sat and listened to me—understanding me because at some point, she had felt the same. She told me that everything would be fine.

I wanted to find out the meaning of her name, Arely. I learned that it means "lion" or "god." Lions are symbols of courage, power, and royalty. They take pride in a family's love. She has these traits. I hope I have them too.

Madelyn Aguilar is 25 and originally from El Salvador.

Love Cures All

SHAMA FATHIMA FAROOK, PLYMOUTH, MN

My name is Shama. I am from India. There we lived in a joint family house. Joint family means an extended family, typically consisting of three or more generations and their spouses, living together as a single household. In my family, there were fourteen people living together. Family is a place where life begins and love never ends. I am blessed with such a family!

This incident happened before I came to the U.S. It was the month of Ramadan. Muslim people fast for thirty days during this month. It was the twenty-seventh day of fasting. That morning, I prepared to take a bath. In India, not all the houses have water heaters to bathe. So in our house, we had the habit of keeping hot water in an induction stove and carrying it to the bathtub.

I followed my usual procedure that day, but when I was carrying the vessel to pour the hot water in the tub, I slipped and fell, crying loudly! I could feel my hand burning as the boiled water fell on my right hand. Hearing me crying, my husband and my family came running. When they tried to remove my wrist bangle from my hand, I could see my skin coming along with the bangle! It was a horrible day for me. I was crying louder and louder since I was feeling like my hand was burning in fire. I could not control my tears even when I saw my two-year-old daughter crying, looking at me.

They took me to the hospital, and the doctor said that I should break my fast since I needed to have a shot immediately. They gave some ointments and antibiotics for the wound. But during this situation, I could literally see how my family suffered, seeing me. They were wounded more badly in their hearts than me! My husband and my whole family were taking care of me so much when I was not able to do my own work. With their love and support, I was able to get well in three weeks. But my whole hand looked reddish in color. It took nearly six months for my skin to look normal. I believe true love can cure any types of hurdles that arise in our life!

Shama Fathima Farook is 30 and originally from India.

Vacation to My Family Home

MERY SANCHEZ, FRIDLEY, MN

I took a two-week vacation in November. My family and I went to Ecuador and we had a great time there because my mother and my husband's parents and grandmother live there.

We took a plane to Miami and another plane to Guayaquil, Ecuador. After landing, we had to drive three and a half hours to get to my town where I grew up. My town's name is San Jose.

I was very excited to see my mom after three years. We cried just thinking about COVID-19.

We thank God nobody got infected and hope for the best for everyone. I hugged my mom and I told her how scared I was and how lucky we feel that nobody in our family died. I am so glad we are still alive. I felt sad and very lucky.

We had a great time eating, dancing, drinking, and I drank a lot. It was fun! It was a great time to be back with my family.

My mom has a farm. She has cows, pigs, hens, and many little chicks. It was so cute to hold them for a little bit. My daughter rides a horse and she loves doing that. Also it was raining. Some days we had to walk to the farm, and some days we could have a car.

It was a very short time for me, but I loved going back to my family home.

Mery Sanchez is 35 and originally from Ecuador.

My Beautiful Life

MARTHA JARQUIN, ST. PAUL, MN

I came to this beautiful country with my husband on March 1, 2019. He has lived here for fifty years. His mother brought him here when he was ten. We live in an apartment. We live alone. We both have no children, but we have made many friends here.

Martha Jarquin is 50 and originally from Nicaragua.

When You Need to Be Strong

MARCELA ACOSTA, ROSEMOUNT, MN

I moved to the USA when I was fourteen years old. I became a mother at the age of fifteen. Becoming a mom was hard because I didn't speak English or know how to drive. My husband worked the night shift and slept during the day. When I found out I was pregnant, I got scared thinking about how I was going to take care of my baby. I didn't have any of my family close to me.

I had a tiny and beautiful baby girl. We named her Cynthia Janet. I had to learn how to be a mother all by myself. When she was three years old, I moved to Minnesota to live with my older sister while my husband worked on the fishing boat. When my daughter started school, we began to have additional problems due to our language and cultural differences. There were not many Latinos in the school and the teachers were racist. I couldn't communicate with the teachers because of my limited English.

Once I moved from my sister's house, my daughter started at a new school. As a child, my daughter helped me a lot with translating and interpreting. Although it was hard for me to help her with my limited English, I have always been proud of her. Her dream school was St. Olaf College and she talked about it a lot in high school. I watched my first daughter grow up; she applied and was accepted to St. Olaf College.

She graduated and moved to St. Paul where she worked with the former governor of Minnesota, Mark Dayton. One day she invited me and my husband to see her office in the Capitol. It was a very nice place and I felt proud that my daughter worked there. But soon after my visit, she wanted to focus on completing her degree as a writer. She left the governor's office and started a new job with the Women's Foundation of Minnesota. This job change allowed her to start grad school.

Now when I see my daughter, I'm proud of her. It makes me think that maybe I was not a perfect mother but I was a good mother for her. I was able to be strong and supported her, with my husband, so she can be where she is today. I sacrificed a lot, but I don't regret any of it.

Marcela Acosta is 42 and originally from Mexico.

My Sweet Grandmother

ZINA DEMLIE, NEW HOPE, MN

My grandmother lives in Ethiopia and she is ninety-eight years old. She is very beautiful, healthy, and strong. She is still doing some activities like cooking, cleaning, going to church, and gardening. Most of the time she spends her time at church, praying for the world and everybody. She has nine kids and forty-four grandkids. She is happy about her family and she said, "I am lucky and blessed in this world because I have a big family, thanks to God."

We have had a big party two times a year at her house during Ethiopian Christmas and Easter holidays. On that day, she gives us good advice about our future life, like to focus on education, to have good marriage life, to raise our kids with good manners and social life, and how to spend money, et cetera. She had different types of life experience. She shared her life experience for all families, and we have learned many things from her.

Unfortunately, now I am living in U.S. and I can't go there to attend the holiday parties. Last time I went there was 2020. We are lucky to have this grandmother. She loves us unconditionally. Sometimes when I talk to her by video call, she says, and I quote, "Please come and see me before I pass." When I think about her, I cry because I love her very much, and she is my everything.

Zina Demlie is 32 and originally from Ethiopia.

Friend

RAJA MUSTAFA, SARTELL, MN

Samar is my best friend. We were neighbors and grew up together, that made us share all things in our life like playtime, school, food, and picnics. When I got married, I moved to Syria. However, we kept in touch and saw each other every two or three years. Samar is a good, kind, and open-minded friend who I trust all the time.

Raja Mustafa is 62 and originally from Jordan.

Memory from Home

HAE NAY PAW, ST. PAUL, MN

When I lived in a Thailand refugee camp Mae Ra Moe, I was young. I was ten years old when my dad taught us how to work. I am older than my siblings and my dad taught me first and instructed my brother Dah Eh Say and my sister Hser Nay Paw, but my little brother was too young. His name is Kaw Nay Say.

When I was fourteen years old and I knew how to work, I went with my friends, so I did not need my father. I could go alone with my friends Moo Ku Wah, Poe Love, Poe Hser, and Naw Christ. Every Friday morning, me and my friends said, "Let's go work," and we were so happy. We always went because we needed money to buy a snack when we got to school. I usually went to work every Saturday, but we left home on Friday after school because it was too far to walk to the village.

When we were in the village, we found someone to hire us. When they hired us, they also gave us a house for sleep. We were so happy when we could work. On Saturday, we started work at 7 a.m., worked all day and after like 5 p.m., we got the money and went back to our home. When we went to work, we removed and picked the scutch grass with our hand, and nettles too.

In the village, people do grain, chili, and many vegetables. Sometimes we planted rice. My father also had a garden and we hired people to work for us too. We loved to plant many vegetables, and chilies.

We also found bamboo shoots in the forest with my friend, sister, and brother, usually after school on weekdays. Sunday, we went to worship in the church. Sometimes we went to swim in the long river. This river is not safe to swim but many people love to swim in this river. Many people died in this river too.

After we worked, we also picked up the vegetables for eating and brought them to our home. I felt so cheerful and happy but sometimes I felt so tired too. This I will never forget in my life. One day, I will go back and see my old home, and all my old friends, and see how many changes happened since I was there.

Hae Nay Paw is 21 and originally from Myanmar.

My Life

SAFIA ADEN, ST. PAUL, MN

I was born in Somalia. My family is big. I have three brothers and three sisters. My mom and dad have passed away. My country was in a civil war. My brother paid for everything we needed after my parents died. I helped my family by cleaning the house, cooking, and washing clothes.

I am married and have one daughter. My first job in the United States was a bus aide. The second job was at Target. Now, I am working at Walmart in Roseville.

I study English at the Hubbs Center for Lifelong Learning. My plan for the future is to go to college so I can be a math teacher in a middle school. My life is very, very good in the U.S. because I am healthy, have free education, and a good job.

Safia Aden is 47 and originally from Somalia.

My Pregnancy

TOMASA ROMERO, FRIDLEY, MN

I didn't know I was pregnant.

I was feeling sick. I had nausea and headaches. I went to the hospital, to the emergency room. Also, they didn't know that I was pregnant. It happened twice. Then they put me through the scanner tube to look at my head and my neck. They did a pregnancy test because you can't go through the scanner if you are pregnant. They found that I was pregnant.

They told me I was pregnant. I was surprised! I didn't believe them.

My headache is gone and I have my little baby now!

Tomasa Romero is 32 and originally from Mexico.

Ride the Buffalo with My Brother and His Friend

XENG HA, ST. PAUL, MN

When I lived in Laos, I was young. I was ten years old. My brother was twelve years old, and his friend was twelve years old too. My brother's name is Tong and his friend's name is Yeng. My family, we have five buffaloes. My brother was with his friend and me. We study in the same school. Tong and Yeng are close to each other because they study in the same grade and classes together. I study a different grade and classes. Every day after we finish school, we always go tend the buffaloes in a field together.

One Sunday, we had no school that day. We are planning to go tend the buffalo all day. Tong prepared some breakfast and some food for us for lunch. Then we started herding the buffaloes to the field. When we arrived, we let the buffalo graze on the field freely. At the field, there were two fishponds. We enjoyed swimming in the ponds while the buffalos were grazing. When the buffaloes are thirsty, they come to drink and bathe in the ponds. After we were done swimming, we went and had lunch at a hut. We ate and watched the buffalo roam and joked and goofed around.

In the evening, we were tired, and the buffaloes were full, so we decided to herd them back home. My brother and his friend would ride the buffalo home. Tong and Yeng got on and rode a buffalo together. I saw this and I wanted to join them, but I was too short. Tong said, "Get on the wooden fence and wait for us." My brother told me, "When the buffalo gets close, you jump onto his back, okay?" I said "Okay." Tong was in the front and Yeng was in the back with a space for me in the middle. I jumped onto the buffalo when it got close to me, I accidentally bumped and knocked my brother's friend off the back of the buffalo. He fell and cut his chin on the wooden post! I was so scared because I caused it. We went home quickly and got it treated with medicine.

After the incident, Yeng still went to tend the buffalo with us, but he never rode the buffalo with us anymore. I'm still scared when I think about it to this day.

Xeng Ha is 22 and originally from Laos.

My Good Friend

NTXHI VANG, ST. PAUL, MN

When I was young, I had a friend whose name was Pa Yao. She was my first friend. We grew up, went to school, and lived together in KM20 village in Laos.

Pa Yao and I liked to sing songs when we walked to school. We learned new things from each other. She was a nice person, she was an artist, and also her parents were very nice, too!

Her mother planted a lot of vegetables in their garden. On Saturdays, my friend and I went to sell vegetables at the market. Sometimes she came to help me water my plants, we ate dinner in my house, washed our clothes, and did our homework together. We studied together from first to fifth grade. After that, I went to my next grade, but she didn't because Pa Yao and her family had to move to another village. I felt very sad and she was too. That year I was alone, and I had no friends. I missed her so much.

A few months later, I heard some bad news from her parents. Pa Yao passed away because she was sick. I didn't believe that because she was only thirteen years old. I couldn't go to see her one last time because my parents weren't home and nobody took me there. I was very sad about that.

After many years, I got married and moved to the U.S. I'll never forget her. She is always in my heart.

Ntxhi Vang is 27 and originally from Laos.

Soulmates

ODILIA PEREZ, ST. PAUL, MN

This story is about my friend and me. She does not have my blood or my last name, but she is my sister from the heart. She has always been with me through thick and thin and has always supported me. I always appreciate the time she spends with me. I feel blessed by her friendship. She is unique.

Now she lives in Atlanta. Although distance separates us, she is always in my heart. She is a true friend. I miss her when I need to talk with someone about my problem or anything else. For example, I miss her when I am feeling sad.

The most curious thing is that we were both born under the sign of Taurus. Her birthday is April 21 and my birthday is April 29. We used to celebrate our birthdays together. I love April. It is my favorite month.

Odilia Perez is 35 and originally from Guatemala.

My Friend

BER DI, ST. PAUL, MN

His name is Moe Poe, village name is Tea Moo Ta. He is living in St. Paul, Minnesota right now. He doesn't have any brothers and sisters. He lives with his aunt and cousin. He was a good student so he graduated high school last year. His house is close to me so if he comes to visit me, he doesn't drive his car. If he goes to the park, he calls me every time. He also taught me how to drive a car and how to go to the freeway. He is funny, honest, and kind. He speaks English well because he lived here for eight years. His favorite color is black. He is shorter than me and also he is skinny. Last year he felt so happy because he got a new car. He is my friend and I feel so happy too.

Ber Di is 23 and originally from Thailand.

My Life in America

SAMRAWIT WOLDETENSAY, RICHFIELD, MN

I feel young.

I have two kids, a girl and a boy. My daughter is four years old. My son is ten months old. My husband has a really good personality because he always supports me. My country is Ethiopia.

I have two sisters and two brothers in my country. My mom is in Ethiopia too.

My favorite foods are injera and shiro.

I enjoy exercising sometimes.

I want to learn more English because English is used everywhere in America.

In my country, we have a special coffee ceremony. All tourists like it.

I wish my children very good knowledge and success. Always I want to support my children because I love them very much.

Samrawit Woldetensay is 35 and originally from Ethiopia.

Mexico and Family

BIVIANA COLIN, RICHFIELD, MN

I really like Mexico because my mother, my father, and my grandfather are there. I have two brothers and two sisters. Three are in Texas and one is in Mexico. No one is here in Minnesota.

One brother and one sister came to Minnesota for my daughter's baptism and third birthday last summer. My uncle and aunt came from California. My cousin came from Georgia. It was a big party.

I like Mexico because there I played basketball every weekend. My husband also likes basketball. There we played.

Another reason I like Mexico is because there it is not cold like in Minnesota. I like the nature of the countryside with the animals, the rivers of water, and the climate.

Biviana Colin is 24 and originally from Mexico.

My Grandmother

KADIRA KAHIN, ST. CLOUD, MN

When I was seven years old, I lived with my grandma and my mom. My grandma was sick with cancer. One day, I was at school. When I came home, no one was there. I looked everywhere in rooms, kitchen, living room, but nobody was there. Then I went to my uncle's house near my home and he told me what had happened. My grandma was in the hospital. Next day, my sister, my brother, and I stayed at my uncle's house. My grandma died after two days. I felt so sad because my grandma was nice to me and I loved her so much.

Kadira Kahin is 24 and originally from Ethiopia.

An Important Friend

BATULA OMAR, ST. CLOUD, MN

The most important person in my life is my friend Kendra. We met through an acquaintance who was my friend and her friend too. We became very close friends. We lived together for many years. She helped me when I was having a rough time there. She is my hero. God sent her to me. We were so happy living together with her kids. She had her own children and I was helping to raise the kids. Then I became a godmother for her children. We never called each other only friends. She is like a sister to me. She even told her other friends that I'm her sister. That's why she is very special to me.

After all those years we lived together, I decided to move to St. Cloud and she decided to move to Las Vegas. We contact each other, we talk on the phone, and text. We are not living in the same state, which is a little sad, but we still have a good relationship.

Batula Omar is 43 and originally from Somalia.

My Favorite Object

ANABELLE GONZALEZ, WATIE PARK, MN

My name is Anabelle. The most important object for me is the sheet in which my daughter was taken from the hospital when she was born. My daughter's grandmother gave it to me because in her family, all the first grandchildren have used it at birth. It is a bit run down because it has been used by many children in the past.

Anabelle Gonzalez is 22 and originally from the Dominican Republic.

My Daughter Ami

KADIATOU CAMARA, MINNEAPOLIS, MN

Ami is my first kid. She is six years old and is a sweet little girl.

Ami is tall, brown, very smart, and beautiful.

She is always smiling and loves questions. Anything she sees, she asks questions about.

She loves rice with tomato sauce, banana, ice cream, cookies, and candy. She doesn't like milk.

She loves sports like biking, gymnastics, running, and jumping.

Ami likes being with people. She is helpful and friendly.

She is scared of mice, bugs, and ants. She likes fish and cats.

When she is home, she often sings and draws and sometimes helps me to clean the house.

She likes to play with her brother and sister, and watch TV too. Her dream is to be a doctor.

I love her so much, and I want to teach her to be respectful and a great person.

Kadiatou Camara is 38 and originally from Guinea.

I Like America

KA LER, FULDA, MN

My name is Ka Ler. My daughter's name is May Paw. There are three people in my family.

I came to the U.S. on August 8, 2012. I came to live in Fulda, MN. I go to school and am learning the English language. My ESL teacher is good and I love her. All the people in Fulda are nice. I go to the food shelf every month. I love the food shelf people. They are very nice.

My daughter, May, graduated from high school in 2020 with honors. She went to college and is now a surgical nurse in a hospital.

I am sick a lot. My doctors are very good. I am happy to be in America, to have good doctors and good friends. God bless you.

Ka Ler is 50 and originally from Thailand.

Cattleya Orchid

ANONYMOUS, BURNSVILLE, MN

When I was around thirteen years old, I was reading a book about flower plants. Then I came across the name of Cattleya and I loved it and investigated more about the orchid. It is queen of the orchids for its color, for its texture, for its meaning. The white orchid represents justice, prudence, and wisdom. So I chose it as a name for my future daughter because of everything that name meant. Years later, I had a daughter and I chose to name her Cattleya.

A Very Important Person

RUKIA HUSSEIN, ST. CLOUD, MN

A very important person in my life is my mother because she gave birth to me. She gave me life. She took care of me and she fed me. She is my hero. What she gave me in my life I can't give her back because she made me who I am today. She is my everything in the world. My mother is one of the best moms in the world. Even when I did something wrong, she never yelled at me. She talked to me slowly. She's always by my side.

My mom is the strongest person I know because she is a single mom with eight kids in the USA without any help. She took that challenge and turned it into a beautiful thing. My mom made something out of herself because now she has her own business. She faced a lot of problems since we moved to the United States. She had no help from family members and she spoke no English. Having no support meant working extra hard. It was hard for her in the beginning, but after many years, we're grateful for how life is treating us now. I love her more than everything!

Rukia Hussein is 39 and originally from Somalia.

My Hero

SARTU AHMED, BROOKLYN CENTER, MN

This person that I am going to write about is very special to me, my mom. My mom had twelve kids, but six passed away. She married my dad at about thirteen. Unfortunately my dad passed away and left the other six kids and my mom behind.

After my dad died, we struggled so much. We lived in the villages so we grew corn, and we had cows, sheep, and goats. My brother was not old enough to do all of these because he was born after the three girls. My mom's first option was to step in to be a dad and mom to raise these six kids. Sometimes we went through a whole day without food.

A week after my dad died, my mom got really sick and ended up in the ICU. No one thought that she was going to survive, but *alhamdulillah* (thank God) she did survive. After a couple of months, my mom was completely healthy. She left the house very early in the morning, bought eggs at a cheap price, and then sold them for more money for food for us.

One of our neighbor guys came to my mom for my sister's hand in marriage. My mom had no option but to say yes because we still needed a man to help us with the farmlands. This was my mom's little break since my sister's husband was handling things.

After a year or two, my mom heard some good news from my uncle who lived in the U.S. for more than thirty-five years that there would be an opportunity to come to the USA. Everything was new to us. We had no choice but to learn a new language. It took me approximately five years to learn English and get my diploma. I decided I was going to step in to help my mom so she could at least get a big break. My brother and I pitched in some money and bought the house for her down in the cities. My mom used to live in the villages, but now she lives in the cities. My mom is now the happiest person ever. I have always appreciated how much she gave up to take care of us, and it makes me so happy to know she is now able to enjoy her life.

THANK YOU SO MUCH, MOM, YOU ARE MY HERO.

Sartu Ahmed is 36 and originally from Ethiopia.

Our Blessed Son

ANONYMOUS, FARMINGTON, MN

I got married on February 14, 2001. I had three children from my previous marriage and my husband did not have children. Since I had three children, he said our family was complete. Before I got married, I told my husband that I couldn't have children anymore because I had my tubes tied when I delivered my youngest son in 1997. Everything was going great with our life together until I wanted to have another child with my husband in 2005.

He told me he didn't want any more children. He said, "We already have three kids." However, I insisted and eventually managed to convince him. Once we were ready, I went to Mexico to have an operation to untie my tubes. This is what needed to be done, so I could get pregnant again. My doctor only gave me a ten percent chance of becoming pregnant again. Even with these low odds, I had a lot of hope that I could get pregnant again. I had the complicated surgery on November 26, 2005. Thank God, everything went well. In April of 2006, I was pregnant again after nine years of having my tubes tied.

I felt especially blessed to have the opportunity to carry another child. I wished to have a girl, but we were given a beautiful baby boy. He was born on December 13, 2006. This day was important to me because it is the day after the Virgin Maria's birthday of December 12. Jesus's mom's birthday is a celebrated day in Mexico for almost all Catholic people like me. This added to my feelings of being blessed with my second son. My husband was surprised and couldn't believe our good fortune. Our family is complete and perfect. We now have two girls and two boys. Our luck has continued and we are also grandparents of a beautiful girl. I am always a very positive person even if everything looks very difficult. This positive outlook has given me good fortune in my life.

My Friend Huikui

QIONG SUN, ST. CLOUD, MN

Huikui and I met each other twenty-two years ago. We lived in the same dormitory and went to the canteen together and we studied together. We were best friends in my school time. She was a smart and helpful girl. She often helped everyone in our classroom. She especially helped me learn computers and math, and she reminded me to call my parents every weekend. She always made me laugh when I felt sad, this is why I always have many memories of her. Now, I often dream about her. Though we are not often in contact with each other, I hope we can see each other soon. She is the best friend in my life.

Qiong Sun is 40 and originally from China.

My Friend

RUMANA MOHAMED, FRIDLEY, MN

Iftu is my close friend. She is a beautiful, sweet, and hard-working person. Iftu is married and has two kids, a boy and a girl. We mostly go out and visit each other's homes. We work in the same place. Then I changed my job to a different place. When I did that, she was happy for me but at the same time she wasn't. We aren't working together any more, so now I'm missing her.

Rumana Mohamed is 29 and originally from Oromia.

My Grandmother

RUTSEL RAMIREZ, ST. PAUL, MN

The most important person in my life is my grandmother, because she raised me and she made me who I am today. She taught me about respect, economic independence, and that I have to be strong in difficult times. My grandmother is so brave, hard-working, and strong, but she is also sensitive. She is all in my life. Every day, I feel so bad because she is seventy years old and now I'm so far from her, from my home. I miss her every day of my life. I love her so much that I cannot explain it.

Rutsel Ramirez is 24 and originally from Venezuela.

Back Home

AYAN DIINI, RICHFIELD, MN

This year l was so happy because l visited my family back home. l did not go back since I left over sixteen years ago. l missed my mom and my brothers and sisters so much. I was working hard and l couldn't save enough money to buy a ticket because it is expensive. But this summer my daughter and I were able to travel with the help of my husband.

I saw my mom, my brothers, my sisters, other family, and many relatives. I saw my oldest family member that lives in that city. We call him Awoowe. He is very smart. He memorized the whole Quran and everyday he reads it. He goes to the Masjid five times a day for praying.

I was glad to see them all. We traveled to another city to meet my mother-in-law, father-in-law, sisters, and brothers. We were so happy to meet our families and we are back to Mogadishu and we went to see Liido Beach and had fun. I would love to go back again.

Ayan Diini is 36 and originally from Somalia.

My Best Friend

WAJEEHA FAQEERZAI, ST. CLOUD, MN

A friend is one of the most precious gifts from God. In this world it is very difficult to find a good and wise friend. I am very fortunate to have a very good and true friend.

Wajeeha Faqeerzai is 27 and originally from Afghanistan.

About Me

SHAQUITA TAYLOR, ST. PAUL, MN

I grew up in Chicago and learned a lot of things. I've had friends that came and left. I've watched my great-grandparents leave this world, even though I was really close to them. I had good days and bad days. There were times when my siblings and I would go outside and play until the streetlights came on. We would play jump rope or have a dance party. There were times when my mom and sisters would leave me alone because they felt like I was too little to go anywhere with them. They would get their nails and hair done while I stayed at home with my brothers.

We went to Mississippi: just my dad, grandad, brothers, and I. We had a firework shoot-out that caused my brother to get shot with a Roman candle in his chest. My grandad had fallen out of his chair and everybody had to help him back up in his chair. When we left to go home my little brother had gotten bit by a mosquito on his leg. When I got home, there were a lot of things going on. My sisters and I went to my auntie's house to go back-to-school shopping and get coats, shoes, and book bags. We went to my other auntie's house and we played a game, cooked, and went skating. When winter break came up, I went to my grandma's house and I didn't want to go home. I was forced to go home and when I got there, everybody was talking about a fight, but I was focused on getting ready for school instead of a fight.

Growing up, school was the best place to be because I didn't get in trouble, and I had good grades in all my classes. I remember my library teacher giving me purses and talking to me to keep me from getting into trouble. Over the years, everything changed when we moved and I had to leave all my friends that I grew up with. I had to change schools and help my little brothers with their homework. Growing up, I wasn't a girly girl because I didn't have anybody to show me how to be one.

Shaquita Taylor is 26 and originally from Chicago, IL.

My Grandmother's House

TIFFANY EDMOND, ST. PAUL, MN

My grandmother's house in Madison, Mississippi was full of jokes, laughter, and smiles that filled up the whole room. Grandmother's cooking was on Sundays when everyone would come and sit around my grandmother and listen just to hear her fuss and give people a piece of her mind if they had done wrong. Grandma would give words of encouragement. My sister, my brother, and I lived with our grandmother after our mom passed when we were very young. I was only three years old. Grandmother was always there for us even when it did not seem like it. Grandmother was special because she was love. Love was always there in my grandmother's house.

Tiffany Edmond is 39 and originally from Madison, MS.

Important People in My Life

MARIA ELENA MORALES, MINNESOTA

Paloma is important because she is my daughter and she is as a star for me. Luis is important because he is my son, and I always wanted a son.

Lupe is important because she is my mama and she forms a special piece of my life. Guadelupe is a very important person for me. She was born in 1960 in a small town. She began to work when she was very young. For me, she is my big star, my favorite person.

Maria Elena Morales is originally from Mexico.

Peace Poem

JHOONN GENAO, MINNESOTA

Peace is like God.

Peace is like the family.

Peace with my house.

Peace with my company.

Peace is within Navidad.

Jhoonn Genao is originally from the Dominican Republic.

A Visit with My Mother

SHAMSO OMAR, MINNEAPOLIS, MN

When I was thirty-three years old, I lived in Saudi Arabia, and I came back home to Somalia. I saw my mom after fifteen years away. My mom that time was so, so happy to see me, and me too. I cried and my mom cried too. My mom said, "Thank you, Allah, I saw my daughter before I died." My mom and I talked for a long time. She asked me about Saudi Arabia. "Are people in Saudi Arabia nice? How do you feel?" I said, "People in Saudi Arabia are very nice. I feel good. A little bit sad because I didn't see my mom and my dad and my sisters for a long time."

I brought my daughter Safa with me. Safa was four years old. My mom saw my daughter, and she hugged her and kissed her a lot. My daughter knew my mom because every day I talked to my mom on the phone. Safa said, "Grandma, I'm very proud to see you." My mom said, "Me too. I was scared I would never see you."

I stayed with my mom fifteen days only. It was not enough time. That fifteen days, I felt like I was five or ten years old because every single day my mom said, “Come sit with me. I want to see your face.” She hugged me. She and I made together my favorite childhood foods, like spaghetti with sauce and then bananas.

After fifteen days, I came to the United States. Then my mom died after three years. I felt very, very sad because I never saw my mom again.

Shamso Omar is 44 and originally from Somalia.

Family

MARIETTA EASTMAN, MINNEAPOLIS, MN

My family: My daughter.

She's precious to my heart. When she was a toddler, she was always a bright light in a room. She put joyful smiles on everyone's face she encountered.

She would dance at three years old, I'm sure since then. She had rhythm, she had rhyme. She loves, she cares, her heart is so tender it's like fragile glass, it would break. If she saw someone hurt, now! She's overcome horrific obstacles in life, it's made her even stronger, but still admitting her weakness humbles her more.

She's beautiful, her dimples are her personality. Always laughing, uplifting. She, Natasha “Solider Woman,” is the ultimate gift from above.

Marietta Eastman is 59 and originally from Rosebud, SD.

An Important Person

ANONYMOUS, WEST ST. PAUL, MN

One of the most important people in my life is my dad. I think he is one of the most intelligent people I have ever met. I learned almost all I know about life from him. He is so serious and has a particular behavior. He is so strict, but always laughs and teases all our family members. He has always been an example for all the family, almost all of my family members have told how honorable my dad is and how responsible he has been since he was a kid. His family and my mom's family really admire his courage and determination to reach all his goals. He shows the honorable way to become a good father, brother, son, uncle, friend, and husband. He has a lot of bad things like all people, but that doesn't define him. That's why I admire my dad. He is and will always be one of the most important people in my life.

Mom

MUHUBO DUHULOW, ST. PAUL, MN

My mom is important to my life. My mom loves me because I'm her first child. She loves me more than my other siblings. My mom is important to me and I love her more than any other person in this world.

My mom is happy all the time. She is a very quiet person. She likes nice dresses and she likes nice colors. She loves me and my children. I remember when I was young, my mom, my dad, and I went to the movies. My other siblings stayed home.

Thanks, Mom!

Muhubo Duhulow is 62 and originally from Somalia.

I Love Christmas

NANCY ROCIO VINTIMILLA, RICHFIELD, MN

My mother came from Ecuador last Wednesday. She will stay fifteen days. My brother is coming from New York today, on Monday. He will live with us for two months.

He works in New York, but he has two months vacation because he worked for ten years with no vacation. He has lived in New York City for twenty years.

I have seven brothers and no sisters.

I love snow and the dream. I love Christmas. I love presents.

My mom doesn't like snow. My mom says, “What happened to the trees?”

My son's birthday and party are on Thanksgiving this year.

About twenty or twenty-five people will eat Thanksgiving food and birthday food at the party. They will have a little buffet with white rice, turkey, chicken, beef, salad, yogurt, pita bread, and lamb, including Greek food. My ex-manager is Greek. We worked at a restaurant together. My husband will cook all the food.

On Friday, we will use our points and stay at a hotel with a casino and a swimming pool.

Tuesday is garbage day so every week, my three-year-old son will sit in the window all day, waiting to watch the garbage trucks come and pick up the garbage.

Nancy Rocio Vintimilla is 36 and originally from Ecuador.

Important People in My Life

MARIA DOLORES VAZUEZ, MINNESOTA

Some important people in my life are my parents, sons, husband, brothers, sisters, friends, teachers, and nephews.

Ricardo and Oliver are important because they are my sons.

Ricardo is important because he is my husband.

Marid and Jeremias are important because they are my parents.

Nelly Rocio, my sister, is important in my life. She is very special to me. She is sick and that makes me very sad.

Maria Dolores Vazuez is originally from Mexico.

Ingrid, Maureen, and Laurie

INGRID HANSEN, CRYSTAL, MN

Years back, when I was a young girl in San Diego, I had two good friends named Maureen and Laurie. I don't remember how we met, I just remember always being together and being good friends right from the start. I do remember Maureen's birthday because it was just twelve days before mine. The three of us had so much fun, laughter, and good times back when we were young. In high school, we were pretty wild, and we would sneak into college parties where there were bands. Back in those days in California, we had a lot of freedom to do things like that! There were so many artists and musicians and fun times everywhere in California back then.

Like any friends, Maureen, Laurie, and I would sometimes disagree about things like boys, but we always stayed friends, even after I had a stroke on December 24, 1986 when I was only twenty-three years old. My stroke was severe, and I lost so much: I lost my vision on my right side; my right hand was affected, and now I use my left hand to draw and paint; it's difficult for me to speak as easily as I used to, but I can still sing. It's all coming back slowly. My whole life changed, but Maureen and Laurie stayed my friends. I have a photograph of the three of us having fun as teenagers. I also have a photograph of the three of us in 1990, after my stroke. When I look at those photos, I feel happy. My memories of the good old times come back to me, and I feel myself moving up and getting better. Slowly, slowly, every day, I'm moving up and getting better.

Ingrid Hansen is 59 and originally from San Diego, CA.

An Important Person in My Life

OHNMAR THIDA, ST. PAUL, MN

Three years ago, I met someone in a refugee camp. We are from the same homeland (Myanmar), but we met each other in a Thailand refugee camp. Now he lives in Thailand and he is studying at Chulalongkorn University.

One day in the afternoon, we have Subject Specific Training (SST) for teachers, and I was eating lunch in the school. When I was eating, I saw a man come to me and ask me, "Are you Ohnmar Thida?" and I said, "Yes." Then he introduced himself, "I will be your new trainer for this training." I didn't expect this man will be my new trainer because he is younger than I thought and I think, "My new trainer will be around thirty-three or something." I was surprised and laughed at him. He also laughed. His name is Andrew. He has brown skin, eyes, and hair, and he is tall. His body looks a little big and fat. He is intelligent. He taught me how to use grammar correctly and he told me what I should learn about English skills. I learned from him about "how to see someone in a positive way," and forgiveness. He supports me to be self-confident. He always encourages to me to be brave. We are not from the same parent, but we are like siblings. He is such a brother from another parent. We are so close to each other. His age is the same as mine, just older than me by three months. He is a good person, like an elder person. He is a polite person and an honest person.

Now, we live in different countries. But I hope we can see each other again. I miss my brother.

Ohnmar Thida is 22 and originally from Burma.

Don't Speed

ABDI MADEY, ST. CLOUD, MN

One of my boy relatives and I were working at a restaurant. A few hours later, the boy said, "I want to take a break." I said, "I want to take a break too." He said, "Okay, but I want to take a motorcycle and ride it." I said, "I will take a bicycle then." We started to go. When he rode the motorcycle, he just drove through the football field, but kids were playing in there. Unfortunately, he hit the ball while he was speeding. Then the motorcycle was hijacked and suddenly he got injured. He broke one of his arms and his neck, and we took him to the hospital.

Abdi Madey is 42 and originally from Somalia.

My Life

HASSEN AHMED, ST. PAUL, MN

I was born in Somalia in 1957. I graduated high school in 1978. I was a teacher in an elementary school for seven years. I got married in 1984. We have ten children. After seven years, I started a little pharmacy business. The government was destroyed in 1991 and the civil war began. Tribes were fighting for power. I moved my family to an Ethiopian refugee camp in 2008. We stayed there for seven years.

We moved to the USA on December 10, 2014. When I came here, I started an assembly job and English classes at the Hubbs Center for Lifelong Learning. My goal is to get a GED and go to college for nursing.

Hassen Ahmed is 64 and originally from Somalia.

My Best Friend

ENDA ROSEWENDA, ST. CLOUD, MN

My best friend Dillah retired from her job last year so now we can hang out. She was my classmate in senior high school forty years ago. We helped each other when we needed it. Dillah always gave me a souvenir when she went to another city and I did the same. We always remember birthdays by calling or giving gifts. I know her children well. When Sarah, Dillah's older daughter, got married, I helped her.

Enda Rosewenda is 60 and originally from Indonesia.

My Special Namesakes

ANNA QUINTERO, MINNEAPOLIS, MN

When I was little, I felt like the black sheep of the family. I had certain traits and peculiarities that made me believe that I was a little different, special, or simply rare. Let's start with the fact that my parents and my brother have curly black hair and light green eyes, and I, well, I have straight brown hair and brown eyes. Additionally, the girls in my family wanted to play with Barbies and dolls growing up, but I just wanted to ride my bike around the neighborhood. Also, all my cousins wanted their hair long, but I always asked my aunt to cut my hair to my shoulders. But perhaps the most special thing about me is my name.

My parents wanted me to be unique, and with my name, they really achieved this. I was born in Colombia in the 1990s, and at that time (and today as well), it is normal to name your children in honor of a grandparent, an uncle/aunt, or maybe a famous person, but I was named after three people: I was named in honor of my grandmother Ana Maria, and I have not only inherited her name, but also her big heart and her love for the kids. I have also been named in honor of my uncle, Manuel Antonio. He is a carpenter, and together we are very creative. My third namesake is my dad's favorite actress, Valentina Rendón. She was one of the best representations of how beautiful Colombian women are, and I am as well. My name is Ana Manuela Valentina. Yes, I have three names. I used to feel like an outsider in my family, but as the years passed, I began to feel like the girl with the three names, not the black sheep of the family. I am proud of it.

Anna Quintero is 24 and originally from Colombia.

My Daughter

BILKISA ABDALLA, BURNSVILLE, MN

I am thankful to know my daughter. She is generous with her time in the school. Maryam helps to read a book to her classmate. When we go to the park, if kids ask her to play, she will go play with them. Maryam does not hoard her toys. She shares her toys to play with her friends. She likes to share her skills with her friend reading books. Maryam is a very generous person helping to write journals with her groups in the classroom. I am a happy mom knowing that my daughter helps another person who needs help. When I didn't know how to write English grammar, someone helped me to write better. Today, I am proud to say that I have a daughter who can make a difference for others who need help like me. I struggled to read English and understand. That is why I am thankful to God for giving me my daughter.

Bilkisa Abdalla is 43 and originally from Ethiopia.

Friends I Have Loved

CHOUA LOR, ST. PAUL, MN

When I was a kid, I had a friend named Mai Yang. She was my first childhood friend. We were classmates. We sold candy at the school and we got some money to buy books and pencils for us to learn.

After many years, I moved to town. I met a new friend named Xee. We studied together for two years. I liked to do homework with her. She helped me do art and other things. After that, I married my husband.

I came to the U.S. on December 17, 2012. At that time, I didn't study English. I was a farmer. In 2016, I moved to St. Paul and I went to school to learn English. I met my new friend named Ntxhi Vang. We study English, math, writing, and other subjects. We help each other to learn new things. She picks me up every Monday to Friday. We eat lunch together at school.

All the friends that I knew are important to me because they share relationships, love, and care. I will never forget them in my life.

Choua Lor is 29 and originally from Laos.

My Life in St. Paul

SANDRA GUTIERREZ, ST. PAUL, MN

My name is Sandra Gutierrez. I am from El Salvador. I live with my husband, and two children, Nahomy, age seven, and Alexa, age two, and my two sisters, Dori and Griselda, and three brothers, Alvara, Maros, and Walter. I have been in the U.S. for nine years. I work as a cook in a Mexican restaurant. Mexican food is different than food in my country. I work forty hours a week.

My favorite holiday is Christmas because my whole family gets together to celebrate. I am happy to be living in this country.

Sandra Gutierrez is 33 and originally from El Salvador.

My Mother's Story

SOPHEAP KEO, FARMINGTON, MN

This is my mother's story. She told it to me when I was young. It happened around the year of 1960, before I was born. Her story was about a plot of land that a rich man wanted to steal from her. My mother told him that it belonged to her, but the rich man thought she lied. He did not believe her because the plot of land was located in another province than my mother lived in. He said my mother's document was not real. Later, that argument was sent to court.

After the court viewed her case, the court sent a letter to tell her that she needed to attend the court hearing. At that point, my mother had a difficult time because she did not know how to read the Cambodian language. Unfortunately, only a few people who lived in her rural village could help her to read that very important letter. They lived very far away from her house. My mother had to take a lot of time to ask them for help, but she never gave up. She continued on even though her relatives suggested she stop arguing with the rich man. They thought poor people never win court cases. To this my mother replied, "No," and she told her relatives that the land was her land and she did not steal it from anybody. She asked her relatives, "Why should I be afraid of going to court?" She felt very brave and continued, "If I do not win at the lower court, I will go to the highest court." She knew sometimes the court made decisions based on subjective bias. But in this case, she was sure the documents, which her grandparents gave her, would prove her case. Although my mother had many struggles, she finally won the court case and got her land back.

From that day, my mother always advised people to be encouraged and felt they should not be afraid when they were faced with an event like hers. Despite what my relatives told her, my mother believed in herself. She would say, "When we have enough evidence, we will win, then the rich people will not always succeed."

Sopheap Keo is 58 and originally from Cambodia.

My Life Story

HEI MOO, FULDA, MN

My name is Hei Gay Moo. I came from Thailand. When I lived in Thailand, I lived with my parents, brother, and three sisters. My parents and older sister and brother still live in Thailand. I have a sister who lives in Worthington, MN. I like Thailand but we didn't have opportunities there.

I have my family. I have one son and two daughters. I have a good husband who works for a trucking company. My family lives in Fulda, Minnesota. My family likes Fulda. Fulda is a small town. My children are happy every day.

I am a student in an ESL class. I have a good teacher for me. Thank you, America, that my children have an opportunity to study in Fulda.

Hei Moo is 27 and originally from Burma.

Important People in My Life

HECTOR CARRILLO, MINNESOTA

My wife is important because she is the love of my life.

My sons are important because they are my friends and the reason for my life.

Lord Jesus is important because he is the light of my life, my help in difficult times. Before he arrived in my life, I had nothing. He gave me all that I have today: happiness, a home, a son, and money.

Hector Carrillo is originally from Venezuela.

My Husband

HABIBO HUSSEIN, BURNSVILLE, MN

My name is Habibo.

I'm thankful for my husband.

He is working hard to get money and helps with everything.

Habibo Hussein is 31 and originally from Somalia.

My Best Friend

PATRICIA VILLAGOMEZ, COLD SPRING, MN

Ana is my best friend. She is always there for me. The first time I met Ana was in church thirteen years ago. We enjoy cooking together. We talk and laugh all the time. Ana helped me with driving lessons and I appreciate that so much. I feel grateful to have a good friend in my life.

Find a faithful friend, it's like finding treasure.

Patricia Villagomez is 42 and originally from Mexico.

Journey to My New Home

AMY TONG YANG LEE, OAKDALE, MN

When my husband Brian and I wanted to move from Burnsville into a new house, Brian wanted a home with a large living room and house that was nice. We found a house in Oakdale. It has a large yard and is in a quiet neighborhood. The house stayed quiet. My home has five bedrooms and three bathrooms. My husband Brian and I are so happy to have found this house. The rooms are perfect for Brian and I with our children and my uncle. We each have our own room to stay in.

In the large yard, I planted a little garden. When summer came, I grew vegetables, onions, and cucumbers. We have renewed the roof, repaired the furnace, and we painted. The neighborhood is nice. Every year, the neighbors bring me flowers and plant them for me at my front door. Every holiday, they bring presents to my children. We are very lucky to have such good and kind neighbors. So today Brian and I, with my children, stay in the house that Brian dreamed of.

Amy Tong Yang Lee is 32 and originally from Laos.

My Mother

DAWN DEUTCHMEN, ST. PAUL, MN

I am writing about my mom. Her name was Leona Mae Deutchman. Her mom, my grandmother, was Elrida Deutchman and her father, my grandfather, was Paul Deutchman. They were from Drake Avenue in Windom, Cottonwood County, Minnesota.

My mother Leona had twenty-seven sisters and brothers, none of them were twins and these were all single pregnancies. My mom's family disowned her because she had mixed race kids in Minneapolis. I don't know how old she was.

My mom took great care of us five girls by working and being there when my dad was not. She also helped me with my son whose name is Stephan Luther Walker. When she got sick with a cold I took care of her.

Dawn Deutchmen is 47 and originally from St. Paul, MN.

Me and My Stories: Fiction and Folklore

Featured Author

Deisy Acosta

LAKEVILLE, MN

Deisy was born in Chihuahua, Mexico. There she trained as a hairstylist. She loves coloring and cutting women's hair. She moved to Minnesota in 2015. Since then, she has studied English in Lakeville. She is married and has three boys. Deisy enjoys cooking for her family and friends. This is her first time writing for *Journeys* and she is honored to participate!

The Mysterious Mannequin

Chihuahua is the state that I'm from. If you go downtown in the city, you can find one of the most interesting mysteries of Chihuahua. It is the most popular bridal dress store in that city, La Pascualita. That store has a beautiful mannequin who has an interesting folktale about it.

Pascuala Esparza was the owner of the store. She had a daughter who was going to get married, but unfortunately, she died on her wedding day. Her mother was so devastated that she didn't let people see her. Mysteriously, after this event happened, on March 25, 1930, Pascuala Esparza had a new mannequin in her store. Many people were talking about it. They were really interested in how the mannequin could look so much like her daughter.

The mannequin is considered to be good luck to shoppers choosing their wedding dress. Shoppers also have said they saw the mannequin's eyes move. The owners say she sometimes changes her dress at night when the store is closed.

The mystery of the mannequin continues. People talk about the mannequin and visit the store to see her.

Deisy Acosta is 32 and originally from Mexico.

Lune Poem - A Nice Day

NAZANIN MIRBEYGI, ROCHESTER, MN

I painted today

My mom made yummy cookies

Today is sunny

Nazanin Mirbeygi is 34 and originally from Iran.

The Dream in Paris

MARY NAVARRETE TABARES, GOLDEN VALLEY, MN

Once upon a time, there was a girl named Bella who was ten years old and lived in the beautiful city of Paris. Her dad, named Geronimo Franchesmo, was thirty-five years old and worked as a writer for the La Croix Newspaper Outlet. Her mother Adelina, who was thirty-two years old, was a seamstress who worked for rich families that appreciated her work ethic. Overall, the family was not rich, but they had a normal life with enough money to feed their family. Each member of the family had their own things to do, which is why the time they spent together was usually during dinner time. Bella always took this opportunity to talk about her dream of becoming a fashion designer. She would recount endless stories of women and men she saw on the street with good fashion sense. Her notebook was where she designed some clothes that were surprisingly good for a child.

On August 12, Bella's parents decided to celebrate their anniversary in a restaurant called Le Paste that was in the rich area of Paris. These luxuries did not occur very often, but a special moment deserved a fancy dinner. During their dinner, they spent time remembering their loving teenage years. Afterwards, they exchanged gifts and decided to head home. During their drive, they noticed a sudden storm starting, but Geronimo insisted on getting home to see Bella. Adelina was worried that an accident could happen, but she trusted Geronimo and she did not insist on staying in a hotel nearby. Subsequently, car accidents started to occur on the side of the road and they began to fear that situation could happen to them. Then, a red car behind them began to speed up trying to pass Geronimo's car. The driver was drunk and could not control his car which caused a giant crash that killed both of Bella's parents.

When some police officers knocked on her door, Bella came out to hear the news of her parents' death. She had become an orphan and she would be placed in an orphanage. The rest of the night she was crying nonstop, thinking about the moments when her parents were alive. She knew then, that if she was taken to an orphanage, she would not be able to pursue her dream of becoming a fashion designer. She decided to escape and found that her only option was to sleep on the streets. The night passed, with cold and pain, and all she had was her sleeping clothes and a piece of cardboard to cover herself.

Some days passed and she met an old woman named Agostina who was once a fashion designer for a well-known brand in France but had become homeless because her clothing department had economic issues. Bella started to become interested in the old lady's story and told her about her dream to work in fashion. Agostina noticed that Bella observed the clothing of the people passing by in the streets, so she introduced her to an old friend who could support Bella in her studies. The old friend agreed to support Bella financially in her fashion career, and enrolled her in the most well-known fashion design school in Paris. Bella was happy to receive the news from Agostina, knowing that she would receive the proper education to make her dream come true.

During the first days at the IFA Paris School, she met students who were wealthy and arrogant towards poor and middle class families. She engaged in several arguments when these students disdained her humble attitude. Bella was full of passion and talent, so many envied her. Some teachers loved her and others hated the fact that she was not of the same social class as the others. But that did not stop her from making her dream come true. The pain she suffered became a learning experience. Years later, she became known as the best fashion designer in Paris.

Mary Navarrete Tabares is 37 and originally from Mexico.

Lune Poem - A Dog

LISA ZHAO, PLYMOUTH, MN

There's a dog.

She is yelling at me.

I yell back.

Lisa Zhao is 33 and originally from China.

A Superstition in Japan

TAKEHIRO JOHNSON, WHITE BEAR LAKE, MN

When I try to avoid bad things in any form, I usually knock on wood. Since I have started to live in the United States, my wife's family has taught me about this. When I lived in Japan, my parents would tell me not to cut my nails at night or unfortunate things would happen. This is not familiar with people living in the United States, and I do not believe it is true now, but as a child I did believe my parents, as did my siblings.

Takehiro Johnson is 27 and originally from Japan.

The Day Jimmy's Life Changed

MEHRYA BEHSUDI, MAPLE GROVE, MN

Once upon a time, there was a homeless man named Jimmy outside on the streets. He walked by a gas station and saw a man named Sam drop his Powerball ticket. He wanted to keep it but he remembered that when you do good things, it always comes back to you. He ran and gave the Powerball back. Sam said thank you and got into his car.

When Sam woke up, he hit the jackpot. He was so grateful that Jimmy gave the Powerball ticket back. He went back to find Jimmy. He found Jimmy by a dumpster. He asked if he remembered him. Jimmy said yes. Sam told Jimmy he won the lottery. He didn't know that Sam was going to give Jimmy half of the money. Once Sam told Jimmy, he got so excited that he hugged Sam. Jimmy thanked Sam and they became best friends.

Mehrya Behsudi is 32 and originally from Afghanistan.

A Folktale of Myanmar

THINZAR EAINDRAY, ST. PAUL, MN

Once upon a time, there was an old couple who did not have a child, although they always wanted one very much. The old man was full of WANDERLUST and while searching for food, he found a big pot deep in the forest. He took it home to put things in. One day, when he and his wife came back from finding food in the forest, they noticed that their house was so clean and there was food ready on the table for them to eat.

A few days later, they decided to pretend to leave the house and watch who was doing these jobs because the situation happened every day and they found it strange. Surprisingly, they saw a teenage girl coming out of the big pot like a magical fairy and doing the household chores. They were both shocked and asked the girl about what was going on. Then they realized that the girl was supposed to take care of the person who picked up her magic pot. Only when her master let her go, then she would be FREE. Despite their desire to have this kind of lovely daughter, they decided to let the girl go because they wanted her to be free.

Thinzar Eaindray is 21 and originally from Maplewood, MN.

Lune Poem - Favorite Season

PAT KIATDILOKRATH, PLYMOUTH, MN

Christmas is coming.

Kids are waiting for Santa.

Most wonderful time.

Pat Kiatdilokrath is 37 and originally from Thailand.

Supersitions

REFUGIO ZARRAGA, MAPLEWOOD, MN

It is a superstition that if you sweep your house at night, you are throwing your money out the door. This is true and why some people are poor. So you only sweep during the day. If you shuffle your feet, you will marry a widow, and if you see a black cat, that is bad luck. Do not open an umbrella inside, it is bad luck. These are some superstitions from Mexico.

Refugio Zarraga is 44 and originally from Mexico.

Lune Poem - Mother's Love

ARACELI HERNANDEZ RAYA, ROBBINSDALE, MN

Love my daughter

Represents: strength, intelligence, kindness, compassion

I feel proud

Araceli Hernandez Raya is 43 and originally from Mexico.

Non-Standard Solutions

ALLA AROSHIDZE, DAYTON, MN

Ben is a young farmer. He has a small farm. He loves his business so much!

His wife recently gave birth to a baby, but she has little breast milk for her baby. She tried to follow all the doctor's recommendations. She ate well and drank a lot of fluids, but it didn't help. It seemed her milk was running out. The doctor threw up his hands and he gave a final recommendation. He advised her to listen to classical music.

Ben's wife started listening to music every day, and in a few weeks, her breast milk increased! It was fantastic!!!

Thinking about this, Ben did not hesitate to order an orchestra for his cows. This news spread all over the neighborhood. Other farmers considered this idea crazy and laughed at Ben. On the day of the orchestra's arrival, all the villagers gathered near Ben's barn. Ben cleaned up his barn during the prior week, but the smell of cow dung did not go away.

When the musicians arrived and realized where they were going to perform, they were shocked and wanted to refuse, but they did it. The concert was amazing! The musicians played as if they were performing in a large concert hall. People applauded for a long time! The farmers and their families have been listening to music all this time, standing at the open barn door. Many of them had listened to classical music for the first time.

The farmers thanked Ben. In a few weeks, the cows start producing more milk. After that, Ben became the most respected farmer in the area and the other farmers have become open to creative non-standard solutions!

Alla Aroshidze is 52 and originally from Belarus.

Journeys 2022 Special Feature: Letters about Literature

In collaboration with the Friends of the Saint Paul Public Library (as the Minnesota Center for the Book), Literacy Minnesota is proud to feature Letters about Literature for a third year.

This fall, we invited *Journeys* authors to submit a written piece on this special Letters about Literature theme. The author in this chapter took the opportunity to select and read a piece of literature, reflect, and write a personal letter to the author explaining how it changed their views of the world and/or themselves.

Letters about Literature helps students practice writing personal narratives, develop authentic written voices, and celebrate the power of reading written work. Educators statewide value the program because it gives students perspective on the ways stories can "bring us to a new understanding, touch our hearts, and see ourselves and build empathy for others."

A Letter to the Author of *Frogness*

JAY LI, ST. PAUL, MN

Dear Ms. Nelson,

Thank you for sharing the story *Frogness*. It unearthed the deep-buried memory of my mirthful and careless childhood.

I grew up in a mountain region similar to New Hampshire in China. Like every typical child living in that environment, I was born with an unexhausted energy, an undaunted curiosity, and a frisky spirit—in other words, I was a troublemaker. I would set foot into nature whenever the opportunity presented itself (just like Sammy and Chocolate did in the story), and a lot of the time, it far from ended up well. Every time I came home from the woods, the dirt-stained face and the mud-smudged shoes made my mom grimace. One time, a bloated leech dangled on my hamstring like a fresh strawberry (which I thought was exactly what it was). My mom cried out the divinest word (God) and cursed out the vulgarest slur (bastard), at the same time. All these familiarities exuded, richer and stronger, when I pored through from one page to another as if the thought of trickling streams flew into a vast lake.

When I read that Chocolate almost had his first taste of frog legs, I could not help but chuckle: it is so hilarious, yet so true! I still recalled after the first sniff of dandelion, my face was choked to blue; I took the first bite of wildberry without considering its edibility or potential poison; I had the first pluck of daisy petals before I learned they are actually makeshift leaves called "Ray;" I tried to get the first snap of a butterfly, but the thwarting force unfortunately smashed it into sticky mash between palms. These silly, yet lovely deeds vividly flashed through my mind, like I was sliding through my Instagram video clips.

In the end, Sammy's dream melted into the frogs' croak and starry sky, while my fancy reverie stopped playing and dragged me back to the cruel reality: the cage-sized cell and iron-bar door. However, the echo of Sammy's felicity rippled through the dim air, and washed away glum emotions. Lying on the bed, my head propped on my arms, I pondered, "If one Frogness could wondrously help me free my mind out of physical confinement, why should I not compose my own Dandelioness, Wildberryness, Daisyness, Butterflyness, and on and on. Let every piece of my cherished memory weave into the magical world of unbridled freedom." With a wry smile, satisfied, I dozed off…into Merriness.

Jay Li is 32 and originally from China.

Visions for a Better World

Featured Author

Julio Esquibel

ST. PAUL, MN

I was born in El Salvador. When I was only three months old, my dad died. After that, we went through a lot of things. My brother and mom, they worked very hard on the land to feed our family. They endured a lot of hunger because we were very poor.

When I was ten years old, we moved to the city and I started going to school. I began to suffer a lot of discrimination from my schoolmates. I suffered a lot of bullying because I didn't play soccer. They always said that to be a man, you had to play soccer. Everything was very hard because they hurt me a lot over time.

Everything started to improve when I was fifteen. My life changed at school. I had good schoolmates and everything was fun.

I moved here on December 6, 2017. I suffered a lot of depression because everything here was different. In my work, my boss humiliated me a lot, and then I got injured at work. I sometimes felt that I wanted to commit suicide. Because of depression, I had to drop out of school. But little by little, I worked on myself and sometimes I still have depression, but I know that everything will be fine in the end and if it isn't, it's because it isn't the end.

"The little seed knew that in order to grow, it needed to be covered in soil, buried in darkness, and struggle to reach the light." - Sandra Kring

An Important Time in My Life

An important time in my life was coming to America, because in my country, people are rude to LGBT people. So I decided to come to America to be free. Life in my country is bad, because it has a very high crime rate and many people get killed. LGBT discrimination is also high. They get harassed because my country is very religious and people think being gay is the worst thing that can happen in the life of someone or a family. They shout ugly things to gay people. Some people get abused by gang members just for being gay.

In conclusion, my life is good in the U.S., free of crime and LGBT discrimination. As Johanna Siguroardo said,"It is absolutely imperative that every human being's freedom and human rights are respected, all over the world."

Julio Esquibel is 21 and originally from El Salvador.

Streetz

ZAYVION EDGERSON, ST. CLOUD, MN

Drugs slanging, guns banging

Product of my environment, so I grew up dangerous

Never resting, always anxious, judges biased, juries racist

My life's insane, my past is crazy, the systemz crooked, and never changing

My sister, she just had a baby, she's on welfare by the way,

Of course, she still lives in the basement,

Never once walked home from school, I ran cause the bullets chased me,

My life's a black hole, once you're caught, there's no escaping,

Grew up on the north side bases, where cops confuse guns with tasers

And still gets pity, with bad replacements

"I hope I get an appeal," Derek Chauvinz prayer

I'm still ****** up they turnt Jamar Clark into an angel

I love my mom to death, but mother **** the mayor

I've watched ten people lose ten trials

I call that modern day enslavement

I'm in Hennepin County, where we are looked at like animals and the trustees are cavemen, I wish I could just say no like "nacey," but I'm surrounded by crack babies, thanks to Ronald Reagan

This statement, I must admit, is penitratin', with heavy elaboration, but with my calculation, some preservation might save the nation, forgive me for being so victatious, but the streetz need, and forever will have a STATEMENT

"STREETZ"

Zayvion Edgerson is 20 and originally from Pine Bluff, AR.

The Worst Happened in 2020

FARTUN MOHAMED, MINNEAPOLIS, MN

In 2020, I was a volunteer helping homeless people and it made me sad to watch them. Why isn't the government helping those people or aren't they the same as those who have a house to live in? I and another group were fighting for homeless people because they need food and a safe place to stay.

Last year, homeless people lived in Powderhorn Park. Everyone brought food, clothes, water, tents, and medicine, too. I met a wonderful lady and I started working with her. She was a social worker. I talked to her and she said, "We need to support them because we need to speak up and let people know who lives next to the neighborhood and hear what we need, something for homeless people." Some neighbors were scared of homeless people.

Some groups sent messages saying we have a meeting today, so all community members came together and supported each other because we are all equal. I wish everyone would help people who don't have a home and protect them from the cold outside and give them warm clothes to sleep in.

The social worker was with me all day and she asked me some good questions like, "What did you think about this situation?" I said, "I hope someday this problem will change and we treat them like other people, equal. The saddest thing was when neighbors called the police on homeless people to kick them out of the park because there was food and dirt everywhere. Neighbors were scared they might come to their houses."

My other difficulty was racism. I hope one day the world changes and people understand that it doesn't matter what skin colors we are. My friend and I asked ourselves why so many black people were killed. They deserve to be like other people who want to live peacefully. Why do white people treat blacks unfairly and shoot them for no reason? I hope one day, they stop racism and have a love for each other.

It's sad to watch kids learn racism from their parents. I hope every single parent teaches their child that colors don't matter at all.

I hope everyone still remembers a quote from

Martin Luther King Jr., "Darkness cannot drive out darkness, only light can do that. Hate cannot drive out hate, only love can do that."

This means, let's support and respect each other.

Fartun Mohamed is 24 and originally from Somalia.

Corruption

ANAYELI SANTOS, BROOKLYN PARK, MN

Corruption exists everywhere. Some people like to cheat to obtain what they want. We can see the corruption in the police, attorneys, and politicians. Some police officers don't do the right things, and instead prefer to make easy money. For example, in Mexico, when they see a driver committing a traffic violation, they do not stop him and give him a ticket, instead they say, "Give me some money, then you can go." The driver gives them money. This is why corruption increases day by day in my country. Also, sometimes when the police arrest drug traffickers, they only threaten the mafia, and take the weapons or some money for their silence.

The drug traffickers and drivers aren't scared of the police because they know the police are negotiable or they can pay off the police for their protection.

Corruption also exists among attorneys in this way. The attorneys like money and like to not really do their job. Sometimes they say we can win your case, give me some money to start, and then they say, I need more money because the case is a little difficult. The person gives the attorney money because he trusts them. Finally, when the client does give more money, the attorney says, "Sorry, I can't do anything," and threatens the other party in the case to get more money from them, promising to lose the case. Some attorneys are corrupt and lie.

How about politicians? In this area, corruption also exists. Many politicians lie to people, make promises because they want to win power, have a campaign, and bring things to "buy" a vote—for example, they might bring food, like beans or rice. They might give money or furniture in exchange for votes. They could even give a home to the people who help them to win the election. When the politicians become president or government leaders, they forget the promises and are not really interested in the needs of people. They don't really want to change and make our country prosperous, they are interested in being rich themselves.

As long as people are corrupt and don't want to do the right thing, there will be corruption. As long as people want to make easy lives for themselves, the corruption will never stop and my country will never change.

Anayeli Santos is 34 and originally from Mexico.

My True Enemy

ELSTON WILLIAMSON, ST. PAUL, MN

That video of Chauvin choking George Floyd with his knee on George's neck, while other officers either participated or stood there, ignoring the pleas from this dying man, was far from the first time I've witnessed white officers do physical harm to a Black man. The simple truth is I've been victimized by, and a witness to these injustices my entire life. Nobody ever seemed to care or believe me until video footage from cell phones started surfacing everywhere. Before that, our cries were either shushed (were our elders afraid?) or ignored.

Watching that video hurt me to my core. Being raised to believe that the police are an enemy of my people, I felt that maybe I was wrong to reject that ideology as an adult. This video seemed to be undeniable proof that the police hate my people. I was blinded again by my pain and the cries of Black Americans. My rational mind can't accept this as truth, though. If I did, I'd be perpetuating the same ignorance, the same hate, that oppressed us all these years.

My opinion is that there's not enough interrelational initiatives between Black and white America. The police as an entity aren't taking their hate out on Black people. The laws being enforced, and some rotten apples, seem to be the source of all this hate. Even as a convicted criminal, I've experienced men and women in law enforcement that I would be proud to call friends. Individuals who just reek of love and compassion. No, they're not my enemy; this system might be; some of their co-workers might be; but a lot of these PEOPLE are true Americans who believe our anthem, "The land of the free." They are good people with a real interest in making our country great.

It's our duty to teach our children that the very idea of stereotyping people is wrong instead of pointing at the rotten apples and saying, "Look at how they all behave," conveniently dismissing every decent individual that looks the same or wears the same uniform. My wife and I teach our children to love and not judge others. If every parent in America tried this, I believe our brothers and sisters that fell victim to the hate that lives in the heart of the rotten apples would still be here with us. Let's learn to love one another, no matter what

Elston Williamson is 41 and originally from Chicago, IL.

Bright Futures

Featured Author

Sondra Keezer
WHITE EARTH, MN

My name is Sondra Grace Keezer. I am twenty-five years old. I am from White Earth Reservation. I have a son who is three years old. His name is Jaxxon Thomas Bittner. I grew up living with my grandma due to my mother and father not being around too much. My grandma's name is Grace, she is eighty-three years old and one of the strongest women I know. She has encouraged me a lot with my music, art, and writing.

I love to sit down for hours and write poems or make music. A lot of my writings or songs have a lot to do with my life. So a lot of my writings or songs have helped me get through some very tough times in my life. My writings or songs is how I get my therapy because I have a really hard time sitting down and talking to someone. I guess you could say that my poetry or music could say or show who I truly am, being that my whole life I've used a series of masks to cover up my true feelings or emotions.

River

We are all born into this River without knowing how to swim;
Eventually keeping the water below our chins...

Sometimes this water is so cold to be in...
Freezing my soul , Solidifying my skin...

No matter how far I see,
My travels never end...

In this River;
We're being carried by the current,
And getting drifted by the wind...

Trying to remember places,
That we may never see again...

We are lost in the thought
that this River should just go straight...
We set goals and desires to control our own fate...

I try to flow with River's natural process,
The way it's supposed to twist and turn...
Isn't that the same way of life; how we learn?

Sometimes I like to float downstream...
I see the beauty of it all, and it feels like a dream...

Sondra Keezer is 24 and originally from White Earth Nation.

We Are Here

A COLLABORATIVE COMMUNAL POEM BY FATOUMA HACHI, DAHABO ABDI, HALIMA ABDI, ARDO DAHIR, ZEINAB HASSAN, AND OTHERS WHO WISH TO REMAIN ANONYMOUS

ST. CLOUD, MN

In response to "Within" by Louise K. Waakaa'igan.

We are humans learning English
within God's creation in America,
St. Cloud, Minnesota.
We are fathers and mothers who are students.
This is not easy. Head hurts. Hard.
Back hurts. Hard, hard.
Are we not meant to be proud, making improvements?

Already we see benefits. Our children can no longer hide
from us behind their perfect English words.
We are learning to understand them.
But we cannot wait for the day
when we can express ourselves better in English.

We hope to speak like our teachers, to read applications
and understand, to write letters, to communicate well
to our American friends.
When will our dreams come true?

Our tears fall down our cheeks into our hands.
Not to be able to articulate to doctors
what our children need—
humiliation.
Sometimes we want to go home to our country.
When will we be understood?
We miss our mothers and fathers back home,
miss the tropical weather of Somalia,
we feel an ache in our hearts,
we feel abandoned.
We older people have lost our friends and country, our culture.

How will our broken hearts ever be mended
without our tribal society?

Who will remember our stories from Somalia
through North Carolina, Buffalo, New York,
South Dakota, Willmar, Minnesota, and into this place?

Children—
we are divided
into separate cars, driven by strangers
to our new place in this new
world.

Parents—
we miss your home.

Neighbors—
we have been afraid.

Allah—
we.

*Poem first appeared in *Sunday Morning Lyricality*, April 2021. Reprinted with permission of the publisher.

The authors are all originally from Somalia.

Wasted Talent

ANONYMOUS, BURNSVILLE, MN

Let's get one thing straight. I'm just a talented artist who never made it. I've been wanting to sing since I was two. But the music business pushed me away. For so many years, I wrote a lot of lyrics hoping it'll get me to square two. I got doors SLAMMED! in my face because I didn't graduate from high school.

I prayed to God every night to help me get a record contract. I tried to connect with celebrities, but all I get is rejects. I've been checking out "Soul Train," "Solid Gold," and "American Bandstand" all the time. I am still shy today because when I try to sing, I hear "SHUT UP!!" I was treated unkind.

I've been struggling for so many years since 1989. The world is cold and I'm getting old. It feels like I'm running out of time. To all musicians and songwriters that never made it, I really feel your pain. We can make something work and we'll have more than fame.

Wasted talent is what I got
Now it's a different ballgame
Since I got wasted talent
My life is not the same.

Future Plans

MATEO CARRILLO, ST. PAUL, MN

My name is Mateo. I have been living in St. Paul, Minnesota for five months. I live in an apartment with my parents and my girlfriend. I don't have kids, but I think I would like to in maybe three years.

I want to learn to speak English so I can go to college in the future. Right now I work in a company making shampoo, conditioner, and other products. In the future, I would like to have my own company. I would like to be able to help my parents.

In the future, I would like to travel and get to know more countries. I would like to be an example for my future sons to follow.

Mateo Carrillo is originally from Venezuela.

Life in America

DAMA ABDULLAHI, ST. PAUL, MN

I came to America on January 10, 2013, from Somalia. I live with my family. I started my first job at Walmart. I worked five days a week from 7 a.m. to 3:30 p.m. Right now, I work at the post office. It is a good job, so I do not want to change jobs now. I am taking English classes at the Hubbs Center for Lifelong Learning because I want to go to college to study to be a nurse.

Dama Abdullahi is 41 and originally from Somalia.

Memory

ANONYMOUS, ST. PAUL, MN

I am from Burma. Because of the civil war in Burma, I moved to Thailand in 2009. I came to Minnesota on February 21, 2019. I took an airplane with my family. I have seven siblings: four boys and three girls. I want me and my siblings to finish high school and get a good education. If we live in this country, we need to get a high school diploma. If we didn't have a good education, we couldn't get a good job.

The 2021 Word of the Year

DUNIA FERNANDEZ, CRYSTAL, MN

A lot has happened in the last two years, some good, some not so good, but we have learned something. Although our lives, activities, and behavior changed after the start of the Covid-19 pandemic, all of these changes have led us to appreciate life more. Therefore, for me, the word of the year for 2021 would be "life."

There are a few reasons why I chose this word. First, through life, we can exist, breathe, feel, and enjoy every moment, although life is not fair and easy sometimes. Also, with life, we can share incredible and special moments with family, friends, co-workers, and the community.

During the pandemic, we have learned to value life as we have never done before. The fear of losing it, or that one of our loved ones will lose it, has made us understand how important life is. This is why people are trying not to get Covid-19. In addition to this, life gives us the great opportunity to impact others with our examples or by simply doing something for someone in need. Being alive today is a great blessing, so we must meditate on what we do with our lives every day.

Dunia Fernandez is 47 and originally from Honduras.

I Am Thankful For

ASMA ABDI, ST. CLOUD, MN

I am so thankful that Allah gave me:

health

family

good kids

a home

resources

friends

and a good husband

I am so thankful that Allah gave me all these things.

Allah, I am so happy and thankful.

Asma Abdi is 48 and originally from Somalia.

My Expectations of America

MEFTUHA ABDELA, MAPLE GROVE, MN

When I was in Ethiopia, I used to think life in America was easy for everyone, even newcomers. I thought that you could get anything you want and change your life easily. I thought you could drive a nice car, live a comfortable life, and shop as much as you want.

This idea came from movies that I watched and I also saw some people from my country who were living in the USA buying new things for their family and changing their families' lives. When they came back to visit Ethiopia, they spent a lot of money and enjoyed themselves. I always used to dream that I would do that with my family one day.

Then, I came to America and saw that what I used to think about having an easy life was incorrect. I learned that people work hard and save their money. People also go to school. But it is possible to improve their standard of life.

Meftuha Abdela is 27 and originally from Ethiopia.

My Goal

NURO SAHWI, ST. PAUL, MN

My name is Nuro Sahwi. I am from Somalia. I came to the U.S. in 2016. I live with my four children and my mom, so I am happy. I take English class, English Language Learner Level B, at the Hubbs Center for Lifelong Learning. My goal is to go to college to be a nurse. Then I can help people.

Nuro Sahwi is 36 and originally from Somalia.

YEM Says

YOU EH MOO, ST. PAUL, MN

{1.} If you're someone who likes to read, you'll be the one who graduates from a school that no one else would know about. That is the "school" of life.

{2.} Do not feel sorry for a poor person because poverty will make us concentrate.

{3.} To improve myself, I have to make a lot of effort and determination.

You Eh Moo is 23 and originally from Thailand.

My Childhood Dream

BERTHA LOPEZ, ST. PAUL, MN

My name is Bertha and I was born in the country of Guatemala in the year 1972. When I was five years old, I went to school and went on to finish sixth grade. I remember my teacher giving me my sixth grade diploma. I was very happy since my dream was to go to college.

In my country, school is not free; we have to pay every month. My teacher helped me get a scholarship to finish my education. However, due to my father not knowing how to read or write, he misunderstood the scholarship and rejected it. Due to the misunderstanding, he thought that he would have to pay for my whole education.

My father was very poor, and he did not have enough money to pay for school. The rest of my nine siblings were only able to finish second grade.

When I came to the U.S., I prayed to God to continue my education. I started my education again at Open Door Learning Center learning English. I am going to continue my education until God gives me strength to finish and accomplish my dreams so that I may help my family in the future.

I hope God gives me more time to tell my story and thank you all who have read my story. God bless you. Thank you.

Bertha Lopez is 49 and originally from Guatemala.

My Life

MOHAMED YOUSUF OMAR, ST. PAUL, MN

I came from Somalia in 2013. I studied in high school up to grade eleven. I have not finished high school yet.

My first year in the U.S. was spent in federal detention waiting for asylum. After that, I started my first job in Denver, Colorado. There are nine people in my family. I have two daughters and five sons. I am a truck driver, so I want to speak good English. I also want to read and write well. These are the goals I am working on now.

Mohamed Yousuf Omar is 45 and originally from Somalia.

Dreaming Is Living

ALLISON CASTILLO, BURNSVILLE, MN

When I was only fourteen, my life changed completely. I had come to have a very rough character and I did not mind hurting those around me. I felt an emptiness in my heart and I thought my life had no meaning. Night after night, I prayed to God that he will help me find meaning in my world. His blessing filled me with spirituality.

Four years passed and I matured. I began to appreciate my mother, asked her forgiveness for all the nights and days that I made her shed tears. I managed to believe in myself as far as I can go. Then, at just eighteen years old, I traveled to the United States of America, which taught me that living is dreaming, that each objective and goal that we set ourselves we can fulfill.

Here, day by day, I fight for my family, to get them forward. I am grateful to God and my mother who was my engine. Now I help people for nothing in return, regardless of race or color.

Allison Castillo is 19 and originally from Ecuador.

Meeting the Prince

SVETLANA KARTAK, ST. PAUL, MN

I believe I can say that every girl dreamt of meeting a true prince. Once I had my chance. Only I was not a young girl. I had two kids and worked on a boat as a tour guide. It was the year of 2003 and in my city of St. Petersburg, Russia, the city celebrated its 300-year anniversary. Prince Charles came there among the other noble people.

It so happened that I, a tour guide, returned from one of my tour boat trips. I saw a huge crowd on the bank of Moyka River at Stroganov Palace, where we had our pier. I walked up and asked what was happening. Prince Charles himself was in the palace! Wow! I felt like it was the moment that you call "once in a lifetime!" The Prince was freshly widowed, and I was divorced. I spoke some English (very little, but who cares?! The language of love is international, for Pete's sake!) and that was my moment! I squeezed through the crowd to the front door and prepared to meet the Prince.

Then my pager (it was the era before cell phones, and we felt really advanced to have pagers) started to buzz. My captain demanded that I be back on the boat because it was already full of tourists. I didn't want to believe this. It was literally not possible that all the boats before ours had filled with travelers and had left. (Later I learned that four of them had left on prepaid tours.) This was my time to go and do my job. On the other hand, there was my "happy ever after," the Prince. He was only a few meters away and somehow I knew we just needed to have our eyes meet…

My pager buzzed and buzzed. And I felt that if I were not back to my boat, I would lose the job, and not only that – I would lose the ability to talk about the city I was in love with. My everyday passion and pleasure – to see hundreds of grateful eyes, meet some famous actors, artists, writers, politicians, and make friends – I would put at risk. I had a good salary with tips to lose.

I still don't know if I did the right thing. In a year and a half, my destiny brought me to America. But it could have been England!

Svetlana Kartak is 56 and originally from Russia.

Goals

CARLA CASTRO, ST. PAUL, MN

My name is Carla Castro. I am from Peru. My family lives in Peru. I don't have children. I am a lawyer in my country. I worked as an auditor for the Peruvian State. I came to the U.S. to learn about a new culture. Now I am a student at the Hubbs Center for Lifelong Learning and am learning about many cultures. I work in a food packaging company. In my free time, I go to the gym.

My goal is to become an assistant lawyer in the USA. But first, I have to learn more English and then study American law.

Carla Castro is 34 and originally from Peru.

Language and Learning

ANONYMOUS, ST. PAUL, MN

I came to the U.S. in June 2013, from Ethiopia. When I came here I had many difficulties. First, there was the language problem. I knew a little English but not enough. It was difficult to talk with some people. Now I go to school at the Hubbs Center for Lifelong Learning to learn English so I can have more opportunities. English is my fourth language.

I teach an Islamic Studies class online in my language, Oromo. The students live in South Africa, Kenya, America, Ethiopia, and Saudi Arabia. Our class meets three days a week for forty minutes. This week we studied respect and sharing what we have with people in need.

I feel living in this democratic country is very, very good. I feel safe here. Many people in the U.S. are honest. For example, my friend left his phone on the bus, and it was returned to him. Now, I feel good and expect the future to be good. I plan to work in medical administration.

The Best Advice

HALIMA YUSUF, MINNEAPOLIS, MN

What is the best piece of advice you have ever received?

The best piece of advice I have ever received was from my teacher. She always says to me, "never give up." This is good advice for me. In the past, in class, it was my habit to say, "I don't know" when my teacher asked me a question. However, now, I try not to say, "I don't know." Instead, I say, "I will think about this question and try to find the answer."

Now, sometimes when I am studying, I feel like giving up, but I remember my teacher's words, and I continue to work and learn. This small phrase has helped me many times in my life, and I think I am a stronger student and person because of my attitude change. "Never give up" is helping me to reach my goals. In the future, if I have children, I will say this same advice to them. I am happy with my teacher's advice, and I will continue to follow it.

Halima Yusuf is 35 and originally from Somalia.

School Challenge

SAID SAID, ST. PAUL, MN

When I was in tenth grade, I remember thinking "What's the point of all of this stuff I'm learning? Why do I have to know how to do calculus or how chemicals combine?" All I knew was that I was supposed to get good grades, even if I didn't understand what I was learning. The importance that was put on grades made the learning seem less important.

I think schools should not use grades and should, instead, focus on making sure students are interested, engaged, and learning. The reason why I think schools should not use grades is because they don't help students learn. When students know they are going to receive a grade, they think only about what they have to do to get a good grade. They don't use the assignment as an opportunity to really learn something about the world, because they know that, in the end, all that will matter for the teacher, for their parents, and for colleges, is the grade they receive.

The second reason why schools should not use grades is because teachers do not use grades consistently. Every student knows that some teachers give a lot of A's and some teachers hardly ever give A's. That seems unfair. Your grade point average can depend on which teacher you have, not on how much you learn or how smart you are. Grades should not be subjective like this. And each teacher has a different way of assigning final grades.The difference between failure and the honor roll often depends on the grading policies of the teacher.

Said Said is 18 and originally from Somalia.

My Hopes and Goals for 2022

MAYLI YANG, BROOKLYN PARK, MN

My hopes and dreams for 2022 back in my home, Laos, is that things will get better soon. I have heard that my Hmong brothers and sisters are sad, worrying, and having difficult situations in their lives. The country has been in a second lockdown for Covid-19.

The big thing is that school has been closed and families don't have good technology to help their children do online classes. Some young people have to quit their education because school was closed for a very long time and some get married earlier than they would have and some still are waiting for school to begin again. This year, New Year's celebrations have been canceled. Young adults are not very happy.

My brothers and sisters hope that the new year will bring better times again for them like a caterpillar turning into a butterfly.

Mayli Yang is 25 and originally from Laos.

What Happened to the Birds

HANA TEKLE, WEST ST. PAUL, MN

Once in a while, I heard the birds singing.
I have good memories of my childhood.
Learning English was so interesting.
I wished I was a nurse assistant.
I could have done with a better understanding.
What happened to the birds singing in the morning?

Once in a while, I hear the birds singing.
My dream is to be a nurse assistant.
Sing! Sing! Sing! from the birds in the morning.
Wake up!
Wash your face!
Get ready for school!
I wish to have a baby.
I try to always do my best.
What happened to the birds singing in the morning?

Once in a while, I will hear my mom's voice.
I don't know when I will meet her.
I wish my mom was with me.
I will try to get my mom here.
I will be ready to face all challenges.
What happened to the birds singing in the morning?

Hana Tekle is 38 and originally from Eritrea.

I Know I Can Bring Love

XENG LEE VANG, ST. PAUL, MN

Once in a while, I heard my parents say, "Do your best and don't worry about us."

I have good memories of staying with my family.

Learning English was difficult and hard to understand.

I wished I could speak English well.

I could have done with a better job.

What happened to my life?

I know I can bring love and happiness to my family.

Once in a while, I hear people talk about how to improve my English.

My dream is to have my own house, a happy life, and have a good job.

No! Don't do that! No! Don't do that! No! Don't do that! From my mother-in-law.

Don't be lazy!

Get up early!

Don't copy bad things from people around you! ...From my parents.

I wish I had a new house.

I try to understand people who live with me.

I know I can bring love and happiness to my family.

Once in a while, I will hear good news.

I don't know when I will visit my family in Laos.

I wish I will have a new baby.

I will try to be a nursing assistant.

I will be ready to go on vacation in the summer.

I know I can bring love and happiness to my family.

Xeng Lee Vang is 27 and originally from Laos.

I Will Try to Communicate

WEDEB GEBREMESKEL, ST. PAUL, MN

Once in a while, I heard my mother say wash your hands.

I have good memories of my friend helping me with maths.

Learning English was very tricky.

I wished I could speak English well.

I could have done with a better school.

What happened to those many hours to pray?

I will try to communicate with everyone.

Once in a while, I hear my family say to walk slowly.

My dream is to finish my English class.

Tweet tweet tweet from the birds outside of my window.

Wear safety shoes.

You must wear a mask.

Tie your hair up.

Learning English is an international language.

I wish I worked as a manager.

I try to come early to class.

I will try to communicate with everyone.

Once in a while, I will hear good conversation with all people.

I don't know when I will visit my homeland.

I wish I was born in the USA.

I will try to get a good job.

I will be ready to play with my friends.

I will try to communicate with everyone.

Wedeb Gebremeskel is 36 and originally from Eritrea.

I Know I Can Be Better

BERTHA RODRIGUEZ, SHOREVIEW, MN

Once in a while, I heard people complaining.
I have good memories of my parents' smiles.
Learning English was a challenge, especially grammar.
I wish I could write and speak English well.
What happened to this world?
I know I can be better every day.

My dream is to speak and write English well.
Woof, woof, woof, from the neighbor dog.
Be respectful with adults.
Study hard.
Ask before take, never steal.
I wish I could fly.
I try to eat healthy every day.
I know I can be better every day.

Once in a while I will hear my grandsons talk.
I don't know when I'm going to see my mom again.
I wish I could fly.
I will try to work next year.
I will be ready to improve my baking skills.
I know I can be better every day.

Bertha Rodriguez is 53 and originally from Mexico.

Life in Minnesota

HUSSEIN ALI, ST. PAUL, MN

My name is Hussein Ali. I was born in Somalia, but didn't grow up there. I came to the U.S. when I was ten years old. There are many differences between my country and Minnesota. When I came to America I was amazed at all the different things I saw. For example, it is amazing how much the weather changes every few months and we have to be ready to buy new clothes for each new season.

I am now an adult attending English classes at the Hubbs Center for Lifelong Learning. When my English gets better, I will go to college.

Hussein Ali is 35 and originally from Somalia.

What I Am Thankful For

AHMED JAMA, ST. CLOUD, MN

This life give me a
house
family
kids
job
health

Allah gave me the ability to know what is right and wrong.

I am thankful to be a Muslim.
I am thankful Allah guided me in Islam.
I am thankful for a prophet to guide me on the right path.

I am a student and teacher for the Prophet.

Ahmed Jama is 54 and originally from Somalia.

Life in St. Paul

JUAN MARCA GOMEZ, ST. PAUL, MN

Hello! My name is Juan. I am from Azogues, Ecuador. I am eighteen years old. I live in St. Paul with my uncles and cousins. I work as a personal assistant in a supermarket Monday to Friday and on the weekend, I work in a restaurant.

I have been in the United States for three months. I am going to the Hubbs Center for Life-long Learning to learn how to speak, write, and understand English better because I want to be able to continue working and be able to communicate with the people next to me.

Juan Marca Gomez is 19 and originally from Ecuador.

Come to Minnesota

YER YANG, ST. PAUL, MN

I am from Laos. I came to the United States in 2010. The first winter to summer, I stayed at home, looked out the window, and waited for my parents to come back home. My parents worked six days a week.

When I came to the United States, I didn't speak English, only Hmong. One day, my parents took me and my sister to the grocery store. I needed to buy a phone card to call back to my country, but I couldn't tell the seller at the store the name of the phone card. I felt very sad for myself.

Now I have been in the United States for ten years. I want to study English because I need to get my GED and find work. I would like to go to college and start my own business.

Yer Yang is 33 and originally from Laos.

The Next Phase

SANGMI LEE, PLYMOUTH, MN

My journey to the next phase in my life started in 2020. At that time, the pandemic was predominantly in the U.S. and it led me to be hopeless and helpless. I couldn't go to any academies or learning centers. I thought that I should give up all my studying.

Meanwhile, my neighbor introduced Open Door Learning Center to me. Teacher Lindsey gave me hope to start and Teacher Jessica made me go forward. Before the long summer vacation, I promised Jessica to move on to Nikki's class and develop my English. Now, I study hard with Nikki and my classmates, dreaming of entrance to a U.S. university. I don't know what will happen to me again, but I'll keep trying on my next journey.

Sangmi Lee is 41 and originally from South Korea.

What Happened to My Fingers?

MARIO ZAPATA, ST. PAUL, MN

Once in a while, I heard my friend say to me coffee no sugar.

I have good memories of the lunch lady asking my name and smiling at me.

Learning English was about books and stories.

I wished I was funny every day.

I could have done with better vitamins for energy.

What happened to my finger movement?

Once in a while, I hear I'm nice and get the store diploma in my community.

My dream is to get my diploma in 2022.

Go to school! Go to work! Go to school! Go to work! Go to school!

Go to work!

Clean shoes inside the house.

Clean the table for dinner.

Clean my teeth in the morning.

I wish Mexican food would change to Chinese food.

I try to understand more English.

What happened to my finger movement?

I will not cry in classes.

I don't know when I will have a cappuccino in the store again.

I wish I could break in my car on Saturday.

I will try to visit Panama.

I will be ready to clean the store.

What happened to my finger movement?

Mario Zapata is 45 and originally from Mexico.

What I Would Put In My Gratitude Jar

HALIMO AHMED, ST. CLOUD, MN

My health.

My beauty.

My job.

A roof over my head.

I have a family that loves me.

If I try to write down how grateful I am I would run out of paper.

My thankfulness would not fit in a jar.

Halimo Ahmed is 53 and originally from Somalia.

I Am a Candle

NIEMAT ELREIDA, ST. PAUL, MN

Once in a while, I heard someone say you are the best and you change my life.

I have good memories of middle school.

Learning English was difficult.

I wished I was still a child.

I could have done with a better friend in college.

What happened to old people?

I am a candle on my road to the future.

Once in a while, I heard someone say you are the best and you changed my life.

My dream is to be a supervisor.

Is mom dead? Is mom dead? Is mom dead? I hear in my head every morning.

Never look at the past.

Never forget the tradition.

Never lose your nationality.

I wish to go to my country.

I try everything that's hard.

I am a candle on my road to the future.

Once in a while, I will hear someone say you are the best and you can change your life.

I wish to find a proper job.

I will try to go to the ocean and to space with my son.

I will be ready to start to change my life.

I am a candle on my road to the future.

Niemat Elreida is 41 and originally from Sudan.

I Love to See My Kids

RUTH FLORES OLIVAR, ST. PAUL, MN

Once in a while, I heard Manchita's bark frequently.

I have good memories of my first baby.

Learning English was so difficult but so fun.

I wish I could spend more time at school.

I could have done with better pronunciation of English.

What happened to my freedom?

I love to see my kids happy.

Once in a while, I hear my boys fighting.

My dream is to get my GED.

Moo! Moo! Moo! From the cows early in the morning.

Do your homework.

Take care of your brothers.

Don't take a long time.

Learning English is wonderful, the best.

I wish I had time to learn English.

I always try to do my best.

I love to see my kids happy.

Once in a while, I will hear my father's voice.

I don't know when I can see my father again.

I wish my family was with me.

I will try to get my GED.

I will be ready to face all challenges.

I love to see my kids happy.

Ruth Flores Olivar is 37 and originally from Mexico.

Choices

WENDY MARTINEZ SAMANIEGO, MINNESOTA

Some of the choices I've made were unexpected. Actually, some of them I didn't choose. When I was a child, my parents played rock 'n' roll in English all the time, so I was learning English accidentally. In high school, English was a requirement, and I was very good at it. So I decided to come to the U.S. and live as an exchange student.

I'm making friends from different countries, I'm getting to know new places, cultures, and lifestyles, and now I'm studying English because I decided to improve it. This will give me more opportunities. Also, I want to learn French, Mandarin, and another language.

Wendy Martinez Samaniego is originally from Ecuador.

I Know I Can Eat

DELY BLANDELLE TADAA, ST. PAUL, MN

Once in a while, I heard my mother say don't go to the neighbor's house.

I have good memories of my grandmother.

Learning English was too difficult for me.

I wished to have a lot of money.

I could have done with a better friend.

What happened to this innocent child?

I know I can eat every day.

Once in a while, I hear my child say he wants to eat.

My dream is to be a governor.

Roar, roar, roar! Hiss, hiss, hiss! Cluck, cluck, cluck! say the lion, the snake, and the chickens.

Don't speak when you are eating;

Don't go to school late;

Don't go to the neighbor's house.

I wish to be a good wife until the day I die.

I try to be a good mother.

I know I can eat every day.

Once in a while, I will hear happiness in the church.

I don't know when I will see my mother again.

I wish to be a governor of the American republic.

I will try to have a hair dresser's shop.

I will be ready to take care of my baby.

I know I can eat every day.

Dely Blandelle Tadaa is 25 and originally from Cameroon.

My Goal

ANONYMOUS, ROSEMOUNT, MN

When I was a child, I was a part of a big family. My parents had four children, and my dad took care of his mother and three younger brothers. He did this because my grandfather passed away while my uncles were very young. I'm sure my parents worked hard to take care of everyone; nevertheless, it was never enough for us financially. One day, I told my mom I wanted to learn how to play the piano, and she replied, "Later, later." After that, I tried not to bother my mom with what I wanted to do because nothing happened to me "later."

Time went by quickly and soon enough, I became a mother of three children. It wasn't easy at all, I worked as hard as my mom and I tried hard to support my kids. Nevertheless, sometimes, I wondered how my kids perceived our life. What were their thoughts about our lifestyle? I wondered because I often felt that we didn't have enough to financially support them. It made me think about my parents. Is it possible they had the same thoughts while they were raising me? So, now I understand, more than ever, about the difficulties their life had while I was young. I am so glad my kids are grown up and all of our families are settled down. Finally, I can afford to take care of myself and do what I like to do. I've started studying English and teaching myself how to play the piano. Now my goal is to keep on doing what I like.

What Happened to Me

PATIENCE ELLIS, ST. PAUL, MN

Once in a while, I heard her say come my dear daughter.

I have good memories of the day you were born.

Learning English was hard but it was good to know.

I wished I could get the chance to be young again.

I could have done with a better chance in life.

What happened to me should not happen to anyone.

Once in a while, I hear people talk about Covid-19.

My dream is to be a nurse.

Ahh! Ahh! Ahh! from the old ladies at the nursing home.

Go to Church on Sunday and read your Bible.

Be respectful to everyone.

Make sure you wash the dishes after eating.

I wish the world will have peace and love.

I try to help old people.

I wish there will be no pain.

Learning English is hard but it's good to know.

What happened to me should not happen to anyone.

Once in a while I will hear her say don't make the bad choices I made in life.

I don't know when I will get another opportunity in life.

I wish l could start life all over again.

I will try to make the right choice in life.

I will be ready to listen and try chances I missed earlier in life.

What happened to me should not happen to anyone.

Patience Ellis is 43 and originally from Ghana.

My History

SONIA VILLEDA, ST. PAUL, MN

I was born in a small village in El Salvador. My mom was pregnant with twins, but she didn't know there were two of us, because she never went to the doctor. So, she was surprised at the time I was born. First came my brother. One hour later, I came out. My mom thought I was the placenta. After my dad died, our mom left me at my godmother's house. She took care of me from the age of eighteen months until I was twenty, when I got married. A year later, I came to the United States with my husband. I felt so bad about my English because I didn't know anything, but I got a job in a plastics company. I worked there for two years. Now I am taking an English class at the Hubbs Center for Lifelong Learning. My dream is to be a nurse or a medical assistant, but for that I need good English. I hope to get better every day and reach my goals.

Sonia Villeda is 32 and originally from El Salvador.

Ethiopia Prevails

BEREKET MESHESHA, ST. PAUL, MN

Hey guys, my name is B. I am from the great and beautiful country called Ethiopia. Living in Ethiopia was not bad. I used to go to school. I lived with my family at our house. The weather, the food — everything was fine. But there is no work after students graduate from college and there is a lot of corruption, so all these things make it hard to be successful in my own country. I still have big hopes for my country that maybe one day everything will be good and stable so I can go back and invest in many fields. For example, agriculture, manufacturing, tourism, and mining use all our natural resources. I want to help create job opportunities for young people. I have a big love for my country. That's why I am talking too much.

Oh, I forgot to talk about myself. So I came to the USA in 2019, on March 8. I remember it was winter time and it was so cold. In Ethiopia, it was not cold and I didn't wear a coat when I was waiting for someone to pick me up. I saw how Minnesota is cold. I used to hear Minnesota is too cold. Now I see it in real life. It was so cold. I had never seen cold weather like this in my life. I stayed in Shakopee for a few months. It was a semi-urban place and I didn't see people that much. There were very few people walking around and it was a quiet place and it was boring.

My life started changing when I moved to St. Paul. I started high school. I met many people. I started speaking English. It was good for me to move here. I started my first job and I started saving money. In the summer, I got my driver's license and I got my first car. I was happy. In 2021, I turned twenty-one so I couldn't go to high school. For this reason, I went to the GAP School so I could keep going forward and improving my English skills and my life. After I graduate from GAP, I want to go to college and get more education. That's all.

Thank you.

Bereket Meshesha is 21 and originally from Ethiopia.

Open Door Learning Center, Muchas Gracias!!!

RUTH ZHANAY CASTRO, PLYMOUTH, MN

I can't believe another year, the second one for me, passed learning and enjoying virtually at Open Door Learning Center. The pandemic didn't prevent us from continuing to improve our English and interacting with instructors and classmates.

I am happy that I'm working again, although I miss the English classes. I still have the great opportunity to be part of the Open Door Book Club despite that I don't have much time to read the great books that we select. My classmates read them very fast.

Our teacher Nikki lets us choose a book from four or five. We can read paperback books, e-books, or listen to audio books. The hour or hour and a half that we talk about the book on Sundays goes so fast. I appreciate that Sheila, a volunteer, stays with me to continue reading the book.

I would like to invite you to be part of our book club in 2022. We meet on Sundays from noon to 1 p.m. and just talk about the book, the meaning of words, or of some sentences. It is fun.

Hasta Pronto!

Ruth Zhanay Castro is 65 and originally from Ecuador.

My True Dream

FLORENCIA FRANCO, FARMINGTON, MN

I came to Minnesota with the objective to become more independent and brave. Now I'll go back to being a stronger person, with new ideas, skills, and beliefs.

This story began on my eighteenth birthday, when I had the opportunity to come to the U.S. and learn English. I was so afraid to travel alone for the first time, but my mom told me to engrave in my heart that I'm the principal character of my life. I understood that I need to be brave and apply directed effort to achieve my goals. I took the chance to come and explore a new country and a new lifestyle. I was so excited to experience the "American Dream." I knew that this opportunity would help me decide what I wanted to do with my future, and where I wanted to live it.

This adventure started when I enrolled in English classes, which was an amazing decision. There I learned several important lessons from the people I met. First my teachers, who were so kind to me, helped me to improve my skills in English, which was my principal goal. Then my classmates, now friends, who were people from all ages (like twenty-five to seventy years old) and from all around the world. Some of them shared with me their hard and poignant stories about their migration to the U.S. Their stories were usually about how they came without their family and with the responsibility of working very hard. This was a very different situation from my story, and I am grateful and conscious about the privilege that I had about the way that I came to the U.S.: with a visa, a family, and a house that was waiting for me.

I've had such a wonderful experience. I've learned a lot about how to continue on even though things can feel discouraging. Thanks to my parents and the extraordinarily strong people (teachers, volunteers, friends, and family) which have enriched my experience. I've realized that my true dream isn't in the U.S. My dream is in Mexico, working for the success and the justice of all Mexicans through politics and law.

This experience has convinced me that we all can achieve our dreams and goals, no matter of gender, age, nationality, or race. Each of us are able and responsible for making our dreams a reality.

Florencia Franco is 18 and originally from Mexico.

My Education

KAWSAR MUSE, MINNEAPOLIS, MN

My name is Kawsar. I am from Somalia. I came from Yemen to the United States. In my country, I went to school for a little while, but I worked many, many hours in my home.

When I came to the United States, I got a job and went to school. I appreciated that in America, they helped immigrants. Now I am going to school at Open Door Learning Center, and I am very happy. When I first came to Minnesota, I studied in St. Cloud in beginning English classes. I am in intermediate classes now. Because of COVID-19, right now I am studying online with my teacher Gayle.

I also really enjoy studying math. I love math, especially geometry. In the future, I want to go to college, and I want to become a counselor. I want to help people, mothers and fathers, get an education.

Kawsar Muse is 44 and originally from Somalia.

Coming to Earth

SUE JANSEN, CRYSTAL AND ROCHESTER, MN

See deep into your birth:

Why did you come to Earth?

Was it truly for love,

As on the wings of a dove?

What then is this love Worth?

Sue Jansen is 73 and originally from Robbinsdale, MN.

Money for a Good Life

THO TRAN, ST. PAUL, MN

For the future, I want to work hard to have my own business because I want to get rich. The business I want is a restaurant that makes Vietnamese food and American food. In Vietnam, I had my own business. I bought small fish and made fish sauce. I made a lot of money. I can't do the fish sauce business in the United States because they don't have the same fish.

Tho Tran is 75 and originally from Vietnam.

I Am a Rain of Emotions

ROSA CARRASCO, ST. PAUL, MN

Once in a while I heard my mom cry and yell again.

I have good memories of my brothers playing together.

Learning English was hard, but interesting.

I wished to be a happy girl.

I could have done with a better home.

What happened to that angry girl?

I am a rain of emotion every day.

Once in a while I hear my husband say "you can do that."

My dream is to see my son grow happy and strong.

Line 61! Line 61! Line 61! in my walkie talkie.

Don't speak when I am speaking.

Take care of your brothers.

Don't open the door.

Learning English is important for the best opportunities.

I wish to reach my goals.

I try to keep calm.

I am a rain of emotions every day.

Once in a while I will hear "I am proud of you".

I don't know when I can have silence in my mind.

I wish to travel with my family.

I will try to be a personal trainer.

I will be ready to speak without fear.

I am a rain of emotions every day.

Rosa Carrasco is 27 and originally from Mexico.

My Days at School

OLENA YURCHENKO, ST. PAUL, MN

My name is Olena. When I was thirty-six years old, I moved to the USA. Every day I go to school at Arlington Hills. I study English with students. My teacher's name is Jess. Lessons last four hours every day in the classroom. Every lesson, we study new topics. I know it will help me write, read, and speak better.

Daily lessons will help me receive my diplomas in the future.

Olena Yurchenko is 36 and originally from Ukraine.

My Life in America

EYI JOHANA, MINNESOTA

I was born in Bogotá, Colombia. I have two sisters and one brother. I came to the United States on February 9, 2021. It has been an adventure. I have known other states. I have also met people from many different countries. Being here brings a change of emotions every day, because my family is far away.

Now, I am working as a nanny. I take care of two children. They are cute and good kids. Sometimes they are not good because they are very rebellious, but I love them. Now, I only hope to end my year with this family and find a new family or change my status to student. I would like to learn English well and look for another career.

Ey Johana is originally from Colombia.

Important Events in My Life

ALEXANDRA, FRIDLEY, MN

Life is so complex that you have to live fully. I have the following remarkable events that have taught me a lot.

To study in the university was a goal that I reached in spite of my poverty. The campus was far away from my house. I used to go to the university with nothing in my stomach every day. I asked for help for low-income people, which they gave me, and the only condition was to get good grades and not fail any subject, which I did. I graduated as a teacher in 2001.

In 2002, I met a man who only with opening his mouth conquered me. Two months later, I got pregnant. Nine months later, on August 16, 2003, my baby was born. From that time until now, he is my light in my life. His father went to the U.S. when he found out about my pregnancy.

In 2007, I decided to live apart with my son. I was tired of my mom. At night, we did his homework. I had nobody to help me. Fortunately, that made me a better mom because before then, my mom did everything.

In 2008, I met another man who came to Ecuador and conquered my heart. Three months later, we married. One day, I received a call from the U.S.; it was a woman who told me that my husband was her husband too. I got divorced eight months later. In 2009, because of my failed marriage, I got depressed. But I thought, "I have my son who needs my support." That's when I chose to get closer to

God.

I started to work in Isaac A. Chico High School. It was fantastic. Here, I met wonderful people; one of them was the principal of the school, Jenny Pesántez. In the same year, I married an old friend who lived in the U.S., Oscar. He had a house where we went to live together. The third year we didn't have any more money, so we went to the U.S.

And now we have been here since March 2021. My son is eighteen. I feel very proud of him. I would like for God to allow me to see my son fulfilled and to see my grandchildren.

My husband and I are happy. I love my family. They are my support every day. Thank God for all these blessings.

Alexandra is 42 and originally from Ecuador.

My Goals

DONY SORIANO, ST. PAUL, MN

I have been living in the U.S. for two years. I lived in Duluth first. It is a great place. Lake Superior is there. I like this city but I don't like winter, because it is so cold. I like summer because I can walk and go to the lakes. My first job in the USA was in a Mexican restaurant.

Now I live in Maplewood. I work as a painter. I have three brothers. We are a great family. My goal is to learn more English every day to be able to communicate better. My life goal is to work hard to buy my own house and go to college.

Dony Soriano is 25 and originally from Honduras.

The Door

RONGYUN RUAN, BROOKLYN PARK, MN

I come from an ancient country in the Far East — China. My hometown is a small county in China. In the twenty-four years since I was born, I had never left my country. At that time, I thought the world was so small, like my room. Whenever I was afraid of being scolded by my parents because of bad grades, or when I accidentally did something wrong, I always hid in my room and closed the door.

At that time, I thought that the door was a good protective umbrella, and its closing made me feel very relieved. However, whenever the door was closed my mother always knocked on the door, and then gently enlightened me. My mother was always so gentle and considerate, so I always felt at ease to open the door to let my mother in.

When I grew up, I left my country and came to the United States. I found that the world is so big. When I joined Metro North to study English, I felt very happy, and everything made me feel very novel. However, when I make a mistake or feel that my English pronunciation is incorrect, I always close my mouth. I have so many ideas to express, but I am afraid. I am afraid that I will feel shame, and I am afraid of being laughed at. I know, I closed the door again.

Whenever this happens, my teachers always encourage me and give me affirmative support and understanding. They teach me patiently and tenderly so that I won't make mistakes again. They will let me know not to be ashamed about the mistake, it's okay. Slowly, I feel like this is my other home. The teachers are like my parents. They gently opened the door of my heart, so that I can receive more knowledge and get to know the world well. After more than a year of study, they worked hard to help me reach my goal. At this time, I know that, in fact, the best peace of mind is to open the door so that you will know a better and far more distant world, instead of closing the door. Thank you, teachers.

Rongyun Ruan is 38 and originally from China.

The U.S. Changed My Life

MARIA ANDRADE, COLUMBIA HEIGHTS, MN

When I came to the United States, I didn't think about what I wanted to do with my life. I didn't think about going to school, but thanks to my brother-in-law, I did. He insisted a lot that I go to school. It is really important in this country.

Learning the language in this country can open many doors for you and help you to have a better future. It is hard for adults to go to school and work at the same time because we have a lot of responsibilities.

I went to this school called CTC, Center for Training and Careers, which was an alternative high school. They gave us the chance to get our high school diploma before turning twenty-one years old. I had the chance to get my high school diploma, but I got pregnant with my oldest daughter and I couldn't make it because she was born in September, just when we had to go back to school. I have attended school for almost fifteen months, and I learned about thirty-five percent of my English skills, but now I'm back to school trying to go farther. This time I want to get my GED and be someone in this life.

Maria Andrade is 39 and originally from Mexico.

Family School

ADRIANA QUINTANA, BURNSVILLE, MN

I started going to family school in 2018. I decided to attend family school because, for me, it was frustrating not being able to understand anything when someone spoke to me in English. Back then, I was coming with my son Dylan. He was in year one of preschool. Together we learned a lot at Crystal Lake School. Now he is in the first year of elementary school at the same school as his older brother Jonathan.

I thank each of the teachers who have been in this learning process. Now it is easier for me to understand what people are talking about and I hope one day to be able to speak the English language better. Now I'm still in family school, but accompanied by my one year old twins, Milan and Ariadnne.

Adriana Quintana is 31 and originally from Mexico.

My Goal

DAMTEW TESHOME, ST. PAUL, MN

I was born in Gondar, Ethiopia. I graduated from Gondar Fasiledes High School. Then I entered military service for twenty years. I am married and have one daughter and three sons.

My daughter brought my wife and me to the United States three years ago. I was working as a nursing assistant in my country and that is my goal in this country. Now I work at the healthcare center on Marshall Avenue in housekeeping and supplies. I am attending an ELL class at the Hubbs Center for Lifelong Learning. My next step will be to study to be a certified nursing assistant (CNA). Then, I will take the test. Finally, I will find a job as a CNA.

Damtew Teshome is 68 and originally from Ethiopia.

My Life - A Poem

DIAHANN DAVIS, CRYSTAL, MN

Everything that grows, I always find ways to make it flow.

I may stumble and I may fall, but God always sees me through it all.

So, I must continue to fight with all my might.

And at the end of it all, everything will be alright.

Diahann Davis is 42 and originally from Brooklyn Center, MN.

Persuasive Writing

MARIELA C., WORTHINGTON, MN

Why is it important to eat fruits and vegetables?

Because fruits and vegetables have vitamins, minerals, enzymes, and antioxidants. The different vitamins and minerals present in plant food help us to strengthen all the cells, organs, and systems of the body. Fruits and vegetables are essential for good bowel function.

Fruits and vegetables give us enough energy. Fruits and vegetables provide us with antioxidants which help us to stay healthy and at the same time delay aging. The best way for vegetables to give us energy is to eat them raw.

Mariela C. is 30 and originally from Mexico.

My Country

BELITZA AGUIRE, MINNESOTA

My country is Venezuela.

In 2019, I arrived at the airport in Miami with my American visa. I was very happy. This was the second time I came. I have three children; two boys and one girl. Today, I give thanks to God for having all of them here with me.

This country is beautiful and full of millions of opportunities for career persons and professionals. I did have the opportunity to study in a class for medical assistants, and now I am looking for a new job. It was here that I learned to drive a car, and now I am doing very well.

Belitza Aguire is originally from Venezuela.

Finding and Creating Beauty: Art Work

Untitled

KAMAL FARDAN, BAYPORT, MN

Kamal Fardan is originally from the U.S.

My Village: Karen Refugee Tham Him Camp

YOU EH MOO, ST. PAUL, MN

You Eh Moo is 23 and originally from Thailand.

A Rooster's Tale

CLARE SIERRA, SAVAGE, MN

Clare Sierra is 65 and originally from Decorah, IA.

Untitled

COLGATE WOOD, ST. CLOUD, MN

Colgate Wood is originally from the U.S.

La Vie en rose

FELICIA GOOSE, BLOOMINGTON, MN

Felicia Goose is 21 and originally from Spearfish, SD.

Untitled

RICHARD PENAZ, ST. CLOUD, MN

Richard Penaz is originally from Monticello, MN.

Cold Night

EH KAW SAY, ST. PAUL, MN

Eh Kaw Say is 18 and originally from Thailand.

Untitled

WAKIYA DEREK LITTLETHUNDER, ST. CLOUD, MN

Wakiya Derek Littlethunder is originally from the U.S.

Ingrid, Maureen, and Laurie

INGRID HANSEN, CRYSTAL, MN

Ingrid Hansen is 59 and originally from San Diego, CA.

Untitled

WAHNITA FELIEN, MINNEAPOLIS, MN

Wahnita Felien is 77 and originally from Preston, MN.

Untitled

KARLIE JACOBSON, ELK RIVER, MN

Karlie Jacobson is originally from Buffalo, MN.

Unforgettable Place

HAY DREE, ST. PAUL, MN

Hay Dree is 21 and originally from Kawthoolei (Karen State).

Index

D

E

F

G

H

I

J

K

L

M

N

O

Journeys Curriculum Unit

Overview

Literacy Minnesota is pleased to offer this curriculum unit to accompany *Journeys*. It is written for an audience of High Intermediate to Advanced ESL learners (CASAS scores 211-235). The learning objectives below are aligned with the College and Career Readiness Standards (CCRS) and the Transitions Integration Framework (TIF). For more information about the CCRS and the TIF, visit atlasabe.org.

In response to COVID-19, we have also suggested activity modifications for the virtual classroom. These modifications are labeled with the tag VIRTUAL CLASS IDEA and were designed to eliminate the need for printing and advance distribution of materials. These ideas rely primarily on the features available on the Zoom platform.

Objectives

After the unit, learners will be able to:

1. Discuss the concept of "storytelling" and its varied roles across cultures.
2. Read and navigate a table of contents, activating prior knowledge, making predictions about content and locating key information in a text. **(CCRS RI.2.5) (TIF LS 1a, 1b)**
3. Identify and analyze examples of literary genres in *Journeys*. Identify the main purpose of a text, including what the author wants to answer, explain or describe. **(CCRS R1.2.6) (TIF CT 1b)**
4. Read *Journeys* texts aloud with fluency, focusing on appropriate speed, accuracy and expression after successive readings. **(CCRS RF.4)**
5. Compare and contrast *Journeys* texts of the same genre using graphic organizers. **(CCRS RI.3.9) (TIF CT 1c)**
6. Use a personal response journal to synthesize and reflect on *Journeys* texts. **(TIF CT 1c)**
7. Write a *Journeys*-style narrative text, using a prewriting/rough draft/final draft process. **(CCRS W.2.3, W.3.4, W.3.5)**

Structure

This unit consists of eight cumulative lesson plans, including ready-to-use activities. Each lesson is designed to be approximately 1 to 1.5 hours long. Teachers are welcome to adapt the lessons to accommodate their unique classroom settings. Since class levels and sizes vary, a range of times is suggested for each activity.

Lesson Contents

Lesson 1: Storytelling

Lesson 2: Navigating a Table of Contents

Lesson 3: Literary Genres in *Journeys*

Lesson 4: Reading with Fluency

Lesson 5: Compare and Contrast Texts

Lesson 6: Culminating Activity: Prewriting

Lesson 7: Culminating Activity: Rough Draft

Lesson 8: Culminating Activity: Final Draft

Tech Tip

To copy handouts from the *Journeys* print edition onto 8 ½ x 11 sheets, use an enlargement ratio of 121%.

Lesson 1: Storytelling

Objective:

Discuss the concept of "storytelling" and its varied roles across cultures.

Materials + Prep:

1. *Journeys*: teacher's copy or class set; 2. Reference copy of the unit's learning objectives (see previous page); 3. Copy and cut Storytelling Mingle Cards (see next page) so each learner gets one card. Note: there are only four questions total, so learners will have duplicate questions.
VIRTUAL CLASS PREP: 1. *Journeys*: teacher's copy; 2. Storytelling Mingle Cards for reference; 3. PDF copy of a *Journeys* text.

Lesson Plan:

1. Introduce the Unit (10-20 min)

- Show and introduce *Journeys* as a book of stories written by Adult Basic Education (ABE) learners across Minnesota. It is published annually; this year nearly 300 learners' stories and poems are in the book.

- Explain that the class will be using *Journeys* to work on some reading/literacy learning objectives. Talk through the objectives in detail if appropriate.

- Explain that as a final project, learners will write their own *Journeys*-style texts; ask them to keep in mind what story of their own they would like to tell.

2. "Storytelling" Warm-up (15-20 min)

- Remind learners that *Journeys* is a book of stories, as well as some poetry. Write the word "storytelling" on the board and define/discuss. **VIRTUAL CLASS IDEA:** Use Zoom's Whiteboard or Google Slides.

- Lead a Think-Pair-Share activity with the prompt: "What do you think of when you hear the word 'storytelling'?" **VIRTUAL CLASS IDEA:** Use Zoom's Breakout Rooms to pair up learners. Then, type the prompt in the Chat.

3. "Storytelling" Mingle Activity (30-40 min)

- Introduce the four questions about storytelling—see the cards on next page.

- Lead the mingle activity: each learner gets one card. They mingle around the room, asking peers the question on their card and answering questions from peers. **VIRTUAL CLASS IDEA:** Use Zoom's Breakout Rooms to place your class into 4 (or fewer) breakout rooms. Before breaking out, assign each group one mingle question and designate a facilitator/reporter for each group. Note these assignments on Zoom's Whiteboard. Then, capture your Zoom screen to save these assignments. Once broken out, share the screen shot in the Chat. (Alternatively, type the assignments in the Chat, without sharing the screen shot.)

- To follow up, facilitate a conversation to discuss and summarize learners' answers to the questions.

4. Free Silent Reading (with any remaining time)
With any remaining time, invite learners to browse *Journeys* and get to know the book. If you only have a teacher's copy, make copies of a variety of pages of the book. **VIRTUAL CLASS IDEA:** Choose a story to read aloud to the class.

Storytelling Mingle Cards

Who is the best storyteller you know? Why?	Who is the best storyteller you know? Why?
Is storytelling important in your family? In your culture? Why or why not?	Is storytelling important in your family? In your culture? Why or why not?
In your culture, are stories told mostly by speaking, writing, or both? What is an example?	In your culture, are stories told mostly by speaking, writing, or both? What is an example?
What are some reasons to tell stories?	What are some reasons to tell stories?

Lesson 2: Navigating a Table of Contents

Objective:

Read and navigate a table of contents, activating prior knowledge, making predictions about content and locating key information in a text. **(CCRS RI.2.5) (TIF LS 1a, 1b)**

Materials + Prep:

1. *Journeys*: teacher's copy or class set; 2. Make copies of the Table of Contents page; 3. Make copies of the Table of Contents Quiz (in-person class version).
VIRTUAL CLASS PREP: 1. *Journeys*: teacher's copy; 2. PDF of the Table of Contents; 3. PDF of the Table of Contents Quiz (virtual class version).

Lesson Plan:

1. Key Vocabulary Word: *Anthology* (10-20 min)

- Show and re-introduce *Journeys* as a book of stories written by MN ABE learners; remind the class that at the end of the unit they will be writing their own stories.
- Introduce and define the vocabulary word *anthology* as "a book or other collection with writings by many authors." Post the word on your word wall, board, Zoom Whiteboard or Google Slides.
- Elicit the contexts in which learners may have heard/used this word. As a class, generate a sentence with the word.

2. Table of Contents/Prior Knowledge and Predictions: Activity 1 (15-25 min)

- Give handouts of the Table of Contents page, and project using a document camera (or, in a virtual class, screen share.) Orient learners to the organization of the Table of Contents for this anthology.
- Model reading the Table of Contents with a partner, making predictions about what types of stories will appear in each section. Model some creative predictions using this sentence frame:
  "I notice a section called ________. I think there will be stories about _____ in this section."
- Ask learners to do this read and predict activity with a partner. **VIRTUAL CLASS IDEA:** Use Zoom's Breakout Rooms to pair up learners. Then, type the names of 1-2 Table of Contents sections in the Chat. Next, type the sentence frame in the Chat. Ask pairs to use the sentence frame to make predictions about the sections you shared.
- Give learners the Table of Contents Quiz (next page). Ask learners to use the Table of Contents to find the answers. **VIRTUAL CLASS IDEA:** Do this activity as a large group. Screen share the quiz, then use Zoom's Annotate to fill in the answers as you discuss them. Ask learners to chat their answers or "raise their hand" in Zoom.

3. Table of Contents/Prior Knowledge and Predictions: Activity 2 (10-15 min)

- Model reading the Table of Contents individually, marking the sections you're interested in with a * and the sections you're wondering/confused about with a ?
- Ask learners to read and mark their own Table of Contents page. **VIRTUAL CLASS IDEA:** screen share the Table of Contents page. Instead of using a handout, ask learners to make notes in their notebook on the topic above.
- Assess interest in each section by asking them to "vote with their feet": read the name of each section, and ask learners to respond by standing up to indicate high interest, a "so-so" gesture for medium interest and sitting down for low interest. **VIRTUAL CLASS IDEA:** use Zoom's Nonverbal Feedback feature to assess interest.

4. Free Silent Reading (with any remaining time). See Lesson 1 for notes. Remind learners to pay attention to which stories resonate with them, and what stories of their own they might want to write about. **VIRTUAL CLASS IDEA:** choose a story to read aloud to or with the class.

Journeys Anthology
Table of Contents Quiz (modified worksheet for virtual class)

Table of Contents

---

1. What page does the "In the Past" section begin on? ________

2. What page does the "Bright Futures" section begin on? _________

3. What is the name of the section that begins on page 47?

____

4. What is the name of the section that begins on page 117?

____

5. How many pages is the "Close-Knit Connections" section? _________

6. How many pages is the "Me and My Stories" section? _________

7. What section do you think will have stories about experiencing life in a new place? What words in the section title make you think this?

Journeys Anthology Table of Contents Quiz (traditional worksheet for in-person class)

1. What page does the “In the Past” section begin on? ________

2. What page does the “Bright Futures” section begin on? __________

3. What is the name of the section that begins on page 47?

____

4. What is the name of the section that begins on page 117?

____

5. How many pages is the “Close-Knit Connections” section? __________

6. How many pages is the “Me and My Stories” section? __________

7. What section do you think will have stories about experiencing life in a new place? What words in the section title make you think this?

____

____

____

Lesson 3: Literary Genres in *Journeys*

Objectives:

Identify and analyze examples of literary genres in *Journeys*. Identify the main purpose of a text, including what the author wants to answer, explain or describe. **(CCRS RI.2.6) (TIF CT 1b)**
Use a personal response journal to synthesize and reflect on the *Journeys* texts. **(TIF CT 1c)**

Materials + Prep:

1. *Journeys*: teacher's copy or class set; 2. Make copies and cut Genres Matching Cards, one set per pair (next page); 3. Make copies of *Journeys* texts: choose one text per genre; 4. Make copies of *Journeys:* Which Genre? handout (next pages).
VIRTUAL CLASS PREP: 1. *Journeys*: teacher's copy; 2. PDF of the Genres Matching Activity (virtual class version); 3. PDF of three *Journeys* texts of different genres;

Lesson Plan:

1. Key Vocabulary Word: Genre (10-20 min)

   - Review the vocabulary word *anthology* from the previous lesson.
   - Introduce the vocabulary word *genre* as "a type of writing with similar form, style or topic." Post the word on your word wall, board, Zoom whiteboard or Google Slides.
   - Elicit the contexts in which learners may have heard/used this word. As a class, generate a sentence with the word.

2. *Journeys* Genres: Activity 1 (10-20 min)

   - Explain that you'll be studying five different literary genres that appear in *Journeys*: Autobiography, Narrative Essay, Descriptive Essay, Verse and Folktale.
   - Lead the genres matching activity: each pair gets a set of cards (5 vocab words, 5 definitions); they match each genre with the correct definition. **VIRTUAL CLASS IDEA:** Screen share the matching activity worksheet. As a class, read through each definition and use Zoom's Annotate to match each one to the correct vocabulary word at the top. Write in the correct vocabulary word next to each definition. Give learners time to copy the definitions into their notebooks.
   - Follow up by checking comprehension of the genre definitions. Add the words to your word wall, board, Zoom whiteboard or Google Slides.

3. *Journeys* Genres: Activity 2 (30-45 min)

   - Select a short text from *Journeys*. Read the text as a class. Ask learners: "What was the author's purpose for writing this text?" Decide together which genre this text belongs to and why.
   - Select three or more texts of different genres from *Journeys*. Give learners copies of the "*Journeys:* Which Genre?" handout. Ask learners to work in pairs, reading the texts and completing the genres analysis. **VIRTUAL CLASS IDEA:** Select two or more texts of different genres. Use the Chat to pose the two key questions for analysis: "What genre is this text? Why?" Then, screen share the first story. Read the story as a class and discuss the key questions. Repeat with as many stories as is appropriate.
   - In the "my notes" section of the worksheet (or in their notebooks), suggest that learners note any ideas for their own texts, and remind them that the class will be writing their own *Journeys*-style narrative texts soon. Follow-up by checking comprehension in the large group.

Genres Matching Activity (modified activity for virtual class)

Genres:

autobiography narrative essay verse

descriptive essay folktale

Definitions:

1. A text that describes a person, object, event or place with many details, so the reader feels like they are there or makes a strong connection.

2. A fictional story where magical characters learn a lesson, often passed down by storytelling traditions.

3. A text about the author's own life or history.

4. A poem (may or may not rhyme)

5. A text about one event or experience that was important in the author's life, usually sharing a lesson learned.

Genres Matching Cards (traditional activity for in-person class)

Cut out the individual cards to prepare for a matching activity.

Genres	Definitions
autobiography	A text about the author's own life or history.
narrative essay	A text about one event or experience that was important in the author's life, usually sharing a lesson learned.
descriptive essay	A text that describes a person, object, event or place with many details, so the reader feels like they are there or makes a strong connection.
verse	A poem (may or may not rhyme)
folktale	A fictional story where magical characters learn a lesson, often passed down by storytelling traditions.

Journeys: Which Genre?

Text Title	What genre is this text? Why?	My notes

Lesson 4: Reading with Fluency

Objectives:

Read *Journeys* texts aloud with fluency, focusing on appropriate speed, accuracy and expression after successive readings. **(CCRS RF.4)**
Use a personal response journal to synthesize and reflect on *Journeys* texts. **(TIF CT 1c)**

Materials + Prep:

1. *Journeys*: teacher's copy or class set; 2. Make copies of two *Journeys* texts for fluency practice; 3. Make copies of the *Journeys* Personal Response Journal handout for each learner (next page).
VIRTUAL CLASS PREP: 1. *Journeys*: teacher's copy; 2. PDF of two *Journeys* texts for fluency practice; 3. PDF of Personal Response Journal handout.

Lesson Plan:

1. Key Vocabulary Review (10-20 min):

- Return to the key vocabulary words from Lessons 2-3. Use a vocabulary review activity to reinforce new vocabulary acquisition.

2. Reading Fluency Activity 1 (20-25 min)

- Choose a *Journeys* text that fits most learners' fluency level.
- Explain the purpose of fluency practice: today we'll read a text multiple times to practice reading accurately (with few mistakes), at a good speed (not too fast, not too slow) and with good expression (including pausing in the right places). This will help us become better readers and be more comfortable reading aloud.
- Model reading the text aloud to the class. Ask them to follow along, paying attention to your speed and where you stop to pause. After you read, answer questions learners have about the text.
- Lead a choral reading of the same text. Debrief to ask if they noticed the pauses and expression.
- Read aloud in pairs: one learner reads the text aloud; the other listens. Then they switch roles. **VIRTUAL CLASS IDEA:** Use Zoom's Chat to send a document with the text. Then, use Zoom's Breakout Rooms to break learners into smaller groups. Before breaking out, ask for 1-2 volunteers in each group to read the story aloud. (Allow extra time and model how to navigate from the breakout room to the chat and how to open the document.) Once in small groups, allow time for the volunteers to read aloud to the group.

3. Reading Fluency Activity 2 (20-25 min)

- Choose a new *Journeys* text that fits most learners' fluency level.
- Share (or screen share) the text with the class. Model a think-aloud, scanning the text for punctuation and the phrasing/expression conventions for each: commas, periods, question marks, etc.
- Read the text aloud to the class, with everyone tracking the text signals. After you read, answer questions learners have about the text. Next, lead a choral reading of the same text.
- Repeat the pair reading (or virtual class modification) from Activity 1.
- Ask if anyone would like to read the text aloud to the class.

4. Personal Response Journal (with any remaining time). Give each learner a Personal Response Journal handout. Explain/model the activity and ask them to write a response. **VIRTUAL CLASS IDEA:** Screen share the handout. Ask learners to write their response in their notebooks.

Journeys: Personal Response Journal

Instructions:

1. **Choose** a reading from today that interested you the most.

2. **Choose one** of the Response Questions to the right.

3. **Think** about the question, then **write** a few sentences in response.

Response Questions:

1. What connections did you make with this text? They could be from your experiences, others' experiences, or other texts.

2. What do you wonder after reading this text? Why?

3. What are some other titles for this text? Which one do you like best? Why?

4. What sentence(s) are the most important in this text? Why?

Name:______________________ Date: ___________________

Text title: ____

Response to Question Number ____:

____

____

____

____

____

____

____

____

Lesson 5: Compare/Contrast Two *Journeys* Texts

Objectives:

Compare and contrast two *Journeys* texts of the same genre using graphic organizers. **(CCRS RI.3.9) (TIF CT 1c)**
Use a personal response journal to synthesize and reflect on the *Journeys* texts. **(TIF CT 1c)**

Materials + Prep:

1. *Journeys*: teacher's copy or class set; 2. Make copies of two *Journeys* texts, making sure they're of the same genre; 3. Create a handout with comprehension questions about the two texts and make copies; 4. Make copies of the Venn Diagram handout (next page); 5. Make copies of the *Journeys:* Personal Response Journal handout (previous page) for each learner.
VIRTUAL CLASS PREP: 1. *Journeys*: teacher's copy; 2-5. PDF versions of materials 2-5 listed above.

Lesson Plan:

1. Read and Summarize the Texts (30-45 min)

- Introduce the two texts, explaining that they are of the same genre.
- Ask the class to read both texts. After reading, they answer the prepared comprehension questions. **VIRTUAL CLASS IDEA**: Choose two texts that are short enough to read them both as a large group.
- Review answers to the prepared comprehension questions as a class. Ask learners to point out where they found answers to each question in the text(s).
- Make a T-chart on the board with the names of the two texts at the top. Ask learners to scan the texts individually, noting a few key ideas in each text. **VIRTUAL CLASS IDEA:** Use Zoom's Whiteboard to make a T-chart. Then, use Zoom's Chat feature to send a document with the texts, so learners can refer to the texts during the large group discussion. Alternatively, use Zoom's Simultaneous Sharing: If you have a volunteer, class assistant or advanced learner: ask that person to pull up the text and share their screen, so the class can see the text and the T-chart at the same time.
- As a large group, discuss the ideas they noted. Through discussion, arrive at a consensus about the two or three most important ideas in each story. Note these in the T-chart.

2. Compare and Contrast the Texts (30-45 min)

- Ask for an example of one thing that's similar about the texts and one thing that's different.
- Next, model how to fill out the Venn Diagram with one thing that's similar and one thing from each text that's unique/different.
- After you model, ask learners to pair up and work together to fill out the Venn Diagram. **VIRTUAL CLASS IDEA**: Use Zoom's Annotate to fill out the Venn Diagram as a large group.
- Follow-up with a large group discussion, eliciting learners' responses to the activity.

3. Personal Response Journal (with any remaining time). Give each learner a Personal Response Journal handout. Explain/model the activity and ask them to write a response. **VIRTUAL CLASS IDEA:** Screen share the handout. Ask learners to write their response in their notebooks.

Compare and Contrast Journeys Texts

Text 1: ____________________ Text 2: ____________________

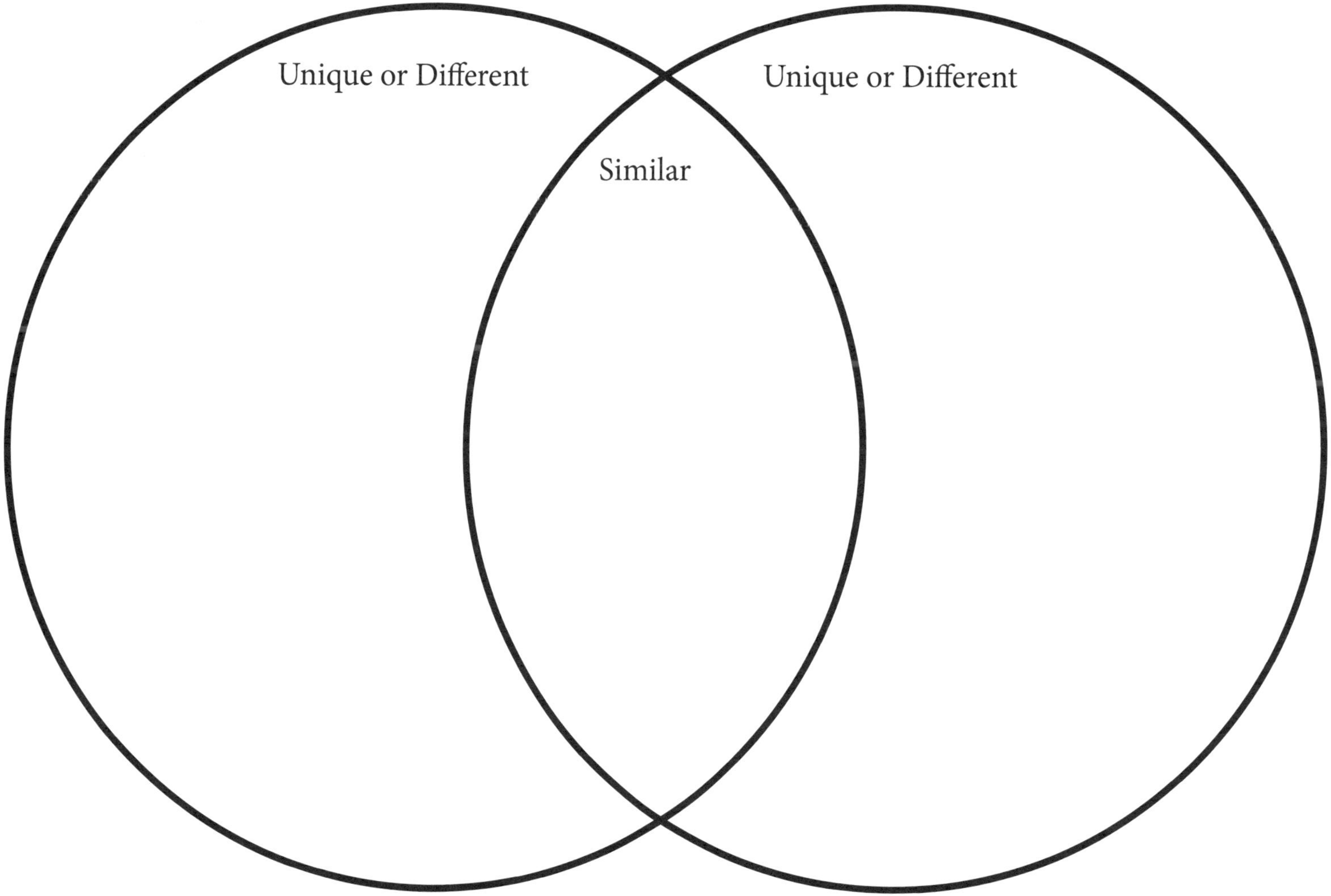

Unique or Different

Similar

Unique or Different

Lesson 6: Culminating Activity, Prewriting

Objective:

Write a *Journeys*-style text, using a prewriting/rough draft/final draft process. **(CCRS W.2.3, W.3.4, W.3.5)**

Materials + Prep:

1. *Journeys*: teacher's copy or class set; 2. Make copies of two examples of *Journeys* narrative texts; 3. Make copies of the Prewriting Narrative Essay Graphic Organizer (next page).
VIRTUAL CLASS PREP: 1. *Journeys*: teacher's copy; 2. PDF of two *Journeys* narrative texts; 3. PDF of the Prewriting Narrative Essay Graphic Organizer.

Lesson Plan:

1. Identify Descriptive Details in Narrative Essays (20-30 min)

- Introduce the two texts, explaining that they are of the same genre. Review the definition of a narrative essay from previous lesson.
- Write this question on the board or virtual whiteboard: What words does the author use to describe?
- Read each text aloud. Ask learners to think about the question as they listen and answer the key question with a partner after you read aloud. **VIRTUAL CLASS IDEA**: Skip the partner discussion and talk as a large group.
- After learners have answered the question, elicit examples from the class. Write descriptive details on the board, Zoom whiteboard or Google Slides. Ask learners to add to the list with their own ideas.

2. Identify Signal Words in Narrative Essays (20-30 min)

- Now, write this question on the board, Zoom whiteboard or Google Slides: What words does the author use to tell the order things happen in?
- Ask learners to read both texts again on their own. Ask learners to think about the question as they read and answer the question with a partner after they read. **VIRTUAL CLASS IDEA:** Skip the partner discussion and talk as a large group. OR, if level-appropriate: share a document containing the texts through Chat, so learners can refer to the texts during their discussion. Then, type the discussion prompt in the Chat. Next, use Zoom's Breakout Rooms to break learners into smaller groups and ask them to discuss the prompt.
- After learners have read and answered the question, elicit examples from learners. Write signal words on the board, Zoom whiteboard or Google Slides. Ask learners to add to the list with their own ideas.

3. Pre-Writing Activity (20-30 min)

- Introduce the Prewriting Graphic Organizer to the class.
- Model completing the graphic organizer by filling it out together, using one of the sample texts you read. Be sure to include descriptive details and signal words.
- After you model, invite the learners to think of their own story and complete the Prewriting Graphic Organizer on their own. Ask them to share their completed graphic organizer with a partner.
VIRTUAL CLASS IDEA: Instead of using the handout, ask learners to note their prewriting ideas in their notebooks.

Prewriting Narrative Essay Graphic Organizer

What is the story about?

Who is in the story?

What **descriptive details** help to tell the story?

What happened **first**?
One day,
In (year),
To begin with,

What happened **next**?
Next,
After awhile,
Later,

What happened **last**?
Finally,
At last,
In the end,

What did you learn?
I learned that...

Lesson 7: Culminating Activity, Rough Draft

Objective:

Write a *Journeys*-style text, using a prewriting/rough draft/final draft process. **(CCRS W.2.3, W.3.4, W.3.5)**

Materials + Prep:

1. Prewriting Graphic Organizer, completed as a sample from previous lesson; 2. Optional: Make copies of the Narrative Essay Paragraph Frame (next page).
VIRTUAL CLASS PREP: PDFs of the two items listed above.

Lesson Plan:

1. Prewriting Review (10-15 min)

- Ask learners to locate their Prewriting Graphic Organizers (or notes in their notebook) from the previous lesson. Give them a few minutes to review their work, then a few minutes to share their ideas with a partner. **VIRTUAL CLASS IDEA:** Use Zoom's Breakout Rooms to pair learners up.

2. Rough Draft (30-45 min)

- Share the sample Prewriting Graphic Organizer from the previous class. Model transferring the story details into paragraph form using signal words and descriptive details. Optional: use the Narrative Essay Paragraph Frame to model.
- Save this model rough draft for the next lesson.
- Ask learners to transfer their prewriting ideas into paragraph form. Optional: share the Narrative Essay Paragraph Frame handout to support learners.
- Reiterate that at this stage, they don't need to worry about spelling/mechanics. Encourage them to focus on the text's organization and development.
- Give the class enough time to write a rough draft of their stories.
- **VIRTUAL CLASS IDEA:** After learners have written their rough drafts, invite them to type and share their rough drafts with you through email, a Google Doc, a Google Form or another sharing method.

3. Reading the Rough Draft (with any remaining time):

- If there's time, ask learners to read their rough drafts aloud to a partner and make any changes they need to. Reading aloud can help to identify sentences they may want to change.

Narrative Essay Paragraph Frame

This story is about ____

____.

What happened first?

______________, ______________________________

____.

What happened next?

______________, ______________________________

____.

What happened last?

______________, ______________________________

____.

What did you learn?

____

____.

Lesson 8: Culminating Activity, Final Draft

Objective:

Write a *Journeys*-style text, using a prewriting/rough draft/final draft process. **(CCRS W.2.3, W.3.4, W.3.5)**

Materials + Prep:

1. Make copies of the Editing Checklist (next page). 2. Sample rough draft, from previous lesson. **VIRTUAL CLASS PREP:** 1. PDF of the Editing Checklist; 2. PDF or other shareable version of the sample rough draft, from previous lesson.

Lesson Plan:

1. Rough Draft Review (10-15 min)

    - Ask learners to locate their rough draft from the previous lesson. Give them enough time to re-read their text.

2. Introducing the Editing Checklist (15-20 min)

    - Introduce the Editing Checklist, project using a document camera, and model how to review/ edit the sample rough draft which you modeled in the previous lesson, checking for the items on the checklist. **VIRTUAL CLASS IDEA:** Instead of screen sharing the Editing Checklist, screen share the sample rough draft from the previous lesson. Then, one at a time, type each editing question (e.g., "Does each sentence have a punctuation mark at the end?") in the Chat. Model how to review/edit the sample rough draft as described above.

    - Share with learners that they will use the Editing Checklist twice. First, they will review their writing on their own. Next, they will have a partner review their writing (or, in a virtual setting, they will review their writing as a group).

3. Review and Editing the Rough Draft (20-30 min)

    - Ask learners to use the Editing Checklist to review/edit their own rough draft, putting a check in the first column for items that are completed. **VIRTUAL CLASS IDEA:** Ask learners to refer to the editing questions already posted in the Chat (from previous activity) and use them to edit their rough drafts. OR, share a document with the Editing Checklist through the Chat, so learners can refer to it while editing their rough drafts.

    - Next, ask learners to work in pairs to review each other's writing using the Editing Checklist. Give them enough time to review/edit the texts. **VIRTUAL CLASS IDEA**: If rough drafts are typed in a Word Doc or Google Doc, ask a learner to share their screen and ask the class to help edit the story using the checklist. Repeat with as many learners as is appropriate.

    - Give learners a "brain break" after editing.

4. Final Draft (20-25 min)

    - Introduce the final draft process to the class and ask them to write/type a final copy of their text, incorporating the edits identified.

5. Share with Class (with any remaining time)

    - Invite learners to share their texts aloud with the class.

Editing Checklist

1) Read your rough draft aloud, checking for the items below.
2) Have a partner read your rough draft, checking for the items below.

		My Edit	My Partner's Edit
Punctuation	Does each sentence have a punctuation mark at the end? . ! ?		
Capital Letters	Does each sentence begin with a capital letter?		
	Do all proper nouns begin with a capital letter? For example, names and place names.		
Grammar	Is each sentence a complete idea?		
	Can you break up any long sentences into shorter ones?		
	Is there agreement between subjects and verbs? For example, *she has* (not *she have*).		
Spelling	Did you circle words that are spelled wrong or words you are not sure about?		

Notes

Notes

Journeys 2022 Editorial Team

Abby Doty

COPYEDITOR

Abby just graduated from Hamline University last year, majoring in psychology and English with a concentration in creative writing. Outside of *Journeys*, Abby is currently a proofreader for Collegis Education. Abby has recently taken creative nonfiction classes and has fallen in love with the genre! She tries to read and write it when she can. Her career goal for the future is to get more into publishing to see what incredible stories are out there. In her free time, Abby enjoys painting, petting dogs, and fueling her book-buying obsession.

Christine Horner

COPYEDITOR

Christine is a Creative Writing AFA student at Normandale Community College, where she is enrolled in her last semester of classes. She is also a part-time Writing Center tutor at Normandale and is the sitting president of Normandale's Creative Writing Club. She thoroughly enjoys writing and reading poetry. Some of her favorite poets include local Minnesotans Jericho Brown, torrin a. greathouse, and Heid E. Erdrich. Christine plans to pursue a career in either professional English tutoring or editing and publishing. During her downtime, Christine loves knitting, cooking, and playing video games.

Journeys 2022 Editorial Team

Adèle McLees

COPYEDITOR

Adèle is a senior at Macalester College with a double major in French and International Studies, and she is a longtime lover of writing of all kinds. She is interested personally and academically in the lived experiences of immigrants and refugees, and has spent a lot of free time since high school volunteering as a tutor in these communities. In addition to working on *Journeys*, Adèle is completing an honors thesis in which she is analyzing the ways in which three novels that discuss migration from Francophone Africa to France give voice and power to migrants within a society that systematically silences them. Adèle's career goal is to combine her writing and migration studies interests in a practical way. In her free time, Adèle enjoys going for walks, eating with friends, and embroidery.

Majdaah Salaah

COPYEDITOR

Majdaah is a junior at Macalester College, studying Media and Cultural Studies, minoring in English, and concentrating in Legal Studies. She has a deep-seated interest in storytelling and loves engaging with different perspectives and experiences. Majdaah also loves to engage with creative projects, and in her own work, she enjoys manipulating perspective towards something unique and unknown. Her hobbies include watching films, reading YA literature, and playing chess. One day, Majdaah hopes to become trilingual and to publish a novel.

Acknowledgements

Literacy Minnesota extends our heartfelt thanks to our 2022 *Journeys* copyeditors Abby Doty, Adèle McLees, Christine Horner, and Majdaah Salaah, who have dedicated their time and talent to the planning, design, editing and production of this book. Special thanks also to staff Debbie Cushman, Ellie Purdy, Gabriela Nesheim, Heather Cook, Kelly Rynda, and Mariah Wika for helping make *Journeys* a success.

We are grateful for a partnership with the Friends of the Saint Paul Public Library and their generosity in connecting us to Letters about Literature. Letters about Literature was a statewide writing contest for Minnesota students from elementary school through adult education. Our version of the program invites students to read a piece of literature of their choice, reflect on it, and write a personal letter to the author explaining how the piece changed their views of the world and/or themselves. Special thanks to Alayne Hopkins.

Finally, we are deeply grateful to longtime donors Mimi and Todd Burke, who give in memory of Todd's late mother through the Burke Family Fund of the Minnesota Community Foundation. Their generous support helped make *Journeys* possible this year.

About Literacy Minnesota

The mission of Literacy Minnesota is to share the power of learning through education, community building, and advocacy. We believe literacy has the power to advance equity and justice, and we envision a world where life-changing learning is within everyone's reach.

Contact Us

literacymn.org
651-645-2277
700 Raymond Avenue, Suite 180
Saint Paul, MN 55114